Bloom's Modern Critical Interpretations

The Adventures of Huckleberry Finn

The Age of Innocence

Alice's Adventures in Wonderland

All Quiet on the Western Front

As You Like It

The Ballad of the Sad Café

Beloved

Beowulf

Black Boy

The Bluest Eye

The Canterbury Tales

Cat on a Hot Tin Roof

The Catcher in the Rye

Catch-22

The Chronicles of Narnia

The Color Purple

Crime and Punishment

The Crucible

Darkness at Noon

Death of a Salesman

The Death of Artemio Cruz

Don Quixote

Emerson's Essays

Emma

Fahrenheit 451

A Farewell to Arms

Frankenstein

The Glass Menagerie

The Grapes of Wrath

Great Expectations

The Great Gatsby

Gulliver's Travels

Hamlet

The Handmaid's Tale

Heart of Darkness

I Know Why the Caged Bird Sings

The Iliad

Jane Eyre

The Joy Luck Club

The Jungle

Long Day's Journey Into Night

Lord of the Flies

The Lord of the Rings

Love in the Time of Cholera

The Man Without Qualities

The Metamorphosis

Miss Lonelyhearts

Moby-Dick

My Ántonia

Native Son

Night

1984

The Odyssey

Oedipus Rex

The Old Man and the Sea

On the Road

One Flew Over the Cuckoo's Nest

One Hundred Years of Solitude

Persuasion

Portnoy's Complaint

Pride and Prejudice

Ragtime

The Red Badge of Courage

Romeo and Juliet

The Rubáiyát of Omar Khayyám

The Scarlet Letter

A Separate Peace

Silas Marner

Song of Solomon

The Sound and the Fury

The Stranger

A Streetcar Named Desire

Sula

The Tale of Genji

A Tale of Two Cities

"The Tell-Tale Heart" and Other Stories

Their Eyes Were Watching God

Things Fall Apart

To Kill a Mockingbird

Ulysses

Waiting for Godot

The Waste Land

Wuthering Heights

Young Goodman Brown

Edgar Allan Poe's
"The Tell-Tale Heart" and Other Stories
New Edition

Edited and with an introduction by
Harold Bloom
Sterling Professor of the Humanities
Yale University

BLOOM'S
LITERARY CRITICISM
An imprint of Infobase Publishing

Bloom's Modern Critical Interpretations:
"The Tell-Tale Heart" and Other Stories—New Edition

Bloom's Literary Criticism
An imprint of Infobase Publishing
132 West 31st Street
New York NY 10001

Library of Congress Cataloging-in-Publication Data
Edgar Allan Poe's "The tell-tale heart" and other stories / edited and with an introduction by Harold Bloom. — New ed.
     p. cm. — (Bloom's modern critical interpretations)
  Includes bibliographical references and index.
  ISBN 978-1-60413-388-2 (acid-free paper) 1. Poe, Edgar Allan, 1809–1849—Criticism and interpretation. I. Bloom, Harold. II. Title. Series.

  PS2638.E39 2009
  818'.309—dc22

                                        2008054307

Bloom's Literary Criticism books are available at special discounts when purchased in bulk quantities for businesses, associations, institutions, or sales promotions. Please call our Special Sales Department in New York at (212)967-8800 or (800)322-8755.

You can find Bloom's Literary Criticism on the World Wide Web at http://www.chelseahouse.com.

Contributing editor: Pamela Loos
Cover designed by Takeshi Takahashi

Printed in the United States of America
IBT EJB 10 9 8 7 6 5 4 3 2 1

This book is printed on acid-free paper.

All links and web addresses were checked and verified to be correct at the time of publication. Because of the dynamic nature of the web, some addresses and links may have changed since publication and may no longer be valid.

Contents

Editor's Note

My notorious introduction brought upon me the wrath of the Poe Society, but I admit that Poe is inescapable though a vicious stylist in all his work.

Critics however mostly delight in Poe, as do common readers, so I am merely a voice in the wilderness. Daniel Hoffman generously admires all the famous tales, while Walter Stepp studies the double in "The Cask of Amontillado."

A feminist reading of "The Tell-Tale Heart" is ventured by Gita Rajan, after which Henry Sussman boldly gives us postmodernist Poe.

We return to the "moral insanity" of "The Tell-Tale Heart" by Paige Matthey Bynum, while Shawn Rosenheim shrewdly examines Poe as detective fiction.

Death and the reader are concerns for Johann Pillai, after which we once more march onto "The Tell-Tale Heart" with Brett Zimmerman.

"The Fall of the House of Usher" is observed by John H. Timmerman, while Richard Kopley then concludes this volume by interestingly tracing "The Tell-Tale Heart"'s influence on Hawthorne.

HAROLD BLOOM

Introduction

I

Valéry, in a letter to Gide, asserted that "Poe is the only impeccable writer. He was never mistaken." If this judgment startles an American reader, it is less remarkable than Baudelaire's habit of making his morning prayers to God and to Edgar Poe. If we add the devotion of Mallarmé to what he called his master Poe's "severe ideas," then we have some sense of the scandal of what might be called "French Poe," perhaps as much a Gallic mystification as "French Freud." French Poe is less bizarre than French Freud, but more puzzling, because its literary authority ought to be overwhelming, and yet vanishes utterly when confronted by what Poe actually wrote. Here is the second stanza of the impeccable writer's celebrated lyric, "For Annie":

Sadly, I know
I am shorn of my strength,
And no muscle I move
As I lie at full length—
But no matter!—I feel
I am better at length.

Though of a badness not to be believed, this is by no means unrepresentative of Poe's verse. Aldous Huxley charitably supposed that Baudelaire, Mallarmé, and Valéry simply had no ear for English, and so just could not hear Poe's palpable vulgarity. Nothing even in Poe's verse is so wickedly

1

funny as Huxley's parody in which a grand Miltonic touchstone is transmuted into the mode of Poe's "Ulalume." First Milton, in *Paradise Lost*, 4.268–273:

> Not that fair field
> Of Enna, where Proserpine gathering flowers
> Her self a fairer flower by gloomy Dis
> Was gathered, which cost Ceres all that pain
> To seek her through the world;

Next, Huxley's Poe:

> It was noon in the fair field of Enna,
> When Proserpina gathering flowers—
> Herself the most fragrant of flowers,
> Was gathered away to Gehenna
> By the Prince of Plutonian powers;
> Was borne down the windings of Brenner
> To the gloom of his amorous bowers—
> Down the tortuous highway of Brenner
> To the God's agapemonous bowers.

What then did Baudelaire hear, what music of thought, when he read the actual Poe of "Ulalume"?

> Here once, through an alley Titanic,
> Of cypress, I roamed with my Soul—
> Of cypress, with Psyche, my Soul.
> These were days when my heart was volcanic
> As the scoriac rivers that roll—
> As the lavas that restlessly roll
> Their sulphurous currents down Yaanek,
> In the ultimate climes of the Pole—
> That groan as they roll down Mount Yaanek,
> In the realms of the Boreal Pole.

If this were Edward Lear, poet of "The Dong with the Luminous Nose" or "The Jumblies," one might not question Baudelaire and the other apostles of French Poe. But the hard-driven Poe did not set out to write nonsense verse. His desire was to be the American Coleridge or Byron or Shelley, and his poetry, at its rare best, echoes those High Romantic forerunners with some grace and a certain plangent urgency. Yet even "The City in the Sea" is a touch too close to Byron's "Darkness," while "Israfel" weakly revises Shelley's "To a Skylark." Nineteenth-century American poetry is considerably better than it is generally acknowledged to be. There are no other figures comparable to Whitman and Dickinson, but at least the following are clearly preferable to Poe, taking them chronologically: Bryant, Emerson, Longfellow, Whittier, Jones Very, Thoreau, Melville, Timrod, and Tuckerman. Poe scrambles for twelfth place with Sidney Lanier; if this judgment seems harsh, or too arithmetical, it is prompted by the continued French overvaluation of Poe as lyricist. No reader who cares deeply for the best poetry written in English can care greatly for Poe's verse. Huxley's accusation of vulgarity and bad taste is just: "To the most sensitive and high-souled man in the world we should find it hard to forgive, shall we say, the wearing of a diamond ring on every finger. Poe does the equivalent of this in his poetry; we notice the solecism and shudder."

II

Whatever his early ambitions, Poe wrote relatively little verse; there are scarcely a hundred pages of it in the remarkable new edition of his complete writings, in two substantial volumes, published by the Library of America. The bulk of his work is in tale-telling and criticism, with the exception of the problematic *Eureka: A Prose Poem*, a hundred-page cosmology that I take to be Poe's answer to Emerson's Transcendental manifesto, *Nature*. Certainly *Eureka* is more of a literary achievement than Poe's verse, while the popularity and influence of the shorter tales has been and remains immense. Whether either *Eureka* or the famous stories can survive authentic criticism is not clear, but nothing could remove the stories from the canon anyway. They are a permanent element in Western literary culture, even though they are best read when we are very young. Poe's criticism has mixed repute, but in fact has never been made fully available until the Library of America edition.

Poe's survival raises perpetually the issue as to whether literary merit and canonical status necessarily go together. I can think of no other American writer, down to this moment, at once so inevitable and so dubious. Mark Twain catalogued Fenimore Cooper's literary offenses, but all that he exuberantly listed are minor compared to Poe's. Allen Tate, proclaiming Poe "our cousin" in 1949, at the centenary of Poe's death, remarked, "He has several styles, and it is not possible to damn them all at once." Uncritical admirers of Poe should be asked to read his stories aloud (but only to themselves!). The association between the acting style of Vincent Price and the styles of Poe is alas not gratuitous, and indeed is an instance of deep crying out unto deep. Lest I be considered unfair by those devoted to Poe, I hasten

to quote him at his strongest as a storyteller. Here is the opening paragraph
of "William Wilson," a tale admired by Dostoyevski and still central to the
great Western topos of the double:

> Let me call myself, for the present, William Wilson. The fair
> page lying before me need not be sullied with my real appellation.
> This has already been too much an object for the scorn—for the
> horror—for the detestation of my race. To the utter-most regions
> of the globe have not indignant winds bruited its unparalleled
> infamy? Oh, outcast of all outcasts most abandoned!—to the earth
> art thou not forever dead? to its honors, to its flowers, to its golden
> aspirations?—and a cloud, dense, dismal, and limitless, does it not
> hang eternally between thy hopes and heaven?

This rhetoric, including the rhetorical questions, is British Gothic
rather than German Gothic, Ossian or Monk Lewis rather than Tieck
or E. T. A. Hoffmann. Its palpable squalors require no commentary. The
critical question surely must be: how does "William Wilson" survive its
bad writing? Poe's awful diction, whether here or in "The Fall of the House
of Usher" or "The Purloined Letter," seems to demand the decent mask-
ing of a competent French translation. The tale somehow is stronger than
its telling, which is to say that Poe's actual text does not matter. What
survives, despite Poe's writing, are the psychological dynamics and mythic
reverberations of his stories about William Wilson and Roderick Usher.
Poe can only gain by a good translation, and scarcely loses if each reader
fully retells the stories to another. C.S. Lewis, defending the fantasies of
George Macdonald, formulated a curious principle that seems to me more
applicable to Poe than to Macdonald:

> The texture of his writing as a whole is undistinguished, at times
> fumbling. . . . But this does not quite dispose of him even for
> the literary critic. What he does best is fantasy—fantasy that
> hovers between the allegorical and the mythopoeic. And this, in
> my opinion, he does better than any man. The critical problem
> with which we are confronted is whether this art—the art of
> mythmaking—is a species of the literary art. The objection to so
> classifying it is that the Myth does not essentially exist in words at
> all. We all agree that the story of Balder is a great myth, a thing of
> inexhaustible value. But of whose version—whose *words*—are we
> thinking when we say this?
>
> (*George Macdonald, An Anthology*)

Lewis replies that he is not thinking of anyone's words, but of a particular pattern of events. Of course that means Lewis is thinking of his own words. He goes so far as to remember

> when I first heard the story of Kafka's *Castle* related in conversation and afterwards read the book for myself. The reading added nothing. I had already received the myth, which was all that mattered.

Clearly mistaken about Kafka, Lewis was certainly correct about Macdonald's *Lilith*, and I think the insight is valid for Poe's stories. Myths matter because we prefer them in our own words, and so Poe's diction scarcely distracts us from our retelling, to ourselves, his bizarre myths. There is a dreadful universalism pervading Poe's weird tales. The Freudian reductions of Marie Bonaparte pioneered at converting Poe's universalism into the psychoanalytical universalism, but Poe is himself so reductive that the Freudian translations are in his case merely redundant. Poe authentically frightens children, and the fright can be a kind of trauma. I remember reading Poe's tales and Bram Stoker's *Dracula*, each for the first time, when I was about 10. *Dracula* I shrugged off (at least until I confronted Bela Lugosi murmuring: "I never drink—wine!") but Poe induced nasty and repetitious nightmares that linger even now. Myth may be only what the Polish aphorist Stanislaw Lec once called it, "gossip grown old," but then Poe would have to be called a very vivid gossip, though not often a very eloquent one.

III

Poe is an inescapable writer, but not a good one. He is, except perhaps for Mark Twain, the most popular of all American authors. The experience of reading Poe's stories out loud to oneself is not aesthetically very satisfying. Greatly improved by translation (even into English), Poe's tales have transcended their palpable flaws in style and diction. As editor of this volume, I am acutely conscious that I am in the critical minority with regard to Poe. Having just reread four of his most famous stories— "The Fall of the House of Usher," "The Tell-Tale Heart," "The Cask of Amontillado," "The Pit and the Pendulum"—I find myself challenged to account for the gap between Poe's worldwide influence and the literary inadequacy of even his best work.

Mythopoeic power in the great Romantics—Blake and Shelley among them—is accompanied by astonishing eloquence. No one—not even a skeptic like me—can deny Poe's strength and fecundity as a mythmaker. The mythic force of Poe's tales, even of his dreadful poems, remains undiminished. Try retelling "The Fall of the House of Usher" to a friend (if you can find one who hasn't read it, or seen a film version!), and I think it likely that you may improve upon the original. The exact words of the story scarcely matter, and yet the fable persists, and continues to enchant millions around the globe. I cannot think of any other author who writes so abominably, and yet is so clearly destined to go on being canonical.

Harry Levin, 50 years ago, observed that Poe's writing "smells of the thesaurus." That was a kind judgment, since Poe's synonyms rarely are appropriate for one another. Poe's partisans excuse him by arguing that he was always in a hurry because of financial pressures, but I doubt that more leisure would have improved his style. I quote, utterly at random, from "The Fall of the House of Usher," and again I urge that you read this out loud to yourself, since that forces one to slow down and listen:

> I have said that the sole effect of my somewhat childish experiment—
> that of looking down the tarn—had been to deepen the first
> singular impression. There can be no doubt that the consciousness
> of the rapid increase of my superstition—for why should I not so
> term it?—served mainly to accelerate the increase itself. Such, I
> have long known, is the paradoxical law of all sentiments having
> terror as a basis. And it might have been for this reason only, that,
> when I again uplifted my eyes to the house itself, from its image
> in the pool, there grew in my mind a strange fancy—a fancy so
> ridiculous, indeed, that I but mention it to show the vivid force
> of the sensations which oppressed me. I had so worked upon my
> imagination as really to believe that about the whole mansion and
> domain there hung an atmosphere which had no affinity with the
> air of heaven, but which had reeked up from the decayed trees, and
> the gray wall, and the silent tarn—a pestilent and mystic vapour,
> dull, sluggish, faintly discernible, and leaden-hued.

That "pestilent and mystic vapour, dull, sluggish, faintly discernible, and leaden-hued" could be marketed as Essence of Poe, if we bottled it. We would do equally well had Poe written: "pestilent and mystic Roderick Usher, dull, sluggish, faintly discernible, and leaden-hued," since poor Roderick is only a vapour, but then so is the entire story. Critics agitate themselves as to whether the Lady Madeline Usher is a vampire, or whether she and Roderick have indulged a taste for incest. Everyone in Poe is more or less a vampire, but characters in Poe, particularly the Ushers, hardly seem robust enough to make love. When the undead Madeline "with a low moaning cry, fell heavily inward upon the person of her brother," that may well have been both their initial and final physical contact, more than sufficient to destroy them both.

Their relationship is as vaporous as the rest of the story, including its narrator, himself very dim.

Still, however I scoff, "The Fall of the House of Usher" persists. Where does one locate its mythic appeal? Poe achieves the universality of nightmare, and that is certainly an attainment, though not necessarily a literary one. We have other authors who have given us peculiarly American nightmares, but only Poe's phantasmagorias export equally well to France and to Russia, to Singapore and to Sumatra. Nightmares are Poe's staple: he frightens children, who discover dreadful intimacies in his worst imaginings. Murderer and victim alike are equally ghastly in "The Tell-Tale Heart" and "The Cask of Amontillado." I remember, as a child, being badly upset by both stories, and frightened out of sleep by the egregiously horrible "The Pit and the Pendulum." Myths of victimage, of being buried alive, of houses falling in upon one, have been more than myths throughout history, and are peculiarly disturbing in our post-Holocaust world. Something primordial in Poe tapped into a universal anguish. Perhaps it is just as well that he wrote so badly; his myths are effective enough to render his readers vulnerable to even his weakest imaginings. I at least would not want a stronger Poe.

DANIEL HOFFMAN

Grotesques and Arabesques

'Of my country and of my family I have little to say,' says the narrator of 'MS. Found in a Bottle.' The teller of 'Berenice' confesses, 'My baptismal name is Egaeus; that of my family I will not mention,' while Poe in 'A Tale of the Ragged Mountains,' writes of his chief character, 'Of his family I could obtain no satisfactory account.'

These anonymous and unfamilied heroes can of course be explained away as the self-projections of their orphaned and disinherited author. Yet this does not sufficiently account for the denial to so many of his characters of a patrimony or a name. Knowing Poe, knowing the *underlying consistency* of all of his work (I italicize the phrase, as he would have done), is there not likely a *philosophical necessity* for certain of his characters to step into our consciousness as though unsired? I thought perhaps Poe kept this reason out of sight in some subterranean chamber, entombed like so many of the victims in his tales, allowing it to work upon us only indirectly as he says allegory best operates. Then, quite by chance—like Monsieur Dupin or the husband of Ligeia or the narrator of 'The Raven'—plucking from the bookshelf of an obscure library (it was the Reference Room in the collections of the Royal Borough of Kensington, in Horton Street, W.8) a volume of unworldly lore, I came, in Porphyry's *On the Life of Plotinos*, upon the following curious passage:

From *Poe Poe Poe Poe Poe Poe Poe*, pp. 205–232. © 1972 by Daniel Hoffman.

> Plotinos, the philosopher our contemporary, seemed ashamed of being in the body.
>
> So deeply rooted was this feeling that he could never be induced to tell of his ancestry, his parentage, or his birthplace.

Birthplace, parentage, ancestry—these are the attributes of body. To the soul they are inessential accidents. And the direction of Poe's mind, the thrust of his imagination is—may I restate the obvious?—away from the body and toward the spirit, away from the 'dull realities' of this world, toward the transcendent consciousness on 'a far happier star.' His protagonists are all attempting to get out of the clotted condition of their own materiality, to cross the barrier between the perceptible sensual world and that which lies beyond it. And so they undertake hazardous voyages, either into the stratosphere or to the moon; or by descending into dungeons and vaults in the earth; or down maelstroms in the sea toward the center of the very world. Others cross the bourne between our life and another by breaking through the barrier of silence and speaking from beyond the grave. Some achieve this posthumous eloquence as the result of a mesmerical suspension of mortality; some, consuming inordinate amounts of laudanum, take the trip on drugs. Still others have already arrived at the desired condition of immaterial existence and speak to one another, in 'Colloquies' and 'Conversations,' as disembodied shades.

But for those Poe stories in which the characters are still alive, it may be inessential, indeed distracting, to establish a recognizable place as the locus of the action, as it is to provide the participants with a realistic station in life or a family. How many of Poe's tales (bar 'The Gold Bug' and 'A Tale of the Ragged Mountains') can be said to take place in the South, or for that matter in the United States, or, by the evidence of their texts, in the nineteenth century? Still, I do not propose that *all* of his fictions are suspended in time and unfixed in locus. In many both place and time are indeed specific. These on inspection prove to be either his detection tales (which most concertedly of his serious fictions do explore a real world), or his grotesques. Satire, the prevailing grotesque tone, is for Poe a lower exercise of the imagination than those fictions which discover the truths of the soul.

Hence the buffoonish tone of those sketches which treat of dull realities. Hence the tone of excitation, the breathless terror and ecstatic fixation in those tales which explore the soulscape rather than the social milieu in which a soul is fated to exist.

Everyone knows that Poe himself points to such a division between his tales by giving his volume in 1840 the double title, *Tales of the Grotesque and Arabesque*. Poe scholars agree that A. H. Quinn correctly identified the source of these odd terms in Poe's critical vocabulary as Sir Walter Scott's essay, 'On the Supernatural in Fictitious Composition,' *Fortnightly Review* (1827). Much has been made over the exact meanings of 'arabesque' and 'grotesque,' and whether we can apply them only to the tales in the 1840 volume or use them as pigeonholes in which to sort out all of Poe's fictions. Although Poe in his criticism is forever, as we have seen, making rigid distinctions, this particular pair of terms has made for as much confusion as clarification of his intentions. A reordering of the works is in order.

I take 'grotesque' and 'arabesque' to indicate two fundamentally different intentions on the part of the fictioneer. Roughly stated, a grotesque is a satire, an arabesque a prose equivalent of a poem. The terms themselves, as used by Scott—and presumably by Poe—derive not from the vocabulary of literature but from that of art, decor, architecture. In this they resemble that parent term, Gothic, of which they are, for Poe, subdivisions.

In an art work, *grotesque* signifies the depiction of monsters in an elaborate, foliated setting; while *arabesque* refers to an intricate pattern, geometric in design, which does not reproduce the human form—this latter element deriving from the Mohammedan injunction against the reproduction in a work of art of that divine image, the human body. *Arabesque* thus links Poe's practice as a writer of Gothic tales with the desired condition toward which his imagination ever impels him: renunciation and transcendence of the body. It connects also with his interest in that other Romantic craze, Arabiana, already touched on in such poems as 'Al Aaraaf' and 'Israfel.' The intricacy of pattern in an arabesque corresponds to Poe's desire, or need, to reveal by complex and elaborate concealments of his theme. There is no *human form* anywhere in Poe's arabesques; but their intricate patterns of abstraction create a synthetic and harmonious—though often horrifying—experience, a consistency.

When a compulsive theoretician of literary form draws the terms of his distinctions from another art, the fact seems both worthy of notice and an invitation to inference. There is evident an irreconcilable difference in both the intention and the mode of operation between a work of fiction and a pictorial or three-dimensional art form. A fiction, as Poe elsewhere says repeatedly enough, requires a plot, indeed hinges upon its plot; and what is plot but the management of a human action in time? But painting, architecture, décor—the arts to which the terms *grotesque* and *arabesque* are more properly applied—have nothing to do with plots or actions, they are concerned with the arrangements of elements in space. Such arts are essentially static, devoid (usually) of human content, and constitute expressions by a shaping aesthetic sense of its chosen materials. The reasons may readily be inferred why Poe's fictions so often resemble *tableaux vivants*, his *tableaux vivants* so readily becoming *tableaux morts*.

* * *

I propose to disregard Poe's use of these terms only for the tales in his 1840 volume, but rather to regard them as indicative of two of his principal commitments of the imagination in his fiction. (Always excepted from these considerations are his tales of ratiocination, in which, to be sure, elements of both the grotesque and the arabesque appear.) By an inductive analysis of Poe's stories, such as he himself (I would like to think) might desire us to make upon his *oeuvre*, I intuit the following criteria for his tales of the Grotesque and the Arabesque. (Henceforth I shall capitalize them as generic nouns, as Poe did in his title.)

A Grotesque is not debarred from representing a real person, but it must do so in a caricature, making monstrosities of realities. Consequently we discover that all of Poe's Grotesques are set in contemporary time, and many are satires of recognizable persons and events. (E.g., the send-up of General Winfield Scott in 'The Man That Was Used Up'; the put-down of the Gold Rush in 'Von Kempelen and His Discovery'; the attacks on contemporary government and philosophy in 'Some Words with a Mummy' and 'Mellonta Tauta.') Poe's Arabesques, however, are set in unspecified time and in imaginary places (as is true of 'Ligeia,' 'The Fall of the House of Usher,' 'Berenice,' etc.). In the Arabesques there are a very few characters—a narrator, two or three others—but the Grotesques may have a cast of a dozen characters or more, although there is no effort to give these personages more than one dimension.

Although the two modes seem mutually exclusive, Poe on examination proves often to have written an Arabesque and a Grotesque on the same theme. His variable sense of gravity enables such divagations to appear in his work. How often haven't we wildly swung between ecstasy and revulsion, between hoax and revelation, between flapdoodle and the sublime! Some may think this proof of Poe's instability, his inability to control his tone. Or perhaps his Imp of the Perverse leads him to mock in Grotesques the achievement of his own Arabesques, as though to put his work beyond the reach of parody by others. Consider. What is 'A Predicament,' that preposterous parody—ostensibly—of a *Blackwood's* story, but a parody—in fact—of Poe's own (and as yet unwritten) 'The Pit and the Pendulum'? And speaking of his 'Imp of the Perverse,' what other than that Imp made him turn the other way and write 'The Angel of the Odd'—a laborious spoof of a simpleton prone to take too many drams, who comes thereby to the frustration of great expectations. Yet again, what is 'Some Words with a Mummy' but a send-up of the very theme taken seriously in 'Mesmeric Revelations,' although to be sure that itself was a hoax to begin with—a hoax of serious intent. But then again, *all* of Poe's hoaxes have a serious intent, somewhere. 'Thou Art the Man' is such a hoax (the narrator knowing the solution all the time), and it is a version, in the mode of frontier humor (the native Grotesque) of the detection theme presented more seriously, more skillfully, and in a more cosmopolitan vehicle in 'The Purloined Letter.' 'The Masque of the Red Death' is one of Poe's most memorable Arabesques, parodied, so to speak, by a Grotesque on the very same theme, 'King Pest.' And, as the present chapter will indicate, other such pairs of linked dissimilars include 'Eleonora' and 'Loss of Breath'; 'Ligeia' and 'The Spectacles'; 'The Cask of Amontillado' and 'The Premature Burial.'

What characterizes the Arabesques is their exploration of extreme psychological states—the narrators or chief characters are often madmen, or persons who undergo some excruciating suffering of the soul. Insofar as the Grotesque is a mode of satire, it depends on a rationalistic view of experience as the norm against which the recorded monstrous defections be measured; but in the Grotesques the ratiocinative power leads not to the perception of ecstasy, as in the tales of detection and exploration, but rather to the exposure of the idiocy of the monstrous world.

Yet a further inference from Poe's duplicity in the treatment of so many of his themes is this: Chief among his themes is duplicity itself. The doubleness of experience. How can we tell the reality from its mirror, the world from its picture in a work of art, the image from the image of the image? Poe, whose entire enterprise is a desperate effort to *unify* our existence on this suffering globe of shards, himself sees that all of our passions, intuitions, thoughts, are susceptible of inversion, may become their opposites, so that ecstatic transcendence may be lodged in the heart of a hoax. Identity itself, the very vessel of perception, may be fatally flawed, fatally broken in twain. One of Poe's themes is the fate of the man haunted by his own double, his anima, his weird. Which is the real consciousness, the 'I' who speaks or the doppelgänger who pursues him?

Seeing Double

Had I not been thus prolix, you might either have misunderstood me altogether, or, with the rabble, have fancied me mad. As it is, you will easily perceive that I am one of the many uncounted victims of the Imp of the Perverse.

Thus speaks Hoaxiepoe in his earnest guise as truthsayer. It is evident, if only from the sentences just quoted, that the author is aware of deep cleavages in his own self—or, in the terminology of his time, in his soul. He appears, to himself as well as to others, as both sane and mad; as both a civil workaday person who keeps appointments and earns his wages, and as a victim of the Imp of the Perverse. This Imp, it will be recalled, is that principle which compels us to 'act, for the reason that we should *not*. . . . Nor will this overwhelming tendency to do wrong for the wrong's sake, admit of analysis, or resolution into ulterior elements. It is a radical, a primitive impulse.'

Poe speaks here with unexampled knowledge of the hidden self within the self. In 'The Imp of the Perverse' he summons the courage so to expose his secret sinfulness only because, like J. Alfred Prufrock, he speaks from across a bourne from which no traveller returns: it is his gallows confession, his confession of his confession of his motiveless crime, a crime which had been perfect except for his double compulsion to perform that which he should not do: first to murder his victim (no details are given as to any injury the victim may have done him), then, 'as [he] reflected upon [his] absolute security,' to confess—to rush down the street crying aloud his guilt—which had otherwise been undetected. Curiously, the mode of the murder's commission was suffocation: he substituted for his victim's night-candle a poisonous candle of his own devising. Curiously again, when apprehended, 'I turned—I gasped for breath. For a moment I experienced all the pangs of suffocation. . . .' Everything is doubled, as the punishment fits the crime.

Who, or what, is this Imp of the Perverse but a portion of the ego separated out from the rest, which seeks the destruction of that from which it is separated? The fact that it may seek its own destruction too does not deter it from its calamitous purpose. Life is on a collision course with death; the death-wish betrays, whenever it can, the life instinct. This seems madness, the mind undoing its own self-protective calculation by an uncontrollable, 'a radical, a primitive impulse.'

This impulse is so primitive, so uncanny, so terrifying that in 'The Imp of the Perverse' it appears only as a malignant force impelling the protagonist. He cannot objectify it as a character. But if this impulse to undo one's own security be considered in a comic rather than a terrifying aspect—as comedy is so often the obverse of terror—it can easily be objectified in a ridiculous guise. Stripped of its terror, it can make us—make author also—laugh, though to be sure its effect upon the self from which it has separated itself is every bit as disastrous as was that of the Imp of the Perverse, whose grotesque double is the Angel of the Odd. In Poe's sketch of that title, the protagonist—the primary self—is a perfectly ordinary *homme moyen sensuel*, to whom appears a ridiculous personage who comments upon his thoughts and plies him with drink. This Angel of the Odd, speaking in the Dutch dialect Poe had borrowed from Irving for 'Hans Pfaall,' is a personage constructed from a rum puncheon, kegs, bottles and a funnel. At his urging the narrator gets so drunk that he snoozes past the hour on which his fire insurance expired. Having missed the deadline for signing its renewal, he awakens to discover, naturally enough, that his house is on fire—and now he becomes temporarily blinded, is deserted by his fiancée, decides upon suicide, dives into a river, changes his mind, then rushes over a precipice—from which he is saved by his 'grasping the end of a long guide-rope, which depended from a passing balloon.' This is perhaps more silly than amusing, yet what does it burlesque but the very themes of self-destruction and escape from reality which elsewhere comprise the ballast of Poe's more serious tales?

Between them, 'The Imp of the Perverse' and 'The Angel of the Odd' state in outline form, as it were, many basic postulates of Poe's *donnée*: the division of the self, the destructive opposition of the death-wish and the life-wish; fear of death, blindness, suffocation (all, as Freud repeatedly shows, surrogate forms of castration-fear and fear of impotence); the unanticipated eruption of aggressive impulse, and of self-incrimination; the incurable addiction to drink (or drugs) which speeds the self-destructive impulse on its way; and the wish-fantasy of escape from all of these predicaments.

* * *

Some of this obsessive material becomes clear, because handled with masterful intelligence, in the story 'William Wilson.' The name William Wilson, as the narrator tells us, is a *nom pro tem*. The chosen disguise reveals that its bearer is, in his own view, self-begotten: he is William Wilson, William son of his own *Will*. He has, that is, willed himself into being—willed the self we meet, the one that survives its murder of its double. It's not entirely clear whether, at the end, as William Wilson sees his own bloodied face in a mirror where a moment earlier no mirror stood before, he does survive the murder of his doppelgänger, or whether he speaks his lurid confession from beyond the grave. If he survives, he does so in a condition of madness which his exacerbated prose style embodies and reveals:

> Let me call myself, for the present, William Wilson. The fair page lying before me need not be sullied with my real appellation. This has been already too much an object for the scorn—for the horror—for the detestation of my race. To the uttermost regions of the globe have not the indignant winds bruited its unparalleled infamy? Oh, outcast of all outcasts most abandoned!—to the earth art thou not forever dead? to its honors, to its flowers, to its golden aspirations?—and a cloud, dense, dismal, and limitless, does it not hang eternally between thy hopes and heaven?

These, as W. H. Auden was the first to notice, are the accents of lunacy—these triple iterations, these rhetorical inflations, these rhodomontades in which luxuriates an abandoned soul—accents which Poe gives his narrator as a means of establishing his character. True, in the body of the tale William Wilson does not rant and rave in three-decker clauses. Indeed, he tells his doomed screed with a reasonableness, a clarity, a perspicuous control of his own narrative which cannot fail to involve the reader in his fate. Unlike the narrator of 'The Tell-Tale Heart' ('why *will* you say that I am mad?'), the possibility of his own dementia never occurs to William Wilson. He is sane, he is cool, he is fully aware of his own doings. But there is one circumstance in his life he can only report, for he himself does not understand it. It is an urge to do evil: 'a sudden elevation in turpitude whose origin alone it is my present purpose to assign.'

What follows is the autobiography of 'William Wilson.' Its chief events are recognizably based upon two periods in Edgar Poe's own life, his boyhood schooldays at Stoke Newington in England and his misadventures at the gaming tables while a student in the University of Virginia. But these schoolboy remembrances are conflated in a tone and style of Byronic intensity. Indeed the shadow of Byron tinges this tale, for, as Arthur Hobson Quinn points out, Poe drew upon Irving's sketch 'An Unwritten Account of Lord Byron' (published in 1836) in its design.

Little did Poe know it, but in 'William Wilson' he made *so easy* Griswold's mission of calumniating his character! Not content with reproducing in William Wilson's history these two well-publicized episodes from his own life, he also assigned to his fictitious narrator *his own birthday*! The 19th of January, 1813. Or, in its first printing (1839), the 19th of January, 1811. (Poe kept moving his birthdate forward, in successive magazine biographies, in order to seem younger than he was. So, it appears, did William Wilson.) But to be scrupulous about it, Poe didn't actually say that it was *William Wilson* whose birth-date coincided with his own. He makes William Wilson say that 'My namesake was born on the nineteenth of January, 1813 [or 1811]— and this is a somewhat remarkable coincidence; for the day is precisely that of my own nativity.' By this time, William Wilson, the bully and scourge of the other boys at Dr. Bransby's dismal school, is himself the victim of the one among them who resists 'the imperiousness' of his disposition. This lad, by yet another singular coincidence, is also named William Wilson. (I shall hereinafter call him Wilson[2]).

William Wilson is tormented daily as Wilson[2] coolly imitates his manner, dress, and speech, though the one defect, the only one, in Wilson[2] is that he cannot speak louder than a whisper. Nevertheless, '*His singular whisper, it grew to be the very echo of my own.*' What is further curious is that none of the schoolboys but Wilson himself seems aware of the mocking and sarcastic harassment inflicted upon him by Wilson[2]. William at last is driven to try to murder his tormenting double: he approaches, by stealth, at night, the sleeping Wilson[2]. As he looks upon his victim he feels 'a numbness, an iciness of feeling . . . gasping for breath. . . .' For he is struck by the identity of the victim's appearance with his own. He flees, quitting the bedchamber, the school, this phase of his life.

Quickly to sum up the rest of the tale, William Wilson passes from Dr. Bransby's through Eton, from Eton to Oxford, by now possessing 'rooted habits of vice . . . soulless dissipation.' Now he arranges to cheat a lord of his patrimony with a fixed deck of cards. (No doubt Edgar here remembers his own *losing* at cards while at Virginia, in consequence of which debts he had to leave the University.) Just as he is about to clinch the trick, there seems to enter the dimly lit room that familiar stranger who is his nemesis. 'Who and what was this Wilson?—and whence came he?—and what were his purposes? Upon neither of these points could I be satisfied. . . .' William Wilson is his own obtuse narrator. Though he thinks himself as clever as might a Monsieur Dupin, he never acknowledges what is obvious to the reader—what Poe had made inevitable by giving this tale for epigraph these lines (which he made up, T. O. Mabbott says, but attributed to Chamberlayne's *Pharronida*),

> What say of it? what say CONSCIENCE grim,
> That spectre in my path?

Wilson[2] exposes William Wilson, forcing his immediate departure from Oxford in disgrace. But, he learns, '*I fled in vain. My evil destiny pursued me as if in exultation*,' pursued him to Paris, to Vienna, Berlin, Moscow. At last, William Wilson attends a masked ball in Naples, intent upon seducing the young wife of the Duke his host. There, too, in a costume exactly like his own, masked in black as he himself is, he sees his nemesis approach. In a frenzy Wilson drags his double into a little antechamber, and 'getting him at mercy, plunged my sword, with brute ferocity, repeatedly through and through his bosom.' Looking up, he discovers now a mirror where the wall had heretofore seemed blank, and 'as I stepped up to it in an extremity of terror, mine own image, but with features all pale and dabbled in blood, advanced to meet me with a feeble and tottering gait.' But no—

> It was Wilson; but he spoke no longer in a whisper, and I could have fancied that I myself was speaking while he said:
> '*You have conquered, and I yield. Yet henceforth art thou also dead—dead to the World, to Heaven, and to Hope! In me didst thou exist—and, in my death, see by this image, which is thine own, how utterly thou hast murdered thyself!*'

Utterly murdered thyself! What is CONSCIENCE, after all, but that part of the ego which regards the rest as an object *which it can judge*. The part so regarded is the less developed, the more infantile, regressive, narcissistic. The more primitive, the more uncontrolled, incivil, aggressive. But how can the evil-doing part of the ego survive the murder of its own judging half?

'William Wilson' is perhaps the most vivid and memorable of Romantic tales of the divided self. In its psychological probing, and in the success of its objectifying the twin irrepressible impulses *to do evil* and *to judge oneself*, it makes Stevenson's *Dr. Jekyll and Mr. Hyde* seem naïve. For how much closer to the inadmissible truth is Poe's resolution than Stevenson's, who makes the better of the two selves destroy its evil-doing double. In Poe's own country the only thing like 'William Wilson' is by that other demon-haunted genius, Mark Twain. But where Poe's tale is taut with demonic intensity, there is a wonderful hilarity in 'The Facts Concerning A Recent Carnival of Crime in Connecticut,' in which Mark Twain, tortured by his Calvinist conscience, outwits his tormentor—and murders him. Then he is free to slay enemies, cheat widows, and freely indulge that wayward, mischief-loving self whose life had been a perpetual pang of suffering thanks to Conscience.

But in Poe's 'William Wilson' the duplication of the self is more complex, the emotional logic more complicated. If William Wilson's double is his conscience, he is also his Imp of the Perverse. Which is to say that each half of the split ego has its own Imp of the Perverse—Wilson himself is such an Imp to Wilson, the first Wilson revelling in obliquity in acquiescence to a deep impulse in himself which outrages the moral imperative represented by Wilson[2]. On the point succeeding in his outrageous vices—bullying the schoolboys, tricking Lord Glendenning into cutting a marked deck, seducing the Duchess Di Broglio—what makes Wilson fail but the betrayal of his impulse to evil by his equally uncontrollable impulse to judge himself? No wonder he has no hope of Heaven at the end, for whichever Wilson he acts as, the other will arise to torment him. All the more damning because there's no vestige in Poe's tale of the damnatory Calvinism which in later life drove Mark Twain to the point of despair. When the Imp of the Perverse triumphs and rules unchallenged, as at the end of 'William Wilson,' that much of the self which survives is condemned to madness in the house of woe.

Murder!

Despite the strength of the death wish among Poe's characters, only in one tale does any of them literally commit suicide. In 'The Assignation' (one of Edgar's earliest Arabesques, begun as a parody of the *Blackwood's* type of Gothic tale), there are not one but *two* suicides: the Prince Mentoni and the Marchesa Aphrodite both perish by their own hands, at the stroke of the same hour on the clock. As the clock ticked on, Poe became more circumspect and skillful in the treatment of his pervasive theme. He puts a mask upon red death, as it were, and contrives at least two disguises for the self's will to destruction: (a) by dividing the ego into a self and a double, he enables one to murder the other in a dramatization of the suicide-wish; (b) without resort to such doubling, Poe contrives that the self undergo obsessive and repeated, *but involuntary*, mortal dangers, particularly by accidental and premature entombment. Such is the heavy burden of his putatively factual-autobiographical sketch, 'The Premature Burial.'

But there's yet a third device in Edgar's handling of his guilty secret and his secret guilt. To wit, (c), in which he doubles his character and then arranges for one self to *murder the other by burying him alive*. Such is the case, most memorably, in 'The Cask of Amontillado.' To understand, as fully as we must, who does what to whom, and why, when Montresor leaves Fortunato chained to the one wall with another, newly plastered, before him, let us consider Poe's affection for the motif of the premature burial. (It will recur also in 'The Black Cat,' and 'The Fall of the House of Usher'; and, with variations, in 'Berenice' and 'Ligeia.' We have already seen Poe's fondness for conferring death-like states upon the living, as in 'Monsieur Valdemar' and 'Mesmeric Revelation,' as well as for bringing the dead back to life, as in 'Some Words with a Mummy.')

'There are certain themes,' he writes, 'of which the interest is all-absorbing, but which are too entirely horrible for the purposes of legitimate fiction. . . . To be buried alive is, beyond question, the most terrific of these extremes which has ever fallen to the lot of mere mortality.' This 'ultimate woe' requires that 'the severity and majesty of truth sanctify and sustain' the author's presentation thereof. In this way Poe invokes the cloak of truth-telling, as had Defoe, Swift, and Richardson before him, for subjects and motives so different from his. What ensues in 'The Premature Burial' is a catalogue of suppositious occasions on which an unfortunate person, thought to be dead, was buried alive. Some were rescued from their vaults or tombs, one or two were later disinterred and discovered in the postures of horrible awareness of their terrifying predicaments: '. . . Thus she remained, and thus she rotted, erect.'

At the last, the truth-teller tells of his own experience, of which the foregoing were but simulacra. Being subject to epileptic seizures, it is not surprising he should be obsessed by the fear of being buried while in a trance. He even has had his family vault 'so remodelled as to admit of being readily opened from within.' No wonder he has made a scrapbook of every occurrence the world over of the accident he most fears. On one occasion—the last which his tale recounts—he seemed to awaken in a closely confined wooden space, all dark . . .

> there came suddenly to my nostrils the strong peculiar odor of
> moist earth. . . . I was *not* within the vault. I had fallen into a trance
> while absent from home—while among strangers—when, or how,
> I could not remember—and it was they who had buried me as a

dog—nailed up in some coffin—and thrust, deep, deep, and for ever, into some ordinary and nameless *grave*.

This seems as horrifying as the worst of the other predicaments Poe has bestowed upon his tortured narrators—groping in the pit, lying bound beneath the pendulum, whirling in the maelstrom, being stabbed by one's double. It is just here, at this point, that 'truth' intervenes, to turn horror to mere nightmare and to restore the bright light of rational exposition to a circumstance too dreadful for the soul to bear. The narrator of 'The Premature Burial' screams and attracts the attention of strangers who 'restored [him] to the full possession of [his] memory.' Now he recalls that he had gone to sleep in the narrow cabin of a sloop bearing a cargo of garden mould. It was no more than that, and the terror is completely explained away. His tortures, he concludes,

> were inconceivably hideous; but out of Evil proceeded Good; for their very excess wrought in my spirit an inevitable revulsion. My soul acquired tone—acquired temper. I went abroad. I took vigorous exercise. I breathed the free air of Heaven. I thought upon other subjects than Death. . . . I read no 'Night Thoughts,' no fustian about church-yards—no bugaboo tables—*such as this*. In short, I became a new man, and lived a man's life.

Poor Eddie. What this rather labored sketch is trying to tell us is, 'I *wish* I could thus easily rid myself of these obsessive hallucinations.' Calling 'The Premature Burial' a bugaboo tale, Eddie admits that he cannot shake himself free from the long shadow, the gasping breath, the feeling of fatal and foetal enclosure.

If he cannot be free from it, though, he can figure out *how best to make use of it* in his ratiocinative-ecstatic-horrific tales. By means of whose telling he can all but control the terrors that shake him to the marrow of his soul.

Doomed to live in his own time, Poe had to be his own alienist. In 1844 there was no physician in America who could have given Poe a better understanding of his terrors than he himself so painfully arrived at. A century later he could have read about such things in Dr. Karl Menninger's study, *Man Against Himself*. He might have found a real-life counterpart to the sufferer in his own 'The Premature Burial':

> One recalls the extraordinary career of Harry Houdini (Ehrich Weiss) who was particularly fond of extricating himself from apparently inextricable situations,

and here Menninger quotes from an article about Houdini in *The Psycho-analytic Review*,

> straightjackets, all manner of manacles, chains, handcuffs, prison cells, chests, hampers, glass boxes, roll-top desks, and even iron boilers. With his arms thoroughly secured he leaped from bridges, suspended head downward by block and tackle he loosened himself from meshes of constricting apparatus. He allowed himself to be chained and buried in six feet of earth, to be locked in steel vaults, to be nailed in huge packing cases. Once, breaking free after an endeavor lasting over an hour, he said, "The pain, torture, agony, and misery of that struggle will forever live in my mind." His variations on the escape act were endless, nothing being too bizarre, tedious, or difficult so long as the principles of a constraining force were present.

Was there ever so close a reenactment of Poe's most horror-struck fantasies? Houdini's escapes recapitulate the predicaments of Poe's hapless balloon-ists, the fears of his epileptic, the fates of his voyager Pym and of Madeline Usher. Of Houdini, Menninger continues,

> His most dramatic escapes were from coffins buried underground and from chains while under water.

But what does it all mean? Why did Houdini seek out, as though impelled by some principle of perversity, situations so claustrophobic and predica-ments so difficult of egress?

> Coupled with this, unconsciously, is the fact that he had an extraordinary attachment for his mother which strongly affected his entire life . . .

And the author in *The Psychoanalytic Review* opined that 'almost every stunt staged by Houdini represented a form of pseudo-suicide.' Now, Menninger himself concludes that

> We have no right then to dismiss the significance of a particular method of committing suicide [or pseudo-suicide] as meaningless. In the light of clinical experience we know with a fair degree of definiteness what some of these symbols, and hence these methods, mean. . . . Such fantasies may be accompanied by a strong sense of

guilt and there is a well-known (concomitant) conception of the womb, or entry into the womb, as being something terrible. This we recognize in the nature of the mythological representations of entering life hereafter—the dog Cerberus, the terrible river Styx, purgatory and so on.

Alas the poor psychotic imagination, to which everything that counts for anything becomes both itself and its opposite: Death is an image of birth, birth of death, and suicide and murder partake of each other's character in the throes of the struggle between Eros and Thanatos, the id and the super-ego, the self and the world.

* * *

'The thousand injuries of Fortunato I had borne as best I could, but when he ventured upon insult, I vowed revenge.' So begins the narrator of 'The Cask of Amontillado,' who, like the Ancient Mariner in Coleridge's *Rime*, has but this one tale to tell—and that fifty years after the event. But what injuries Fortunato had done him, or what insult, he never reveals. These offenses are as mysterious, as shrouded, or—as we now say—as repressed as the crimes committed by the mysterious stranger in Poe's sketch 'The Man of the Crowd'; as rancorous and secret as the wound given Monsieur Dupin by the Minister D—. All we are given is this miscreant's name: Fortunato. The injured party who revels in the perfection of his revenge is Montresor.

Mon*tresor*. *Fortun*ato. Are these not synonymous? When Montresor leads Fortunato down into the farthest vault of his family's wine cellar, into a catacombs of human bones, is he not, like William Wilson, conducting his double thither? My treasure, my fortune, down into the bowels of the earth, a charnel-house of bones.

But if Fortunato is Montresor's double, he is not, like Wilson, his conscience. Indeed, Fortunato appears a pathetic adversary. When first seen—as in the *dénouement* of 'William Wilson' and 'The Masque of the Red Death,' it is during carnival—he is wearing motley, cap and bells, and is quite drunk. No difficult thing for Montresor to play upon his enemy's vanity as a connoisseur of wines (Fortunate would seem already a victim of the Imp of the Perverse, masquerading as the Angel of the Odd). Montresor easily cajoles him down into the vault to taste his newly purchased Amontillado. As Montresor feverishly walls up the crypt into which he has chained the hapless Fortunato, the last sound he hears is the jingling of his bells. At this, he says, 'My heart grew sick—on account of the dampness of the catacombs.' For fifty years no mortal has disturbed his handiwork, the wall of bones and stones behind which the remains of Fortunato, still

chained to the rock, stand now. (Like the unfortunate lady in 'The Premature Burial,' he has rotted erect.)

But has not Montresor walled up himself in this revenge? Of what else
can we think, can he have thought for the past half-century, but of that
night's vengeance upon his enemy? His freedom to do otherwise stands
chained in the dank vault with Fortunato.

A somewhat different thesis is maintained by Mme Bonaparte. She
finds the wine-cellar—the long, dark, dank tunnel of human remains—to be
an obvious, indeed an importunate, symbol of the maternal womb and the
entrance thither, and Montresor, leading Fortunato ever deeper to effect his
execution, is committing the murder of his father-figure in the act of possessing the mother's body. The fact that the names of the two characters are
interchangeable synonyms may seem to buttress this assertion.

Come to think of it, how can we deny the thesis? But, on thinking
further, how can we accept it as a full exposition of the narrator's horrible
purpose, his malignancy, his compulsion fifty years ago so to act, his obsession now to confess his action? Considering the persons, circumstances, and
objects in this very brief tale in connection not only with the universal significations which psychiatric studies place upon them, but also the equally
universal significations they attract to themselves as members of Poe's *oeuvre*,
some further notions come symbiotically into play.

If, as I maintain, the two are doubles, it is doubtless of some moment
that one, Montresor, is in full possession of his wits, acts ruthlessly according to his premeditated plan, and exercises aggressive and total power over
the other. That other, Fortunato, on the contrary is from the start befuddled
by both vanity and inebriation; acts on sudden impulse; assumes good will
where Montresor is malice incarnate; and suffers as the passive, total victim of his adversary's malign cunning. The aggressor is presented as aggran-
dized by his victory, the victim as already degraded and ridiculous (as well as
pathetic) in his sufferings.

His ridiculousness is symbolized by his costume: 'The man wore motley.
He had on a tight-fitting parti-striped dress, and his head was surmounted
by the comical cap and bells.' These are the bells whose jangling is the last
sound Montresor hears from behind the wall of Fortunato's tomb. Now, the
cap and bells are of course everywhere acknowledged as signs of the Fool, but
why is the Fool so crowned? The cap needs no description—we immediately
see it as the bent conical foolscap of tradition, perhaps with a pompom, tas-
sel, or bell at the very tip, while the bells would likely be bunched in clusters above each of the wearer's ears. Anyone familiar with the Fool's antics
in folk pageantry will not miss his personification, particularly around the
head, of the male member. The Fool is man's lustful nature made absurd and
comical. If Fortunato is Montresor's double or the image of his father, he is

made to appear ridiculous in motley because he also represents the all but irrepressible stirrings and strivings of Montresor's own sexual nature. Thus 'The Cask of Amontillado' is, whatever else it may be, a screed of psychomachia, in which the calculating intellectual principle cleverly tricks, entraps, immobilizes and extinguishes the body. What were the injuries and insults of Fortunato upon Montresor? Among others, they include the denial by the former to the latter of that transcendence, that beatitude, which cannot be known to the soul still harassed and enslaved by passion.

So by interring Fortunato, Montresor at once has symbolically slain his own father and rival for his mother's affection, and forever interred his own passion, his own fertility, his own vitality. This narrator has indeed acted in accordance with—has indeed become—his Imp of the Perverse. But is he liberated thereby to experience the transcendent bliss which the insults of Fortunato had denied him? Not a bit of it. He too is dead to the world, immobile, chained to the rock of his one guilt-ridden act of aggression against Father and Self. This is the horrible truth he did not learn until he had experienced it.

And how appropriate it is that such a dreadful aggression against the self be enacted in a place which cannot but suggest the mother's womb, in its aspect of the terrifying: a charnel-house of bones, the family vault. Here is the undoubted source of Montresor's/Fortunato's being.

Poe seems as fixated as his Montresor, but not as successfully has the author himself interred his own vitality-principle. If he tells essentially the same tale over and over, he yet tells it differently every time. This must be the distinction, in art as in life, between symbol and real action. Symbolic action can repeat itself with variations till the end of time, but a real act of this obsessive kind is as much a prison for the actor as was Montresor's murder of his double, than which he has no other tale to tell.

Madness!

There are no parents in the tales of Edgar Poe, nary a Mum nor a Dad. Instead all is symbol. And what does this total repression of both sonhood and parenthood signify but that to acknowledge such relationships is to venture into territory too dangerous, too terrifying, for specificity. Desire and hatred are alike insatiable and unallayed. But the terrible war of superego upon the id, the endless battle between conscience and impulse, the unsleeping enmity of the self and its Imp of the Perverse—these struggles are enacted and re-enacted in Poe's work, but always in disguise.

Take 'The Tell-Tale Heart,' surely one of his nearly perfect tales. It's only four pages long, a triumph of the art of economy:

> How, then, am I mad? Hearken! and observe how healthily—how calmly I can tell you the whole story.

When a narrator commences in *this* vein we know him to be mad already. But we also know his author to be sane. For with such precision to portray the methodicalness of a madman is the work not of a madman but of a man who truly understands what it is to be mad. Artistic control is the warrant of auctorial sanity. It is axiomatic in the psychiatric practice of our century that self-knowledge is a necessary condition for the therapeutic process. Never using the language of the modern diagnostician—which was unavailable to him in the first place, and which in any case he didn't need—Poe demonstrates the extent of his self-knowledge in his manipulation of symbolic objects and actions toward ends which his tales embody.

The events are few, the action brief. 'I' (in the story) believes himself sane because he is so calm, so methodical, so fully aware and in control of his purpose. Of course his knowledge of that purpose is limited, while his recital thereof endows the reader with a greater knowledge than his own. 'The disease,' he says right at the start, 'had sharpened my senses. . . . Above all was the sense of hearing acute. I heard all things in the heavens and in the earth. I heard many things in hell.' Now of whom can this be said but a delusional person? At the same time, mad as he is, this narrator is *the hero of sensibility*. His heightened senses bring close both heaven and hell.

His plot is motiveless. 'Object there was none. Passion there was none. I loved the old man. He had never wronged me. He had never given me insult. For his gold I had no desire.' The crime he is about to commit will be all the more terrible because apparently gratuitous. But let us not be lulled by his narrator's lack of admitted motive. He may have a motive—one which he cannot admit, even to himself.

> I think it was his eye! yes, it was this! One of his eyes resembled that of a vulture—a pale blue eye, with a film over it. Whenever it fell upon me, my blood ran cold; and so by degrees—very gradually—I made up my mind to take the life of the old man, and thus rid myself of the eye for ever.

And a paragraph later he reiterates, 'It was not the old man who vexed me, but his Evil Eye.'

Nowhere does this narrator explain what relationship, if any, exists between him and the possessor of the Evil Eye. We do, however, learn from his tale that he and the old man live under the same roof—apparently alone together, for there's no evidence of anyone else's being in the house. Is the young man the old man's servant? Odd that he would not say so. Perhaps the youth is the old man's son. Quite natural that he should not say so. 'I loved the old man. He had never wronged me. . . . I was never kinder to the old man than during the whole week before I killed him.' Such the aggressive revulsion caused by the old man's Evil Eye!

What can this be all about? The Evil Eye is a belief as old and as dire as any in man's superstitious memory, and it usually signifies the attribution to another of a power wished for by the self. In this particular case there are other vibrations emanating from the vulture-like eye of the benign old man. Insofar as we have warrant—which I think we do—to take him as a father-figure, his Eye becomes the all-seeing surveillance of the child by the father, even by The Father. This surveillance is of course the origin of the child's conscience, the inculcation into his soul of the paternal principles of right and wrong. As such, the old man's eye becomes a ray to be feared. For if the boy deviate ever so little from the strict paths of rectitude, *it will find him out*.

Poe, in other tales, seems to be obsessed with the eye to the point of fetishism. In 'Ligeia' it is the lady's eyes which represent, to her husband, the total knowledge embodied in her person. By synecdoche the eyes become that which he worships. But the old man's eye is endowed with no such spiritual powers. Come to think of it, it is always referred to in the singular, as though he had but one. An old man with one all-seeing eye, an Evil Eye—from the plausible to the superstitious we pass in the text; perhaps further still to the mythical. One-eyed Odin, one-eyed because he sold his other *for knowledge*. Yet the knowledge in a father's (or a father-figure's) eye which a child most likely fears is the suspicion that he has been seen in a forbidden act, especially masturbation, or some other exercise of the libido. That above all seems to the young child to be forbidden, and therefore what an all-seeing Eye would see. Yet this old man's ocular power is never so specified. What is specified, though, is the resemblance of his one eye to that of a vulture.

Vulture, vulture. Everywhere else in Poe's work, in Poe's mind, vulture is associated with TIME, and time is associated with our mortality, our confinement in a body. The vulture-like eye of an aged man is thus an insupportable reminder of the narrator's insufferable mortality. Could he but rid himself of its all-seeing scrutiny, he would then be free of his subjection to time.

All the more so if the father-figure in this tale be, in one of his aspects, a Father-Figure. As, to an infant, his own natural father doubtless is. As, to the baby Eddie, his foster-father may have been. Perhaps he had even a subliminal memory of his natural father, who so early deserted him, eye and all, to the hard knocks experience held in store. So, the evil in that Evil Eye is likely a mingling of the stern reproaches of conscience with the reminder of his own subjection to time, age, and death.

To murder the possessor of such an eye would be indeed to reverse their situations. In life, the old man seems to the narrator an absolute monarch, a personage whose power over him, however benignly exercised, is nonethe-less immutable. Such exactly is the degree to which a murderer dominates his victim. And so it is that the narrator does not merely do the old man in. No, he stealthily approaches the sleeping old man, in the dead of night, and ever so craftily draws nearer, then plays upon his sleeping face a single ray from his lantern. A ray like the beam of an eye. This he does each night for a week—that very week in which he was never before so kind to him during the waking hours, when the old man had his eye working.

> Upon the eighth night I was more than usually cautious in opening the door. A watch's minute hand moves more quickly than did mine. Never before that night had I *felt* the extent of my powers—of my sagacity. I could scarcely contain my feelings of triumph. To think that there I was, opening the door, little by little, and he not even to dream of my secret deeds or thoughts.

This miscreant is full of the praise of his own sagacity, a terrible par-ody of the true sagacity of a Dupin or a Legrand. For what he takes to be ratiocination is in fact the irresistible operation of the principle of his own perversity, the urge to do secret deeds, have secret thoughts undetected by the otherwise ever-watchful eye of the old man. He is so pleased to have out-witted that eye that he chuckles—and the old man stirs, then cries 'Who's there?' The room is pitchy black, the shutters drawn for fear of robbers. Now the old man is sitting bolt upright in bed, 'listening—just as I have done, night after night, hearkening to the death watches in the wall.'

The old man must have realized what was happening, what was about to happen, for

> Presently I heard a slight grown . . . not of pain or of grief—oh, no!—it was the low stifled sound that arises from the bottom of the soul when overcharged with awe. . . . I knew it well. I knew what the old man felt, and pitied him, although I chuckled at heart.

And then, breaking the darkness and the silence, he spots his ray directly 'upon the vulture eye.' 'Now, I say, there came to my ears a low, dull, quick sound, such as a watch makes when enveloped in cotton.' This is the sound, he says, of the old man's heartbeat.

Excited to a pitch of 'uncontrollable terror' by the drumbeat of his vic-tim's heart, he gives a shout, flings wide the door of his lantern, and drags the old man to the floor. Then he suffocates him under the mattress. 'His eye would trouble me no more.'

Now, quickly, methodically, the murderer completes his work. 'First I dismembered the corpse. I cut off the head and the arms and the legs.' Then he places all between the beams under the floorboards. These he deftly replaces so that no eye could detect a thing. He had made care to catch all the blood in a tub. 'Ha! ha!'

Death by suffocation—this is a recrudescence of the favorite mode of dying everywhere else in Edgar Poe's tales of the dying, the dead, and the doomed. Illness is invariably phthisis; what character draws untroubled breath? Such sufferings seem inevitable to the imagination of a writer whose memory is blighted by the consumption which carried off the three women he most loved. But there is yet another reason for the young man's choosing to suffocate the eye which he could not abide. As is true of dreamwork, the vengeance is meted out thrice: he extinguishes the eye, he suffocates the old man, he dismembers him. I think these three terrible acts are disguises of each other.

In its aspect of getting rid of the Evil Eye, this murder is a more intense and violent form of blinding. And the symbolic content of blinding has been self-evident since Oedipus inflicted it upon himself as a partial remission for what the *lex talionis*, more strictly applied, would have required. In striking the Evil Eye of the old man, the young madman strikes, symbolically, at his sexual power. Nor does this contradict the other significations I have suggested for the ocular member. As the source of conscience, of surveillance of the boy's sexual misdemeanors, and as the reminder of his subjection to his own body, the eye derives some of its powers from its linkage, in imagination, with potency.

But what has suffocation to do with this? Only that the inability to breathe is an equivalent of impotence, of sexual impotence. By inflicting this form of death on the old man, the youth is denying his elder's sexual power.

And cutting off the head, the arms, the legs? These amputations, too, are symbolic castrations.

The 'I' is nothing if not methodical. He leaves nothing to chance.

No sooner has he replaced the floorboards—it is now four o'clock—but there is a rapping at his door. Neighbors, hearing a scream, had called the police. He explains that the scream was his own, *in a dream*. Then—why does he do this?—he invites the police into the house, to search and see for themselves, saying that the old man was away in the country.

> I led them, at length, to *his* chamber. I showed them his treasures, secure, undisturbed. In the enthusiasm of my confidence, I brought chairs into the room, and desired them *here* to rest from their fatigues, while I myself, in the wild audacity of my perfect triumph, placed my own seat upon the very spot beneath which reposed the corpse of the victim.

At first all is well, but as they sit, and chat, his head begins to ache, he hears a ringing in his ears. It grows in volume, '*a low, dull, quick sound* . . . *as a watch makes when enveloped in cotton.* . . . hark! louder! louder! *louder!*'

He could escape the Evil Eye, but not 'the beating of his hideous heart.'

Of course it was his own heart which the murderer heard beat. Would he have heard it, had not his Imp of the Perverse commanded that he lead the police to the very scene of the crime? Or was this Imp, whose impulse seems so inexplicable, his own conscience, inescapable as long as his own heart should beat, demanding punishment for the terrible crime he had wrought? Thus he is *never* free from the gaze of the old man's clear blue eye.

WALTER STEPP

The Ironic Double in Poe's
"The Cask of Amontillado"

In Poe's "The Cask of Amontillado," a heraldic emblem offers a suggestive entrance into the story. Descending into the catacombs of Montresor's
failed family, Fortunato says, "I forget your arms." It is one of his numerous
blind, unintentional insults. The proud Montresor, biding his time, blinks
not and replies: "A huge human foot d'or, in a field of azure; the foot crushes
a serpent rampant whose fangs are embedded in the heel."

> "And the motto?"
> "Nemo me impune lacessit."
> "Good!" he said.

The brief scene highlights the major plot dynamics of Poe's great
story: the clumsy insult, Montresor's menacing irony, and Fortunato's further blindness to this irony ("Good!"). Montresor flashes countless "clues"
like the one above before Fortunato's rheumy eyes—signals of his impending doom, but Fortunato does not perceive. The clues are part of the larger
"system" or "demonstration" motif of the story: Montresor, the diabolical
rationalist, systematically demonstrates again and again that the arriviste,
Fortunato, does not *know,* cannot distinguish. Montresor, at the end of his
life, has addressed his narrative to "You, who so well know the nature of my

From *Studies in Short Fiction* 13, no. 4 (Fall 1976). © 1977 by Newberry College.

soul," and it is as if he were performing before some ultimate audience, say-ing "You see? I show him the picture of his own death, and he says 'Good!'" An unspoken corollary of this speech I have imagined for his might read, "And yet, this buffoon, this Fortunato . . . 'is rich, respected, admired; he is happy, as once I was.' *He* is the heir of Fortune!" And so Montresor proceeds to demonstrate the illegitimacy of this heir.

The heraldic emblem represents all the irony of life that Fortunato can-not comprehend. But is it the more interesting, I think, for what it says of Poe's knowledge of his evil protagonist (the two being so often equated in Poe's case). For the emblem suggests a deeper motivation that Montresor does not understand, either, but which Poe seems to have built upon. The Latin verb in the motto makes clear what is clear anyway—that Montresor identifies himself with the golden foot, ponderously triumphing over the lashing serpent. When he holds up the dire image before Fortunato's unsee-ing eyes, he has in mind no doubt the golden legitimacy of his vengeance, a just and unquestionable retribution for the thousand lacerations he has borne in silence. He will tread him into the ground, and indeed he does seal For-tunato in stone.

Such is Montresor's reading of the emblem, it seems reasonably clear; but another reading—Poe's, I think—does not so easily identify Montresor with the foot. The snake is the more obvious choice. Secrecy, cunning, ser-pentine subtlety—these are the themes Montresor demonstrated best of all. And the huge, golden boot fits very snugly the Fortunato that Montresor presents to us—large, powerful, and very clumsy. The larger story shows very well how to read the emblem: a giant has blindly stepped on a snake.

Moreover, to arrive at my main point, the emblem represents a scene of mutual destruction. Allegorically speaking, the foot and the serpent are locked together in a death embrace: neither can escape the ironic bond that is between them. Through this allegory, then, I want to point to the deeper relationship between the two men, a deeper motive for murder, and, finally, a deep, ineffably horrible sense of retribution for the crime. This last may be especially difficult to see, in view of the fact that much of the slow horror of the tale derives from just that sense that Montresor has indeed escaped retri-bution for his deed, that he has acted out his readers' most terrible fantasy: to murder "without conscience." This is the chief burden of his demonstration, told with appropriately dry matter-of-factness. He ends by letting us know he has lived fifty triumphant years since the murder of "the noble Fortunato." My allegory, then, is certainly not Montresor's.

Is it Poe's? I shall say that Fortunato rather ironically represents the familiar Poe *doppelgänger,* and that, as in Poe's earlier, more explicit allegory, "William Wilson," the double corresponds with conscience. (That "with" is a nice hedge for the moment.) The correspondence is unmistakably pat in the earlier story; "Cask" suggests that Poe's command of his theme has considerably deepened in that the double now is a reversed image—a "negative" double, if you will, an ironic double. (Well, all doubles are; I mean something further in that the double is not recognized "as such" by Montresor.) I think most readers have noticed the rather perfect symmetry of opposition between Montresor and Fortunato; most readers should, for that is the chief burden of Montresor's systematic demonstration. Montresor frames a "façade-system" to deny his double, the irony being that he denies him so systematically that he ends by creating a perfect double-in-reverse. The analogy with a photographic positive and its negative is rather exact here—not because life operates so, but because of Montresor's compulsive program, his obsessional wish to demonstrate that "He is not I." Or: "I am not he." The right emphasis ought to emerge from the demonstation to follow.

I think I need mention only a few instances of the systematic opposi-tions that Montresor's procrustean method presents to us, enough to recall its obsessive symmetry. Most importantly, Fortunato is broadly drawn as a character entirely befitting his carnival motley and clownish bells. He appears as the open, gullible extrovert, an innocent possessed of that same ignorant vanity that caused the original fall from grace; he thinks he knows enough to sample the apple the serpent tempts him with. He believes the sacred Amontillado is meant for *him*, but he is a drunkard. Montresor lets us know, certainly not a man of his companion's fine taste. Every delicacy, every pearl of ironic distinction, is utterly lost on this man: "He is not I; I am not he."

But it should be said that Montresor more than once obliquely acknowl-edges that there is more to Fortunato than his portrait is designed to show. Montresor does acknowledge certain sympathies with Fortunato, which point to what is being denied by the rationalist's demonstration. He begins, "He has a weak point—this Fortunato—although in other regards he was a man to be respected and even feared." Here at least, in the beginning, Montresor is quite conscious of his portraiture's limitation, and perhaps that is enough to convince us that he is not himself caught up in his own "sin-cerity"—Montresor's word for his rival's weakness: "In painting and gem-mary, Fortunato, like his countrymen, was a quack, but in the matter of old wines he was sincere." Montresor plays on this sincerity even as Fortunato practices on gullible millionaires. Fortunato is hoist by his own petard, and Poe intimates that Montresor is too, I think; but of course the mine of irony lies deeper with him. If Fortunato's "sincerity" is his connoisseurship, Mon-tresor's is his system. But that is the larger point; here let me emphasize their clearer level of affinity: they are both successful "quacks."

"The rumor of a relationship"—the phrase is from "William Wilson"—sifts out in a few of Montresor's oft-noted "slips." One most touching occurs when Fortunato is near death. Montresor speaks of "a sad voice, which I had difficulty in recognizing as that of the noble Fortunato." The epithet may be taken as an obvious piece of sarcasm in keeping with the general ironic tenor, but I do not find that Montresor allows himself the double-edge when addressing "you who so well know the nature of my soul." Then he keeps to hard, dry understatement of fact. (An exception might be Montresor's final utterance: "*In pace requiescat.*" And even then, if there is indeed a bond between them . . .)

And most readers have noted this piece of apparent rationalization: "There came forth [from out the niche] only a jingling of bells. My heart grew sick—on account of the catacombs." There is also Montresor's failure to satisfy the "definitive" conditions he has set down for himself, the code of honorable vengeance. "A wrong is unredressed when retribution overtakes its redresser," Montresor says, and whether he satisfies that clause is being debated here. "It is equally unredressed when the avenger fails to make himself felt as such to him who has done the wrong." Satisfaction is not debatable here; Montresor fails, for of course Fortunato never knows why he dies. He does not know the avenger "as such." Indeed, his nemesis has gone to great lengths to show that Fortunato is not *capable* of knowing such a man. He merely knows that Montresor has deceived him and that his fortune has run out. To connect with our larger theme, then, Montresor has failed "definitively" to achieve his vengeance in a way that suggests he does not understand its motive much more than does Fortunato. Why *did* he fail? It would have been simple enough to state the formal motive. You have wronged me thus and so; therefore you die. Whether we explain it as a prideful blindness (system always assumed its rationale is self-evident) or as an unwillingness to raise the ambiguous question, the irony of Montresor's "oversight" derives deep from the common substance of the two apparently opposed characters. As the emblem foretold, Montresor is bound with Fortunato and "dies" with him.

But it is the "mocking echo" motif that is the most suggestive of the men's relationship. (I take the phrase from Hawthorne's "Young Goodman Brown," another kind of double story.) Montresor's chosen method of demonstration and torment is to resound Fortunato's innocent words, striking a sinister edge in them known only to himself and his sole confidant, his reader. I am suggesting something further, a strange case of what one might call "murderous identification." I am thinking of the obvious cse of "William Wilson," in which the protagonist learns too late the retribution for slaying one's conscience. Two examples: When Fortunato at last realizes his murderer's intentions, he vainly tries to humor him.

"But is it not getting late? Will they not be awaiting us at the palazzo, the Lady Fortunato and the rest? Let us be gone."

"Yes," I said, "Let us be gone."

"For the love of God, Montresor!"

"Yes," I said, "for the love of God!"

And Fortunato is heard no more, silenced at last by his own words thrust back at him. Certainly the most horrific—because so understated—example of this diabolical doubling occurs immediately preceding this last. While Montresor has been laying the tiers of his masonry, Fortunato has been sobering up and presumably comprehending the imminence of his death; "a low moaning cry from the depth of the recess. It was *not* the cry of a drunken man." This is followed by a long and "obstinate" silence. When the wall is nearly completed, "A succession of loud and shrill screams, bursting suddenly from the throat of the chained form, seemed to thrust me violently back." Montresor quickly puts down his momentary fright and reassures himself of the "solid fabric of the catacombs." Then, "I reapproached the wall, I replied to the yells of him who clamored. I re-echoed—I aided—I surpassed them in volume and in strength. I did this, and the clamorer grew still." I have always wanted to see a skilled actor play that scene; rather, two skilled actors. Fine points matter especially here, to see in Montresor's performance just the fine, ironic blend of "quackery" and "sincerity." Fortunato's dazed agony would be a study, too, as he witnesses the weird spectacle of his devil out-clamoring his victim's agonies—eerie harmonics there. And perhaps in this terrible way, Montresor demonstrates how one defeats the double—by beating him at his own game, doubling *him* up. Just as the subtler quack dupes the lesser, so perhaps Montresor "re-echoes" an "echoer."

Again, the parallel with "William Wilson" helps here. There it was the uncanny voice of the double-as-conscience that was most devastating. *"And his singular whisper, it grew the very echo of my own."* But William Wilson was not so well defended as Montresor; he tried the direct frontal assault and lost. Montresor, it would seem, achieves his triumph by reversing roles with his double, in effect *usurping* the double's occupation. Now *he* becomes the menacing echo and sends his double to the doom meant for himself, as it happened to Wilson.

By systematically denying every impulse represented by "the noble Fortunato," Montresor perhaps restores the perfect, lucid order that prevailed when the Montresors "were a great and numerous family." That is to say, a mental equilibrium, false though it may be, has been restored. I am speculating now that the decline of the Montresor family represented a devastation of disorder to the compulsive Montresor, signifying to him the price of his impulsivity. I suggest this term, of course, because it is the direct antithesis of the cool, controlled character Montresor represents himself to be. I have tried to show Montresor's ambivalence toward the impulsive parvenue, the childlike Fortunato, indeed innocent to the end since he never "knows." As in "William Wilson," Montresor is "galled . . . by the rumor of a relationship," but in spite of the double's "continual spirit of contradiction, I could not bring myself to hate him altogether." Who is "the noble Fortunato"?

In "William Wilson," Poe makes it absolutely clear that the double represents conscience; such a parallel is not clear in "Cask," but it is the case, I think. Fortunato is not the interdictory conscience of "William Wilson," but he is the conscience-related: he is guileless, trusting innocence. It may be misleading to call him conscience, but *his* death is required to slay conscience. If it is not so clear that Fortunato corresponds to conscience, perhaps the blame (or credit) may be laid to Montresor's elaborate plan of denial. If Fortunato is a double-as-conscience, such an idea is not likely to be directly verified by a man whose one great wish is to portray himself as a man—nay, *the* man—without conscience. Indeed, the murder of Fortunato might be thought of as a "test case" to confirm just that notion: a man kills his conscience and rests in peace for fifty years. Surely the horror of Poe's little gem rests on the fantasy of the crime without consequences. If a man might do that, as every boy has dreamed of doing, where is "the public moral perspective"? The disposal of a rival becomes as simple as a child's "omnipotent" wish that he should "go away."

"William Wilson" tells the story of a man who murdered his conscience and thus himself; the same story is at work in "Cask," I submit, but with the great difference that Wilson recognizes his folly, while Montresor steadfastly refuses to. This significant difference is at least one reason why I find perhaps too easily, our own conscientious understanding of the way things ought to be; Montresor is more difficult, he challenges that understanding. He makes claims on us, if we take him seriously, that Wilson does not. Wilson, for all his prodigality, is, after all, "one of us," the difference being of degree. But Montresor, like Iago, stands in the line of Machiavellians who assert that the public moral perspective is but a façade by which knaves are stung and puppies drowned. We may say that Montresor is at heart a tormented sinner like Wilson, but it requires rather than subtlety to show it, and the villain is not likely to own it when we do.

The question of "comeuppance" in the two stories is a measure of their relative subtlety. In "William Wilson," poetic justice is clear if not profound: He slew his conscience and thus himself. Poe clearly emphasizes an allegorical understanding, and his story serves that purpose admirably well. In "The Cask of Amontillado," the same idea is intimated, but much more ambiguously and with formidable qualifications that make its meaning less easily satisfying. That is, though a reader may discern significant chinks in Montresor's armor, the armor remains—for a lifetime, he tells us. The armor represents a powerful lie, and it is important not to underestimate its power. Its felt presence stands in defiance of any mere allegorical, or purely intellectual, understanding. It is disturbing, it sustains the muted horror of this story, and is not easily dismissed, I think, as in James Gargano's formuation: "With a specious intellectuality, common to Poe's violent men, Montresor seeks to escape from his own limitations by outside force. But the force is a surrogate of the self, cozening [the] man toward damnation with all the brilliant intrigue Montresor uses in destroying Fortunato." All which I most potently believe, but I hold it not honesty to have it thus set down, as Hamlet replies to *his* own speech. In the "damnation" of the criminal Montresor, I believe, in theory. Theological grounds being what they are not these days, I might take the case in the good humanistic tradition Gargano espouses. To gain precision and authority, I might go further to document, on psychoanalytic grounds, the suffering that must lie at the heart of "the compulsion neurotic." (I think that is the correct classification.) But, alas, these are general and even problematic premises; they do inform my understanding of Poe's story, but they tend to pale before the immediacy of Montresor's defiant evil. The truth of the story, its meaning, must acknowledge that dilemma of the reader—unless, of course, as is common, we want merely to use the story as a "case" to illustrate doctrine. The slow horror of the story rests ultimately on the reader's ambivalent wish-belief that Montresor did indeed triumph, that he did indeed sin with impunity: that he *did* slay his conscience. When Poe had Montresor address his story to "you, who so well know the nature of soul,"—referring perhaps to the *reader's* role as ironic double—I do not think he intended an easy irony.

GITA RAJAN

A Feminist Rereading of Poe's
"The Tell-Tale Heart"

1

Some contemporary feminists and theorists argue that there is a difference between masculinist and feminist discourse in literary texts. French theorists like Julia Kristeva, Luce Irigaray, and Hélène Cixous follow Jacques Lacan and psychoanalytic theory and trace the unconscious drives exhibited in the discourse of the text as repressed male/female desires. Even though these desires may be contradictory and conflicting, they reveal the position of the speaking subject (male or female) within the discourse of the text. The French scholars, in seeking the overlapping or androgynous places of discourse in the text, assert that males and females engage in differently gendered readings. Kristeva and Cixous argue that sexual identity (male or female) is a metaphysical construct outside the boundaries of the text, while gender identity is based upon cultural notions of maleness and femaleness evidenced in the text. Gender identity is more fluid than the former and makes room for the crucial concept of androgyny that is central to feminist readings in demolishing the rigid patriarchal notion of what is male/female. Androgyny deconstructs crippling binary oppositions of masculinity and femininity by allowing the speaking subject to occupy either or both positions.

From *Papers on Language & Literature* 24, no. 3 (Summer 1988): 283–300. © 1988 by the Board of Trustees of Southern Illinois University.

While sexual identity, and, consequently, discrimination, feature prominently in masculinist readings, French theorists are radically shifting the very nature of the struggle of the sexes by focusing on gender-governed identity. Hence, a feminist reinterpretation of a narrative typically could argue that an unmarked narrator can be seen as female. Such a reading would displace a whole series of masculinist assumptions. In accordance with this approach, I will focus on Poe's "The Tell-Tale Heart," especially its narrator, and argue that the narrator is indeed female. Poe himself never indicates that the narrator is male; in fact, his text offers no gender markings. Readers have assumed that the narrator is male because a neutralized and unmarked term *is* generally granted to be male. This is a trap that the language of the tale innocuously lays before the reader. By positing a female narrator, I propose to dislodge the earlier, patriarchal notion of a male narrator for the story. I argue, instead, that a gender-marked *rereading* of this tale reveals the narrator's exploration of her female situation in a particular feminist discourse. My feminist reading of "The Tell-Tale Heart" profiles the identity of the narrator as filtered through Freud's, Lacan's, and Cixous's theories of narrativity.

2

Psychoanalysis partially bridges the gap between conscious and unconscious thought and language through dream theory. Freud argues that instinctual forces—eros and thanatos—manifest themselves through dreams, and that these forces coexist and continually contradict each other, being intertwined in pairs like love/hate, life/death, and passivity/aggression. However, Freud maintains that people manage to lead ordered lives because they sublimate these forces as desires in dreams through at least two specific mechanisms, "condensation" and "displacement." Freud builds his psychoanalytic theory on human sexuality and desire, seeing the male as superior, in possession of the phallus, i.e., power. A female is inferior for Freud because of her lack of the sexual organ to signify the phallus and the power it symbolizes. In short, Freud's definition of the male and female, locked into this privative power equation, automatically privileges the male and marginalizes the female.

Lacan, in his revision of Freudian theory, fastens upon three principles: desire (the phallus as power), condensation/displacement (the dream as a system of signs), and hierarchy (the male as superior, or possessing power through the penis: the female as inferior, or lacking power).[1] Relying on Roman Jakobson's structural linguistics, he combines these three principles to establish a relationship between language *per se* and conscious/unconscious thought. Jakobson uses language as a model of *signs* to explain human thought and consequent behavior. A sign, for Jakobson, is a representation through language of the relationship between signifier (the physical sound of speech or the written mark on the page) and the signified (the invisible concept that this sound or mark represents). Jakobson's linguistic formulations reveal the doubleness of the sign and the fragility of the signifier (word) and signified (concept) relationship. In effect, he sees meaning emerging in discourse not through the relationship between signifier and signified but through the interaction of one signifier with another.

Jakobson maintains that language is constructed along two axes—the vertical/metaphoric and the horizontal/metonymic. Lacan's matches Jakobson's theory of language with Freud's theory of dreams, positing that dreams are structured along metaphoric and metonymic lines.[2] Lacan claims that the "rhetoric of the unconscious" is constructed on two main tropes—metaphor and metonymy. He equates condensation with metaphor because it is a process of selection, substituting one signifier/word *for* another. Displacement he sees as metonymy because it combines one signifier/word *with* another. For Lacan, unconscious desire, like language, is structured as a system of signs, articulated metaphorically and metonymically in dreamwork and considered as discourse. While in Freudian analysis the focus is on the excavation of the subject's behavior, in Lacan it shifts to language, tracing the path of desire as a sequential power transaction in the discourse of the text. Thus, Lacan reconstructs Freud's behavioral model into a *seemingly* less prejudiced linguistic one by emphasizing the arbitrariness and precariousness of language itself.

Further, according to Lacan, the metaphoric register represents the masculine through the "transcendental phallus," embodying the ultimate power of the signifier as a linguistic mark whose meaning is forever repressed (in the unconscious or the "text") and never attainable. Hence, every subject must engage in a constant metaphoric game of substitution in the attempt to grasp this final desire. In contrast, the metonymic is temporal and sequential; it propels the signifier forward in an attempt to recover the (unconscious) signified through narration. Significantly, Lacan claims that this reaching forward to achieve completeness is a mark of femininity, a feminine marker in discourse. Finally, Lacan concludes that even though language itself is symbolic, the symptom that prompts discourse is metonymic. Thus, the metonymic, feminine, "imaginary" register is the force that propels narrative.[3]

It is at this point that Lacan differs radically from Freud. While Freud assumes that language can completely appropriate and express thought, granting closure in the text, Lacan posits an inherent gap in this relationship, arguing for never-ending narrativity. For Lacan, the sign can never be complete or made whole because a signifier can only point to another signifier, resulting in an unending chain of signifiers we *forever attempt* to bridge through language and thought. Lacan connects language to thought as expressions of patterns of desire, motivated and propelled towards possessing the ultimate sign of power—the "transcendental signified," or phallus. Thus, the transcendental signified belongs in the metaphoric register, and the desire to possess it creates narrativity, which belongs to the metonymic register. Lacan strategically argues that the desire to possess the "transcendental phallus" is universal, both in males and females, and *appears* to collapse sexual difference. But this apparent egalitarianism, I argue, does not in fact work.

A masculinist reading of Poe's tale using Lacan's theory still supports the Freudian notion of the Oedipal myth. However, the Lacanian approach emphasizes sexual difference less than the Freudian approach does. Robert Con Davis analyzes Poe's "The Tell-Tale Heart" using Lacanian principles in "Lacan, Poe and Narrative Repression." He focuses on the latent and repressed levels of the text as a method of locating the nexus of power. Davis argues the act of gazing, whether the old man's or the narrator's, is a metaphoric power transaction between the subject and the object of the gaze. Using Freud's "Instincts and Their Vicissitudes," with its traditional patriarchal dichotomies of "subject/object, active/passive," Davis matches Freud's theme of the "gaze" with Lacan's theory of voyeurism to interpret Poe's tale.[4] Davis highlights the "Evil Eye" as a predominant metaphor in Poe's tale that functions primarily through its power of the Gaze. Building on the theme of the gaze and voyeurism, Davis validates his masculinist reading by arguing that the old man and the narrator are indeed doubles, always already connected by the gaze. He sees both characters as having similar, almost paranoically sensitive hearing and sight, insomnia, and a preoccupation with death. The "eye" of the old man represents the Symbolic Law of the Father, or Lacan's version of Freud's Oedipal complex. Davis argues that in an attempt to escape paternal subjugation, the narrator engages in his own vindictive game of voyeurism. Davis sees the murder of the old man as a cruelly symbolic act of Oedipal mastery: "in choosing to heighten the old man's fear of death and kill him, the narrator controls—just as a voyeur sadistically controls—a situation *like his own*, as if the subject and object could be merged in a mirror phase of complete identification" (255). Davis even argues for a third voyeur in the figure of Death: "Death . . . had stalked with his black shadow . . . and enveloped the victim."[5] This allows him to posit a typical Lacanian triangle, consisting of the old man, the narrator, and Death, and create a constant shift in the power of the gaze through the triple itinerary of the signifier.

Because Davis places the narrator and the old man in the "double" positions connected by the gaze, he sees the gaps in the gaze between the subject and object *and* the gazer and voyeur as forces that produce the narrative, propel the tale forward, and alternately manifest and repress the text. Based on a primarily metaphoric interpretation—the eye as the Symbolic Gaze of the Father—Davis argues for a male narrator who acts as voyeur and exhibitionist alternately. Davis neatly sums up the final scene of Poe's tale as clearly metaphoric by saying: "His [the narrator's] resistance to being seen points to a desire to escape subjugation absolutely and to choose death rather than to become passive while alive" (254). Significantly, Lacan's suggestion that the metonymic dimension of the text is female is absent in Davis's reading. Thus, even though Lacanian readings *seem* to open the door to feminist perspectives, they ultimately only nudge the door ajar.

3

Cixous's feminist approach to psychoanalytic interpretation and her notion of feminine writing provide a fruitful way of sabotaging the masculinist-biased reading of texts. Hence a rereading of Poe's "The Tell-Tale Heart" with Cixous's paradigm offers an alternate gender-marked interpretation. She systematically interrogates existing critical presuppositions, deconstructs them, and advocates a three-step reinscription procedure.[6] First, according to Cixous, one must recognize a latent masculinist prejudice in society, a hidden privileging of the male and marginalizing of the female. Next, one must consciously undo the basic slanting in favor of the male term over the female term at the very nodes of these *seemingly logical* oppositions, such as male/female, reason/feeling, culture/nature, etc. Patriarchy, by creating these oppositions, privileges the first term and lowers the status of the second, forcing the textual subject to occupy either of these positions and accept the power (or lack thereof) that goes along with it. This logic divides each term against itself and makes the whole system of binary (Western) thought rigidly prescriptive. The male, according to this system of thought, can have an identity and value only in juxtaposition to an inferior female signifier and vice versa. Also, in privileging one term over another, the first term sets the norm for the second. More important, oppositional thinking, which is characteristic of patriarchy, forbids a wholeness or a shared existence for any term, focusing on maleness or on femaleness instead of the androgyny that Cixous and other French feminists advocate.

Consequently, Cixous's final step is to combat this problem of division by embracing these oppositions and erasing their differences. This is the "pretext," or background, for the process of *jouissance* that Cixous advocates. The strategy behind jouissance is to discredit the notion of difference by going beyond the idea of constraining divisions, to explore instead the freedom of excess, a utopian vision that subverts the male definition of desire. Patriarchy is based on a system of libidinal economy (a repression of desire both conscious and unconscious that creates meaning in a text). Cixous's jouissance demands a libidinal excess—additions of unconscious meanings through consciously constructed texts. The practical method behind this political feminist position is to create a multiplicity of meanings. In linguistic terms, jouissance creates an excess of signifiers, the freeplay of which will build several levels of meanings, all of which can be validated by the text. These meanings do not depend upon a series of repressed previous ones; they do not impoverish the meanings that come before them through a process of substitution but, instead, enhance each other through a process of addition. An example of this is the notion of androgyny which is central to some feminist readings. Instead of focusing on either male or female voice in the text, androgyny allows the same voice to be male and/or female in various parts of the text, allowing for numerous complementary interpretations.

K risteva, in *Desire and Language*, and Cixous, in *La Juene Née*, argue that the concept of androgyny belongs to the realm of the "Imaginary," which, in Lacanian theory, is pre-Symbolic, or pre-Oedipal, and thus, is before the Law of the Father. While Cixous is explicit in calling this jouissance in the sense of the purely pleasurable state of excess, Kristeva connects jouissance to reproduction. However, they share this vision of utopia, with no boundaries or barriers of any kind, a vision that is based on unlimited joy.[7]

The inherent danger in Kristeva's and Cixous's vision of utopia is their marked privileging of the imaginative/poetic over the analytical/theoretical in feminist writing. Because of their emphasis on emotions rather than reason as the feminine mode, some patriarchal theorists do not treat feminist discourse seriously. Sentimentality is precisely the club that patriarchy holds over the woman to control and deem her inferior. However, there *is* a definite value in adopting Cixous's position of abundance in an effort to invalidate the rigid male parameters and explore the text with an expectation of plentitude and multiple meanings. It is essential to point out that Cixous's notion of jouissance as a pleasure principle is different from Lacan's notion of free space with an abundance of signifiers (or even Barthes's version of the "pleasures of the text"). The latter suggests a chasm with an abundance of repressed, free floating signifiers, while the former gathers up this abundance of signifiers to nourish and cherish separate multiple readings.

Cixous begins by questioning the validity of categories like male/female in both writing and reading texts. She sees these as gaps created by ideological differences propagated by a phallogocentric (phallus- and logos-oriented) interpretive community. Further, she argues that this kind of oppositional thinking is itself aggressive (very much like the male logic and body behind it), because one term in the couple comes into existence through the "death of the other." Cixous, in *La Jeune Née* asks, "Where is she?" (115) in a patriarchal binary thought system that creates divisions like "Activity/Passivity,

Culture/Nature, Father/Mother, Head/Emotions, Logos/Pathos" (116) which is structured primarily on the male/female opposition. An effective way to allow both terms to exist is to ask for a gendered position that both males and females can occupy either jointly or individually within the texts, as speaking subjects. This is made possible through the notion of jouissance, which focuses on the speaking subject with a gendered (hence mobile) identity. Also, this deliberate exploration of multiple meanings would ceaselessly expose the hidden male agenda which is created to silence women.

4

I preface my rereading of Poe's tale with a Freudian analysis, much like that in Marie Bonaparte's *Life of Poe*.[8] However, while Bonaparte's emphasizes the element of primal-scene voyeurism, mine sees the male narrator's retelling of his story/dream as a narration of a rite of passage. "The Tell-Tale Heart" begins by describing the narrator's feelings about taking care of an old man. The old man's disturbing stare upsets the narrator, who decides on an impulse to kill him. The rest of the tale focuses on the narrator's elaborate plan to murder him, and ends with the narrator's confession of the crime. The story has Poe's typical macabre atmosphere and deliberately contradictory syntactical style. By killing the old man, the narrator symbolically castrates him, eliminating him from the text, and hopes to escape subjugation. This allows him to step into the old man's position of unchallenged power. The act of murder reveals the condensed expression of his desire to usurp the old man's place and authority. Similarly, his swing between neurotic and hysteric utterances, repeatedly assuring the reader of his sanity, is an effort to displace the sense of fear that is incumbent upon possessing such authority. At the beginning of the tale, the narrator shelters the old man (love), but ends up murdering him (hate). The narrator's contradictory actions, in an effort to possess ultimate power, are the result of the intertwining of eros and thanatos. The narrator's final confession to the policemen (the substitute father figures) is a combination and sublimation of his desire for power and fear of castration as a challenge to his new power.

The standard Oedipal interpretation is explicit in the climactic bedroom scene that graphically reveals the simultaneous condensed and displaced desires of the narrator. The bed serves to feed the contradictory instinctual urges of eros and thanatos, satisfying the young man's passion while smothering him to death, granting the young man power while nullifying it in the old man. The narrator's imbalanced emotional utterances about being "driven" by the old man's "eye" are symptoms of the condensed desire that make him conceive his elaborate plan of shutting the old man's "Evil eye forever" (303). It is his attempt to usurp that very authority of the old man's surveillance. And the narrator's own deafening "heartbeat" prods him on, leading him from one event to the next in the narrative, revealing his efforts to escape the displaced sense of fear in letting this desire get out of control. While the eye (condensation) represents the narrator's problem through a sense of abstract desire, the heartbeat (displacement) serves as the significant, concrete sense of fear in dealing with this problem. This enables the tale to maintain its ambivalence between myth and reality, dream and nightmare, due to a coexisting tension between metaphor/condensation and metonymy/displacement throughout the narration. In this traditional Freudian analysis, the identity of narrator remains fixedly male.

However, my rereading of the tale includes both a masculinist and feminist approach to the narrator. Using Lacanian principles, I profile the narrator as "speaking subject," presenting the narrator first as male, then as female. Unlike Davis's reading, my masculinist rereading focuses on both the metaphoric and metonymic aspects of the text, moving away from an exclusive "Gaze"-oriented interpretation of manifest and repressed levels of discourse. I treat the eye as a metaphor of patriarchal scrutiny and social control, and the heart as metonymic device to subvert such control. The narrator admits his obsession in saying, "when it [the eye] fell upon me, my blood ran cold; and so by degrees—very gradually—I made up my mind to take the life of the old man, and thus rid myself of the eye forever" (305). The narrator explicitly reveals his anger at the old man's symbolic method of subjugation and expresses his consequent desire to annihilate the old man, thereby negating and usurping his power. Davis too, points this out by showing how the narrator first isolates the gaze, then inverts it, so that he can gaze at and subjugate the old man. The narrator retaliates against the "Evil Eye" by voyeuristically gazing at the sleeping man. Thus, the gaze moves from the old man to the narrator, symbolizing the shift of power between them. Lacan calls this mobility the "itinerary of the signifier" (171) to indicate the constant substitution maneuvers that the metaphoric register undertakes in its attempt to possess the ultimate object of desire—the transcendental signifier.[9] Within Poe's tale, the "itinerary of the signifier" can be graphically traced along the "single thin ray" of light from the narrator's lantern that falls upon the "vulture eye . . . directed as if by instinct, precisely upon the damned spot" (306). Gaining new power through his reversal of the gaze makes the narrator heady, and he cries exultantly that the old man "was stone dead. His eye would trouble me no more" (306).

However, the "itinerary of the signifier," due to its constant process of substitution, does not allow power to rest with one gazer for a long period. The very nature of the gaze, as posited by both Freud and Lacan, is extremely volatile, temporary, and unpredictable. Consequently, in Poe's story the power of the gaze destabilizes the narrator, and it is for this reason that he breaks down and confesses to the mildly suspecting policemen. The police in Poe's tale are the literal representations of societal power, but they are also a metaphor for the Law of the Father in the unconscious. The police-men's gaze, thus, both literally and metaphorically represents the sanctioned authority that the narrator had just usurped from the old man. When they gaze at the narrator, they reverse the path of the gaze, once again throwing him back into the passive object position that is revealed by his hysterical and humiliating confession.

Equally crucial in a Lacanian analysis is the metonymic register, marked by the "heart" in Poe's tale. It exhibits a complicated displacement process working simultaneously on two manifest levels. At one level it represents the narrator's confused emotions, such that the narrator's passions and fears combine and clash, spurring the tale forward. The tale unfolds through the narrator's hysterical utterances, extreme passion (even though the narrator explicitly denies this at the beginning of his tale), obsessive desire, neurotic fears, and pathetic confession. At another level, it represents the physical pounding of the narrator's heart, giving him the energy to kill the old man. On the night of the assault, the narrator remarks: "Never, before that night, had I *felt* the extent of my own powers" (306). Notably, it is the narrator's fear of the imagined sound of the old man's heart, that overwhelming roar, that ultimately betrays him into confessing to the policemen. These two aspects of displacement embodied metonymically in the heart are fused in a strange manner, alternating between hearing and feeling throughout the tale, such that they keep plummeting the narrative onwards. Thus, the sounds in the tale move rapidly from heartbeat to creaking doors, to muffled smothering sounds, to loud ticking watches, and finally pound as unbearable noise in the narrator's head till he articulates his fear through the confused discourse of a hysterical confession.

There is also a third kind of displacement at the repressed level of the text. This is evidenced in the metonymic shift not only between one aspect of the heart to the other, but in a total shift from sound to sight at crucial points in the text. Thus, the metonymic register displaces the narrator's feel-ings throughout the text in various ways. A good example is the elaborate precautions that the narrator takes to direct a single ray of light in a dark-ened room on the old man's eye (sight). When the narrative has been raised to a fever pitch on the night of the murder, the narrator suddenly fumbles with the catch on the lantern and goes into a detailed description of sounds of "death watches," and crickets in "chimneys," effectively displacing reader attention. The displacement and metonymic tactics repressed in the narrative itself act as a marker for signaling the manifest displacement of the narra-tor's fears regarding his uncontrolled and unsanctioned actions. It is here that Lacan's notion of the "itinerary of signifiers" in the metonymic register serves him well. Metonymy, as both agent and trope, by constantly shifting, mediates between thought and language, showing both the instability of this relationship, and its inability to bridge the gap. At the textual level, it highlights the constant forward movement in an attempt to narrate through the rapid and confusing chain of events. It reveals the obsessively fragmented discourse of the narrator, in a painful effort to make meaning, and to make whole this relationship between thought and language. Thus, in my masculinist reading, by using the Lacanian paradigm of a male speaking subject, I reveal the problematic nature of language itself. When the narrator fails, one glimpses—with a strange pathos—the failure of language, too.

In contrast, my Lacanian feminist rereading of Poe's tale, identifying a female narrator, yields an interpretation that is the reverse of the Oedipal myth. Instead of a young man desiring the power symbolized by the Father, *she* is the daughter desiring her father. I will show that Lacan's innovativeness lies in the way he volatilizes the metaphoric and metonymic registers through his theory of the "itinerary of the signifier." Lacan suggests that sex roles as represented by linguistic tropes can be made less rigid. Hence sexual difference can be erased by energizing and mobilizing these linguistic tropes. Metaphor as a trope represents a pattern of desiring and desired where the object of desire is the transcendental signified, or phallus. Metonymy would be the act of seeking and transacting this power through narrative. Thus, Lacan's strategy is to dislocate the fixity of sexual identity, or what he claims is gender identity, through the use of tropes as agents of desire. This would allow both men and women to possess the transcendental phallus, or its metaphoric power; but because of the temporary nature of this power, the very act of possession would be continually deferred and drawn out metonymically in narrative for both masculine and feminine subjects.

Within this framework, the narrator in Poe's tale can be posited as a female rather than a male who desires power. She stalks the old man and father figure for "seven long nights" and kills him in an attempt to escape the surveillance of his Evil Eye. The female narrator begins in the traditional feminine position of a *nurturer*. She takes him into her house and even remarks with dark irony after terrifying him with her nightly ritualistic voyeurism: "I went boldly into his chamber, and spoke courageously to him, calling him by his name in a hearty tone, and inquiring how he had passed the night" (306). But she deeply resents the scrutiny of his eye, feeling abused and objectified by his paternal surveillance. Angered and humiliated by his gaze, she goes through the same maneuver that the male narrator does in reversing the path of this gaze. Unlike the male narrator, her primary desire is to rid herself of the male gaze, or domination. However, in traveling through the gaze's path, she substitutes the first desire for her need physically to possess the old man. In this context, the climactic scene in the bedroom, with its implied sexual overtones, supports a Lacanian feminist reading better than an Oedipal one. In that one moment of possession, she becomes the aggressor; she even assumes a male sexual posture, forcing the old man to receive her, almost raping him, so that "he shrieked once—once only" (305). The scene culminates with her smirk: "There was nothing to wash out—no stain of any kind—no blood spot whatsoever. . . . A tub caught it all" (305). In this one act, the female narrator captures both the masculine gaze and masculine role. Thus, in appropriating the male posture, she even refers to herself in explicitly masculine terms, claiming repeatedly, that her actions are not those of a "madman."

Yet, ironically, the very authority of her newfound power makes her more vulnerable, more of an object of desire by others. Metaphorically, she moves from the position of actively desiring that Lacan allows to both the male and female to the position of being passively desired, one that is traditionally only the female's. It is here that the Lacanian "itinerary of the signifier" betrays her. The movement between male/female roles is ultimately restrictive to the female. Unlike the male narrator who confesses for fear of castration, the female narrator is denied this option. Acknowledging her femininity, she stands before the policemen, stripped of her power in her traditional posture as female, passive, subservient, and accountable to the male gaze—and exposed in the eyes of the Law through the return of the repressed (murdered) father. She begins and ends in a stereotypically feminine posture, the nurturer who has returned to her quintessentially repressed object position.

My feminist rereading with metonymy as focal point again reveals the confined position of the female narrator. The heart as an allegory of metonymy displaces the narrator's fears and desires, working on the two levels already examined, making her obey the dictates of her confused emotions. Further, Poe's text, if reread as narrated by a female speaking subject, indicates that this desire and fear is more frequently associated with a female "voice" than it is with the male's. The female narrator of "The Tell-Tale Heart" focuses on evocations of space and emptiness, which are typical expressions of female consciousness. The narrator claims her fear was engulfing, making her feel as if "enveloped in cotton" (305), just like her "Terrors" which "welled" up in her bosom, "deepening, with its dreadful echo" (304). Interestingly, Lacan's theory of metonymy as the motor of language supports the psychoanalytic view that links the female phobia of emptiness (as a primal corollary to lacking the phallus) with gaps in narrativity that make this tale seem discontinuous and disjointed.[10] Thus, the narrator's confused recounting of her tale is a method of compensating for this emptiness, from the initial display of desire in her heart to the culminating betrayal of that desire, resulting in her agonizing confession.

This feminist investigation into the speaking subject, both male and female, unmasks the hidden male agenda; it also shows that a feminist rereading using only the Lacanian principles of psychoanalysis is problematic. As already shown, the female narrator's voluntary confession to the mildly suspecting policemen reveals her restricted position. As woman, she reoccupies her traditional role as a submissive, victimized object, offering herself up to be scrutinized once more by the male gaze. She can, finally, never aspire to usurp this power or be outside/above the Law of the Father. Ironically, even though a feminist rereading grants the female narrator a temporary masculine, active, subject posture, it undercuts this interpretation in returning her to a traditionally female position by superimposing a judicial and patriarchal closure. Such a feminist reading shows how clearly the female is boxed into a role, making both her sexual and gender identity rigid. A feminist rereading must go beyond the unmasking of such oppression; it must seek alternate positions for the female speaking subject.

Although Lacanian psychoanalysis first creates a division between male/female and then erases it under the guise of gender equalization, it seems to suggest that certain codes of behavior and discourse are allowable *only* to a male. Should a female dare to transgress, she will be punished by the Law of the Father. Consequently, the female narrator is permitted to desire the "metaphoric" phallus as power, but she can never aspire to possess it. And if she chooses to disobey this basic patriarchal dictum, not only will she fail but she must bear the moral consequences. In a feminist rereading of the ending of the tale, the female narrator's marginalization becomes explicit. What was successfully interpreted as a dramatization of the Oedipal *myth* for the male narrator turns to the harsh *reality* of oppression for the female narrator.

A feminist theorist must suspect that this development reveals Lacan's bias in adapting Freud's notion of manifest and repressed texts. At the manifest level, Lacan explicitly advocates sexual egalitarianism, but at the repressed (more influential) level he implicitly subverts it. My feminist rereading of the manifest text is as presented in the above analyses. Yet if one were to reread the repressed text, the Lacanian prejudice against the female would become obvious. I submit that the unconscious, or repressed text, through the pressure it exerts on the conscious or manifest text, shows that patriarchal morality condemns a woman for being aggressive, for desiring power, and ultimately punishes her for achieving this power even temporarily. Both male and female readers of Poe's story have tended to accept the Law of the Father, together with all its arbitrary presuppositions, and grant power only to the male. Thus, the status of the male narrator in Poe's "The Tell-Tale Heart" has remained stable. But if one wishes to transcend this phallogocentric prejudice, one must look elsewhere than Freud and Lacan.

To experience what Cixous explains as jouissance within Poe's text, we must erase the rigidity of metaphor (eye) and metonymy (heart) as separate categories. Instead, a gendered reading of Poe's tale would make the "eye" and the "heart" serve as metaphors and metonymies simultaneously, intermingling and creating multiple meanings. Quite accurately, Cixous's use of tropes can be called gendered, as they have greater maneuverability than Lacan's sexual tropes, which are clearly marked as *metaphor/symbolic/male*, and *metonymy/imaginary/female*. This strategy is Cixous's way of combating Lacan's notion of gender dissemination, which is actually based on a sexual paradigm. Lacan's position is invested with patriarchal biases such that the female term is violated and abused either at the conscious (manifest text) or unconscious (repressed text) level. The "eye" as metaphor has yielded meaning to Poe's text, but reading it metonymically enriches the tale further. The "eye" is the virtual symptom of the female narrator's desire to gain power in a male dominated society. In this context, it energizes the sequence of events in the tale to climax in the narrator's confession. Since killing the old man does not grant her lasting power, she confesses to the policemen and, thus, recirculates her power. Paradoxically, in the confessional scene "she" adroitly forces the male gaze to expose the controlled violence of the patriarchy. Her aggression against the old man is an explicit assault on male domination. Her confession becomes her implicit critique of domination. For a feminist reader, this is gratifying, an expression of solidarity through her exposure of ideology. For a masculinist reader, it is one more reminder of rebellion against patriarchal oppression. Her confession reveals the latent fetters of bondage in a patriarchal ideology, and she *re*reverses the gaze of the policemen by letting it bounce off her objectified body by using the eye as a metonymic instrument. Here the gaze is just one more part in her plan to expose the system. She exchanges the virtual prison bars of the Father's Law for the actual ones of the penal system. Henceforth, she will covertly make her point on discrimination against women through the underlying irony of her tale.

Writhing under the policemen's scrutiny, she protests: "they were making a mockery of my horror! . . . But any thing was better than this agony . . . more tolerable than this derision" (306). This indicates that her first plan to usurp power from the old man had failed, and now she must adopt another, creating a new perspective for the final scene. Her confession, now read ironically and not as evidence of guilt, directs the gaze back into the metaphoric register. It activates her plan for the exposé. For a moment, between her first plan and the second one, the gaze falls on the metaphoric

spectre of the Law. In this sense, the interweaving of metaphor and metonymy, as a slippage of tropes, allows for multiple readings that build on one
another instead of repressing one meaning to manifest another. This is an
example of the jouissance that Cixous advocates as a method of accretion.

Similarly, luxuriating in the jouissance of multiplicity, the "heart"
can be moved from the metonymic to the metaphoric register. As a metaphor, it serves to foreground the tale as belonging to the romance genre,
with all its associations of passion and fantasy. It also allows the tale to be
read as wish fulfillment, a dream in which the narrator as melodramatic
heroine becomes the cynosure in a male arena, the active speaking subject, instead of the fetishized object. She proudly declares: "I foamed—I
raved—I swore" (307), as a way of explaining her frantic attempts to
remain on center stage. This is an enactment of the stereotypical feminine
posture. By obeying the dictates of her heart in committing the passionate crime (exaggerated, no doubt), she dramatizes her execrated position
as woman. Now the female narrator emerges as the martyr through her
confession, also a typical position for the female.

But when examining the text under the light of jouissance, the first
step in reading is to expose such a patriarchal stereotyping. Yet the interweaving of the metaphoric and metonymic registers gives diverse readings. According to the metonymic register (eye), the female narrator is
an active speaking subject who assumes a male gendered identity, but the
metaphoric register (heart) forces her back into the archetypical female
position of martyr. This slip between the metaphoric and metonymic registers is crucial to feminist writing because it reveals the androgyny created by jouissance. Moreover, gendered identity sheds a different light on
the other characters in the tale, too. In the crucial, confessional scene, all
the characters can be read androgynously. The literal keepers of the Law
of the Father, the policemen observe passively while the female narrator is
explosively active. She is the speaking subject, frantically pacing, vigorously thumping the furniture, and energetically talking. She is catapulted
into her final ironic, yet male and active posture by "the beating of his
heart!" (307, italics added). It is the old man's heart, dramatized like a
damsel in distress, that vocalizes the narrator's confession. In the ironic
conclusion of the tale, both the policemen and the old man remain static,
while the female narrator adopts the dynamic and aggressive role, deliberately calling attention to the subservient status of all women. What needs
to be emphasized here is the active androgynous narrator who can be
contrasted to the passive males; her actions should not be mistaken for the
actions for a stereotypical "hysterical" female. This erroneous stereotyping will, no doubt, create a neat niche for the female, but leave the male

position in the discourse vacant. Thus, Cixous's brand of androgyny and multiple readings cancel out stereotypical sexual markings of the text.

Poe's "The Tell-Tale Heart" can indeed be read as the female narrator's own cry from "The soul when overcharged with awe" (304), a tale of escape, but escape into deliberate captivity so that she can articulate a female discourse. She experiments and functions in both the active and passive registers as a speaking subject and passive object. In this venture, her discourse becomes a painful tool of signifying and defining herself within the confines of patriarchy. Through jouissance, interweaving metaphors and metonymies, constantly slipping between the tropes, defying libidinal economy, and creating an excess of signifiers, she inscribes an "other" discourse. This rewriting becomes possible through the complex pattern of gendered tropes that are occupied by both male and female characters in the tale. It is this embracing, this gathering together, not only of the tropes, but also of the characters occupying these gendered tropes, that makes this tale a revelation of feminist rewriting as well as rereading.

NOTES

1. Jacques Lacan, "L'Instance de la lettre dans l'inconscient," *Ecrits I*, trans. Alan Sheridan (New York: Norton, 1977). Lacan argues that metonymy is the "derailment of instinct . . . externally extended towards the desire of something else" (278).

2. Roman Jakobson, "Two Aspects of Language and Two Types of Aphasic Disturbances," in *Fundamentals of Language* (The Hague: Mouton, 1956) 55–82. Lacan matches Saussure's linguistic model with Jakobson's to formulate the signifier/signified and metaphor/metonymy relationship (274).

3. See Jerry Ann Flieger, "The Purloined Punchline: Joke as Textual Paradigm," *Contemporary Literary Criticism*, ed. Robert Con Davis (New York: Longman, 1986) 277–94, who claims that a text through its intersubjectivity acts as a feminine symptom of inexhaustible desire. Toril Moi, in her introduction to *Sexual/ Textual Politics*, discusses Lacan's theory of the "symbolic/metaphoric" and male vector as always coexisting with the "imaginary/metonymic" and female vector in any discourse in an attempt to make meaning within the text. See Anthony Wilden, *The Language of the Self* (New York: Dell, 1975) 249–70, for a discussion of Lacan's symbolic/imaginary registers.

4. Robert Con Davis, "Lacan, Poe, and Narrative Repression," in *Lacan and Narration: The Psychoanalytic Difference In Narrative Theory* (Baltimore: Johns Hopkins UP, 1984). Davis argues that, according to Freud, the act of gazing represents the gazer's status as subject actively engaged in a pleasurable power game with the receiver of the gaze. In the object position, the receiver passively submits to the painful humiliation of the gazer's oppressive surveillance. By incorporating Lacan into Freud's theory, Davis shows that the "Gaze" is composed of three shifting positions of the subject's desire for the Other. Beginning with the gazer in a voyeuristic subject position, scrutinizing an exhibitionist as object, we move to a second, mirror-like stage, where the subject/object of the gaze are replicas of each other. In the final

moment, positions are reversed when the (former subject and current) object returns the gaze. Like the ever-shifting signifiers in language, the gaze is also a never-ending game. Davis's Lacanian interpretation sees the gaze as a mark of desire for the Other that is revealed in the text through intersubjectivity and reciprocal looking. Thus the looker, by looking, loses some of his power through the gaze itself.

5. Edgar Allan Poe, *The Complete Tales and Poems of Edgar Allan Poe* (New York: Modern Library, 1965) 303; cited hereafter in the text.

6. Hélène Cixous, "An Imaginary Utopia," *Sexual/Textual Politics*, ed. Toril Moi (New York: Methuen, 1985) 102–27. Cixous's theoretical paradigm is based on Derrida's deconstructive poetics. This particular three-step reinscription is my synthesis of Cixous's position as expressed in "The Laugh of the Medusa," in *New French Feminisms*, ed. Elaine Marks and Isabelle de Courtivron (Amherst: U of Massachusetts P, 1980) 245–64, and in "Castration or Decapitation?" *Signs* 7 (1981): 41–55.

7. For a more detailed discussion on the nature of patriarchal thought, the concept of sexual difference, and *écriture feminine* see Hélène Cixous and Catherine Clément, *La Jeune Née* (Paris: Union General d'Editions, 1975) 147; Julia Kristeva, *Desire in Language: A Semiotic Approach to Literature and Art*, ed. Leon S. Roudiez, trans. Thomas Gora, Alice Jardine, and Roudiez (New York: Columbia UP, 1980) 239–40; both cited hereafter in the text.

8. Marie Bonaparte, *The Life and Works of Edgar Allan Poe* (1949; London: Hogarth P, 1971).

9. Lacan, "L'Instance" 171.

10. Jacques Lacan, "Seminar XX" in *Feminine Sexuality*, ed. Juliet Mitchell and Jaqueline Rose (New York: Norton, 1982). For Lacan's discussion of women, see 48.

HENRY SUSSMAN

A Note on the Public and the
Private in Literature:
The Literature of "Acting Out"

Literature delights in a blurring of public and private realms often disastrous when it occurs on existential, ethical, psychoanalytical, or legal levels.
Indeed, from a perspective of wish-fulfillment, this confusion between the
public and the private accounts in part for the attraction that literature holds
for its readers. Whereas no small measure of our socialization is dedicated
to the inscription and then rigorous observation of a boundary between our
public self-representation and our private inventions (a dynamic in some
sense akin to the relation between "langue" and "parole"), some of the most
memorable characters (and gods) in literature freely overstep this margin—
with tragic or heroic, but never everyday consequences.

I am of course here speaking to a set of fictive works in which "characters" are, in a variety of ways, "represented." I would nevertheless argue
that within this "body" of literature, however inconsistent and ill-formed
it may be, some of the most seductive works, often playing a formative role
in young readers' gravitation toward literary discourse, are ones in which
important characters traverse the border between the private and the public,
and in which this transgression is then publically registered and addressed.

Is there any meaningful commonality that sustains the bookshelf containing the volumes that have attracted a disproportionate number of, say,
my past students to literary studies? Is it possible to postulate the grounds

From *MLN* 104, no. 3 (April 1989): 597–611. © 1989 by The Johns Hopkins University
Press.

for seminal and formative instances of literary transference? I myself pass from private observation to public debate while avoiding the middle ground of empirical testing when I tell you that, based on my experience, this subset of literary "classics" is heavy on Poe, Dostoyevsky, Kafka, and Camus—and that the attraction of some of their works at least in part hinges on the transition between public and private spheres undergone by certain of the central characters.

To the extent that all of these authors, not merely Poe, take up the phenomenon of the "tell-tale heart," the nearly imperceptible trace of some private murder or other outrage, they tap into roots running deep into the history of literature. The central human figures of Greek tragedies are not merely heroes and heroines; they are defendants as well in legal trials, well in advance of the Josef K. of Kafka's novel. (The "modernity" of Kafka's adaptation in part consists of the extreme idiosyncratic isolation with which a trial can still take place.) And as suggested above, the divinity of the Greek gods in no small measure consists of the freedom they exercise to introject their private "emotions"—disappointments, jealousies, and rages—into their official "portfolios."

As "modern" literature gives increasing credence to private language and personal aberration—and why not, following Benjamin, situate Baudelaire at the horizon of modernity?—measuring the impact of the idiosyncratic within the public sphere becomes increasingly inevitable. Although the following reading of two key instances of this watershed—in Poe and Kafka—is to some degree situated in the thematic domain, it should be noted that important formal and technical innovations in "modern" and "post-modern" literature also impact on the transition from the private to the public in an important way. When we approach the "Hades" or "Nighttown" episode of James Joyce's *Ulysses*, for example, some of the obvious critical issues that come to mind are the following: the incorporation of a topsy-turvy "Walpurgisnacht" episode in an already highly experimental novel, and the collation of widely disparate thematic strands effected by the chapter. Yet hand in hand with the chapter's formal innovations goes the dramatization of some of Bloom's most private and eccentric fantasies, in the form of an exaggerated stage trial. This event furnishes a public forum for Bloom's most secret and embarrassing wishes. It may well be argued that the trial itself, as an actual institution and as it is represented in literature, is a medium for ascertaining, opposing, and punishing instances of acting out[1] performed by individuals. The "Circe" episode in *Ulysses* is merely symptomatic of the trials running rampant throughout modern literature, one of whose major preoccupations then becomes the unresolvable complications resulting from dual citizenship in public and private spheres. The remainder of these remarks will be devoted to two of modern literature's climactic moments in its survey of the border between the public and the private, Poe's "The Tell-Tale Heart" and Kafka's "The Metamorphosis."

"The Tell-Tale Heart" is all of five or six pages long, yet it pursues the figure eight of a doubled trajectory of horror; in this way, it opens up a dimension of infinity. In the senselessness of the murder that it chronicles, this tale shares much with Dostoyevsky's *Crime and Punishment*. The old man who is the narrator's victim "had never wronged me. He had never given me insult. For his gold I had no desire. I think it was his eye! yes, it was this! He had the eye of a vulture—a pale blue eye, with a film over it. Whenever it fell upon me, my blood ran cold."[2] The old man with the uncanny eye, a Sphynx-like eye of blindness and inhuman vision at the same time, causes the narrator a certain anxiety. Or even better—the story begins in a state of terror that precedes any substance that can explain it. The text's very first words run: "True!—nervous—very, very dreadfully nervous I had been and am" (289). Nervousness is already, to paraphrase Hegel, the truth of this text's self-certainty. From its outset, this tale offers us the possibility of explaining it away as an account of a monster, a deviant beyond the table of ordinary behavior. "But why *will* you say that I am mad?" (289). But this "out" is merely a ruse, for the figure-eight of acting out in which the narrator traps himself is not only at the heart of everyday socio-psychological behavior; it is in the very site of literary expression itself.

The ostensible occasion for the narrator's anxiety is an unseeing, unfeeling, uncanny eye. Yet this eye is also the old man's "I," or is it also the narrator's? As a corpse, the old man "was stone dead" (292). In a sense, then, our old man, who already begins in a state of petrification, mocking the vitality of life, only meets his fate in submitting to murder. Our anxious narrator decides that he can quell his terror only by eliminating its purported source, the old man. The murder itself is described at least as much as a death sentence by terrorization and stalking as by stabbing and dismemberment. "And this I did for seven long nights—every night just at midnight—but I found the eye always closed; and so it was impossible to do the work; for it was not the old man who vexed me, but his Evil Eye" (290). The murder does not even succeed in closing the *malòcchio*, because it is always already closed. The narrator acts out his dread by killing its purported source. (In a different sphere, Raskolnikov's murdering the pawnbroker may be said to *act out* certain of *his* Nietzschean social theories and his sense of intellectual superiority.) Curiously, in the Poe story, before the narrator consummates his private affects in the act of murder, he attempts to *transfer* the terror to the victim. The victim must not only die: before dying, the aggressive party's torment must be projected upon him.

The narrator would attempt to quell the *given* affect or structure through a specific action, in this case an act of murder, but this emotional cycle pursues only one loop of the figure eight. For the terror of discovery is every bit the equal of the inability to cope with *Angst*. The acting out of unassimilable emotion promises a certain relief, in this case, the elimination of an uncanny Sphynx or Medusa-like figure; but in the wake of the action, comfort becomes even more elusive, because a counter-terror rears its unforgettable head: the fear that the acting out will itself become public. The narrator's last thought just *before* he precipitates himself on his victim is formulated as follows: "And now a new anxiety seized me—the sound would be heard by a neighbor!" (292). Only initially does acting out present itself as a cure or catharsis; once it has been permitted, once it has been "let out," so to speak, it becomes the basis of a complementary and every bit as persistent anxiety.

We are of course too sophisticated theoretically these days to own that the "substance" of any literary work could be any emotion, such as anxiety, or a psychological manifestation such as "acting out." Far be it from me to fall into such a pit, where I might fall prey to pendulums. What is crucial about the fact that intensely experienced psychological events could compel the narrator to action is less the specific emotion (he could be depressive) or the nature of his action than the *dimensions* that his predicament confuses. The narrator is driven for relief to the public, where he finds none. When he retreats (or rather, is driven back) to the private, the publicity of his solution pursues him there. Poe's tale outlines the confounding of the public and the private that is a very fundamental literary condition. Fictive writing, Poe's story included, may be regarded as an *expression* of the inescapable confusion between the public and the private, just as the narrator's murderous act may be regarded as an expression of his affect, and, correspondingly, the terror of discovery in which the text ends may be read as an expression of the murderous act. We will not follow Poe's ironic direction to dismiss the tale as the depiction of a madman; but the chronicle of acting out, among its other results, powerfully describes the *site* from which literature is produced.

Just as the narrator is anxious before the fact, the old man is, perhaps out of consideration, dead almost before his murder takes place. "*All in vain*; because Death, in approaching him had stalked with his black shadow before him, and had enveloped the victim. And it was the mournful presence of the unperceived shadow that caused him to feel—although he neither saw nor heard—to *feel* the presence of my head within the room" (291). Murderer and victim, like Master and Bondsman in Hegel and detective and murderer in *Crime and Punishment*, share much in common. The phenomenon of "tell-tale heart" breaks out not once but twice in the story, before and after the murder. And both times the narrator assumes that the discernible tachycardia—itself a symptom, an internal variety of acting out—is situated in the old man. But there is no reason for us to follow him here. The nervous heart is projective;

it could palpitate in the narrator's chest every bit as much as in the victim's. "I knew *that* sound well, too. It was the beating of the old man's heart. . . . Meanwhile the hellish tattoo of the heart increased. It grew quicker and quicker, and louder and louder every moment. The old man's terror *must* have been extreme. . . . I have told you that I am nervous: so I am" (291).

At one point in the story, the narrator actually succeeds in leaving behind his terrors. This is during the brief (a matter of lines) moment between the compulsive act itself and the arrival of the police. In celebration of this moment, Poe composes some of the most memorable lines in all his writing: "I then replaced the boards so cleverly, so cunningly, that no human eye—not even *his*—could have detected anything wrong. There was nothing to wash out—no stain of any kind—no blood-spot whatever. I had been too wary for that. A tub had caught all—ha! ha!" (292). This is the one moment in the text when the narrator can allow himself the delusion that he has succeeded *both* in eliminating the source of his disquietude *and* in obliterating all traces of his acting out. The contrast between the unmitigated hopelessness of the character and his inarticulate, self-congratulatory laughter comprises one of the masterstrokes of modern literature. We laugh as well—at the pathetic hopes invested in a tub, at a sordid murder that for one instant promises to be a tale of a tub. The narrator is here in the position of a man who has fallen before he knows it. But his audience sees! And this knowledge is his greatest fear. The narrator "speaks," then, from the position of irony; he, not the old man, is a victim, the dupe of irony itself.

There is a self-defeating quality to the fear of discovery founded, at least in part, on the desire for expression. The act of murder may transform the narrator's initial, unmotivated anxiety into a specific one—dread that the acting out will be discerned. As this story reads, however, the police who have been summoned by a bystander to the scene of the crime are fairly indifferent and obtuse to the clues indicating the narrator's guilt. Expression, publication of the deed, is both what the narrator dreads most and a new possible source of relief. Indeed, the narrator cannot be quieted until he himself has publicized his guilt.

> The officers were satisfied. My *manner* had convinced them. I was singularly at ease. . . . My head ached, and I fancied a ringing in my ears: but still they sat and still chatted. . . . Why *would* they not be gone? . . . Oh God! what *could* I do? I foamed—I raved—I swore! I swung the chair upon which I had been sitting, and grated it upon the boards, but the noise arose above all and continually increased. It grew louder—louder—*louder*! And still the men chatted pleasantly, and smiled. Was it possible they heard not? Almighty God!—no, no! They heard!—they suspected!—they knew!—they were making

a mockery of my horror!—this I thought, and this I think. But anything was better than this agony! (293)

The greatest agony of all for Poe—and it is inscribed in "The Pit and the Pendulum" and "The Premature Burial" as well as this text—is affect without expression. If the officers are blind to the narrator's misdeed and insensitive to his torture, the narrator will set them straight, will complete the communication. In the above passage, the policemen are deaf and blind. The horror of premature burial is less death, an inevitability, than the absence of acknowledgment of one's predicament. In "The Tell-Tale Heart," the policemen, until the narrator disabuses them of the luxury of ignorance, share the obtuseness and lack of sensation characterizing the old man's eye. The narrator punishes the old man by a sentence of death for his inattentiveness; in the case of the policemen, he corrects *their* inattentiveness with a notice that will inevitably result in *his* punishment. But in both cases, inattentiveness to affect, to sensitivity, leads to willed disaster, i.e., to retribution.

By virtue of superior sensitivity, placing the narrator in a category with artistic geniuses and professors, the narrator resides in the space of the ironist. The role of the ironist is to suffer, from the incomprehension and insensitivity of others, but also to gain revenge, to mete out punishment. The ironist traverses the distance from affect to expression by means of acting out. So restricted a privilege is acting out, that wherever it begins there is no end to it, because whoever *observes* it will immediately claim its privilege for herself. This is as true of our socio-psychological relationships as it is in literature. The volatility of acting out explains many situations distinctive for their endlessness: the "unhappy" family or organizational unit; the "feud" spanning generations; the ongoing "hotspots" of world politics—Northern Ireland, the Middle East.

The ironic narrator feels and punishes. These are fine, even pleasurable activities. The weakness of the system is the nonspecificity of feeling and punishment with regard to the subject–object distinction. Feelings may be projected onto others, as when the narrator assumes that the nervous hearts in the tale belong to the living and dead victim; and punishment, as Hegel well understood in the physics that he elaborated for "Force and the Understanding," has an uncanny way of inflicting itself back on the "self." In the basic terminology of psychoanalysis, Freud was also aware of the infinite *transferability* of affect and aggression. It is in this sense that the ironic narrator functions so well both as a sadist and a masochist.

The narrator of "The Tell-Tale Heart" acts out, both in misguided self-interest and *for us* (there is a certain messianism in superior ironic knowledge). The acting out falls within the ambivalent economy of expression. It arises both from a compulsion to express and a dread of apprehension (the cognitive and criminological senses of this latter word are close). Within the framework of the tale, the narrator expresses his preexisting anxiety by the murder and his attempts to mask it.

Yet the tale is itself an expression, of someone or something. Internally, the tale chronicles a certain acting out, which is an inefficient way of coping with the affect that precedes the story, an acting out founded on a confusion of the public and private spheres. As an expression, the tale itself is a manifestation or instance of acting out. Within the assessment of its own status that "The Tell-Tale Heart" provides, "writing out" is but a hair's breadth away from "acting out." To the extent that tales and other artifacts give expression to emotions that have gone unnoticed and misapprehended—remembering that for Poe sensibility in a vacuum is the greatest horror—they come close indeed to actions embodying in themselves the thought or emotion that has not otherwise succeeded in expressing itself. The similarity in status between the "acting out" that the tale thematically chronicles and its own *writing out* is close indeed.

The narrator murders the old man in part to quell an anxiety that has become public at least to the extent that he has become aware of it. He is not satisfied until the act has become publicized, even though it is uncertain that it needs to be. Texts, by the same token, exist in the sphere of publicity, of publication. Texts too are residues of something expressed inadequately elsewhere. An ironic text describing an unnecessary but inevitable murder, which is then unnecessarily made public, where it inevitably precipitates an unnecessary punishment—such a text speaks with intensity to its own status and exigency. Something *compels* actions out and writing out—but this compulsion is far from giving these actions and artifacts any self-explanatory necessity.

From the perspective of literary history, it is most tempting to link Poe's account of the disastrous exigency of expression with the ironically aware moment in which "The Tell-Tale Heart" arises. On some level, Poe's tale does exist in a privileged relationship with the other masterful explorations of irony—by the Schlegels, Kierkegaard, Baudelaire, Flaubert, and Melville—of its age. It is important to note at the same time, however, that the vertiginous play between the public and the private that we find in this text extends well into the twentieth century—where it plays a significant role in distinguishing some of the literature that readers have pursued with the greatest compulsion. Meursault's shooting the Arab on the beach in Albert Camus's *The Stranger* derives its enormous power in part from the obscurity of its motive. The act itself is firmly rooted in the tradition of irony, but it is rendered mysterious and compelling by the absence of context in which its acting out takes place. *The Stranger*, with all the contemporary updating of its emotional and stylistic components, demonstrates the power that acting out, as a literary wish, continues to assert. And then, of course, there is the meditation on the play between the public and private spheres conducted at a far remove from Poe, Joyce, and Camus—by Franz Kafka.

There is a curious satisfaction surrounding Gregor Samsa, the half-man, half-dung-beetle hero of "The Metamorphosis," a satisfaction not unlike the one we experience when we read, "A tub had caught all, ha! ha!" Gregor exists at the very limits of literature. He, or perhaps properly it, strains our credibility to the ultimate degree but inhabits his own space as no other figure could. The intense pleasure of reading "The Metamorphosis"—which is not to say that this story sustains no other emotions—consists in the experience of knowing that literature has opened itself full throttle and has because of this gripped the reader all the more firmly in the track of discovery. Gregor is just right, precisely because he is all wrong.

The question as to when his fate is permanently sealed is the sort of question that sustains critical debate. One could well argue that, in keeping with the other son-figures in Kafka's fiction and the retrospective logic of guilt that Kafka explored so fully, Gregor is ruined from the outset of the story, from the very dawning of his "consciousness." There is much to sustain this position; it is not to be dismissed. I would prefer to explore another hypothesis, however, one more in keeping with Kafka's examination of the interplay between the public and the private: namely, that Gregor's goose is not fully cooked until he, having literally blown his cover,[3] is observed by the middle lodger. Gregor has, in responding to perhaps the final vestige of his humanity, left his hiding-place and entered the room where his sister is playing her violin. Up until this moment, Gregor's monstrosity has been kept a family secret, known only to the immediate family and its servant. When Gregor becomes a public nuisance, the family can no longer tolerate his exceptional status and the exceptional measures, including concealment and dissimulation, that it requires. Whatever the strange turn of events initiated by the metamorphosis means to the family is one thing; when it becomes a matter of public record, the status of the event, and its meaning, changes—terminating the familial contract.

Kafka is, then, in this text continuing his interrogation of familial legacies, obligations, and prerogatives. The family is the setting for Gregor's transformation. It may be that Kafka's other son (and artist) parables have light to shed on this event. The metamorphosis takes place as an ineluctable, involuntary event. Its inevitability may be, however, just a deceptive cover, inducing us to look away from its more subtle qualities. If the metamorphosis is more than a mere fact, if it is expressive of something, then Gregor's bizarre transformation may be another instance of acting out, another place where the private is allowed to venture into the public; as much so as the murder committed by the narrator of "The Tell-Tale Heart."

Gregor's fate is irrevocably decided when that Smith Brother look-alike, the lodger, utters the following words: "I beg to announce that because of the disgusting conditions (*widerlichen Verhältnisse*) prevailing in this household and this family . . . I give you notice on the spot (*augenblicklich*). . . . I shall consider bringing an action for damages against you, based on claims—believe me—that will be easily susceptible of proof" (*CS*, 132). Threatening legal action, this statement assumes the form of a judgment. Once ventilated, the bizarre conditions now defining Gregor's existence justify convening a trial. A trial in fact takes place whenever the private strays into the properly public sphere. All acts of acting out, which facilitate this transition, are adjudicable. Being on trial is a nightmarish predicament, but it offers its attractions as well. Someone is at last paying attention to the defendant, who, if he is anyone other than Meursault, is the possessor of some unique sensitivity or genius. Trials may be regarded as collusions between the punitive institutions of society and an individual's hitherto unheeded cry for attention, for expression. Acting out, and the literature surveying the transference between the public and the private that it effects, are fated to the repetition of their trials, judicial and imaginary.

The judgment that the lodger delivers to the entire Samsa family, not only Gregor, stands anything but alone in Kafka's fiction. Such sentences mark pivotal moments in such texts as *The Trial*, "The Judgment," "In the Penal Colony," and "The Knock at the Manor Gate." Again, we must ask ourselves: If Gregor's transformation is so involuntary (as Josef K.'s indictment is so given), how could it comprise an instance of acting out; how could it express in a dysfunctional but for that reason interesting way some feeling or expression that has found no satisfying form? To answer this, again to suggest that Gregor's mission is not complete until he is *discovered*, we should direct our attention to some of the above-named fictive works, in which the bearer (or vessel) of knowledge happens also to occupy the role of the son.

The figure of the son in Kafka's fiction is hopelessly ambivalent: he is the bearer of awesome responsibilities, often voluntarily undertaken, which at some other level he also despises and resists. The Kafkan son is a pedestrian messiah, one not above his rage and triteness, even if these reactions are elaborately disguised. The brother of "The Knock at the Manor Gate" is sentenced to the ominous fate figured by "half a pallet, half an operating table" (*CS*, 419), even though it is clear that he did nothing to provoke the unusual events (it is not certain his sister did either). The brother is messianic by virtue of his overtly stated innocence; any guilt in the story, and it is not clear that there is any, accrues to him by transference.

The son in Kafka's fiction bears some affinity to the artist. Artists and sons share the sensitivity demonstrated by the ironic narrator in "The

Tell-Tale Heart." In the first half of "The judgment," narrated from the son's point of view (rather than the father's), the son worries about his love-starved and financially destitute friend in Russia; in "The Metamorphosis," the son provides for Grete's music lessons (perhaps this is why even in the end, when it really is too late, Gregor insists on hearing the concert. After all, he's paid for it). The son is capable of hiding a considerable amount of condescension and resentment within this messianic moral superiority, and in keeping with Kafka's imaginative esthetic, these negative emotions can assume some bizarre forms (perhaps this is why the son of "A Crossbreed [A Sport]" feels such an affinity to the kitten/lamb that is a family legacy). In "The Judgment," Georg Bendemann writes of his engagement to the friend in Russia: "just let me say that I am very happy and as between you and me the only difference in our relationship is that instead of a quite ordinary kind of friend you will now have in me a happy friend. Besides that, you will acquire in my financée, who sends her warm greetings and will soon write you herself, a genuine friend of the opposite sex, which is not without importance to a bachelor" (CS, 80). As if the friend, whatever his circumstances, is incapable of any sexual relationship on his own. Later in the story, Georg represents his friend's circumstances to himself: "At the door of an empty, plundered warehouse he saw him. Among the wreckage of his showcases, the slashed remnants of his wares, the falling gas brackets, he was just standing up" (CS, 85). The friend's situation is worse than a case of gas, but it is entirely Georg's projection.

The story goes on, of course, to systematically reverse the ascendancy of this messianic position (Kafka's extreme scepticism regarding this perspective marks the trajectory at which his fictive world is closest to that of Joseph Conrad. Although the latter's fiction draws on much of its power from mythological narrative, in the Barthesian sense, much of its moral outrage is directed at characters who have been taken in and corrupted by their private messianic mythologies, such as Lord Jim, "he was one of us," and Nostromo, "one of us").[4] From the father's perspective in Kafka's story, the divide-and-conquer strategy by which the son has attempted to separate and manipulate the father and the friend in Russia has failed. Father and friend have maintained their contact (enabling the friend to become the son's uncanny double); and the teleological scenario in which the son supplants the father is anything but the case in this story.

In "The Metamorphosis" Gregor's efforts on behalf of the Samsa family have been nothing short of heroic, lulling his parents and sister into a kind of complacency at the beginning of the story. The first good news that Gregor hears after his catastrophe is that his father, unbeknownst to him, has some savings left over from his old business. At the time of the collapse,

> Gregor's sole desire was to do his utmost to help the family to forget as soon as possible the catastrophe that had overwhelmed his business and thrown them all into a state of complete despair. And so he had set to work with unusual ardor and almost overnight had become a commercial traveler instead of a little clerk, with of course much greater chances of earning money, and his success was immediately transformed (*verwandelten*) into good round coin which he could lay on the table for his amazed and happy family. These had been fine times, and they had never recurred, at least not with the same sense of glory, although later on Gregor had earned so much money that he was able to meet the expenses of the whole household and did so. They simply had got used to it, both the family and Gregor; the money was gratefully accepted and gladly given, but there was no special uprush of warm feeling. With his sister alone had he remained intimate, and it was a secret plan of his that she, who loved music, unlike himself, and could play movingly on the violin, should be sent next year to study at the Conservatorium, despite the great expense that would entail, which must be made up in some other way. (*CS*, 110–11)

"Had to get used to it," "no special uprush of warm feeling": these are the phrases we must bear in mind as we interpret the bizarre, seemingly ineluctable insect-transformation as an instance of acting out, a publicizing and notification of the private and inadequately expressed. And indeed, once Gregor becomes an insect, the role of voluntary, but inadequately appreciated family messiah is open to him no more. The story takes care, in its unique realism, to demonstrate the inadequacy of Gregor's new body and voice to his former roles and functions.

In a sense, the unappreciated Gregor has willed his complete failure, in terms of the earlier criteria for his success. The transfigured Gregor occupies a position of total irresponsibility—the marginal and utterly useless space of writing. In a sense, Gregor must go to the length of becoming a dung-beetle in order to openly acknowledge his writing-habit. It is as an allegory of unstated irresponsibility that "The Metamorphosis" becomes an allegory of writing. Gregor still retains certain sentimental attachments and "human" inclinations: warm feelings toward his sister, a fondness at least for her music. As alien as Gregor's transformation may be, the story does provide a rationale for it, in terms of acting out, in terms of a distorted and displaced expression of what has remained private. As in "The Tell-Tale Heart," the public apprehension of this message is tantamount to a speedy and decisive judgment. Gregor's significance is revised in the aftermath of this trial. The revisionist Gregor is as much the occasion for the family's rejuvenation as its depression, just as the guilt-provoking Hunger Artist prepares the way for the panther, whose gratification is so easy and immediate.

Merely by waking up, then, on a fateful morning, Gregor Samsa "acts out," transfigures the values of his existence by externalizing what has been previously relegated to privacy, where it belonged. As a rhetorical as well as biological figure, Gregor hovers in the between-space linking humanity to something radically Other. Gregor is the enigmatic and ambiguous expression of something else, namely Gregor.

For Kafka as well as Poe, then, as becomes painfully evident in the "Letter to His Father," acting out and writing out are intimate indeed. What the figure of the sentimental, humanized dung-beetle is to Gregor, the text of "The Metamorphosis" is to Kafka—a space where the public and private, rigorously quarantined from each other in everyday life, meet; where ambivalence has found a tangible manifestation.

Literature holds out the wish that, at least within its qualified confines, the private can enter the public without devastating consequences. This bridging may well constitute one of literature's most compelling attractions. A carefully chosen and well-formulated literary image can perform this transference at the same time that it constitutes an inexhaustible object for interpretation. Literature gives voice to and assembles images for a privacy that we must divulge only if we want to.

To a large extent, irony is the difference in knowledge that makes acting out possible. Irony is the basis of the claim, whether by the son or the narrator, of superior knowledge or enhanced sensitivity. Ordinarily, we relegate the significance of irony to a merely literary or rhetorical level. Yet if literature is indeed a privileged site for the confounding of the public and the private that takes place in acting out, then irony is not merely a rhetorical figure: irony becomes a structure at the basis of our psychological life. Irony first defines the watershed between knowledge and expression, and then militates for its bridging over, both in the form of acting out and in literary artifacts. The vision of irony compels us, both as individuals and readers, toward the brink where our privacy opens into the public domain. The results are to be found both in the living and in the reading.

NOTES

1. Although the term "acting out" currently enjoys widespread usage as a concept and diagnostic tool in psychiatry, its roots run deep in the classical literature of psychoanalysis. In its original denotation, "acting out" comprises some indirection or short-circuiting that takes place in the process of psychoanalytical transference, affect, for instance, directed at someone other than the analyst. (The

complete original term is "acting out of transference.") After Freud, "acting out" takes on a more general meaning. It goes beyond the psychoanalytical relationship and characterizes instances of indirect and displaced behavior and expression in general. Acting out can therefore assume a myriad of forms: "misplaced aggression," in which fear and anger are not vented at the individual(s) who give rise to them but at some uninvolved, "safer" party; malicious gossip, in which rage takes the form of public character assassination rather than direct, private expression of differences; and various manifestations of "bizarre behavior," e.g. mumbling, talking to oneself "out loud," in which private thoughts are transmitted to the public sphere, but in a deliberately scrambled and problematical form. Freud's meditations on this concept begin in such a 1914 essay as "Remembering, Repeating, and Working-Through," in which acting out receives its initial definition as a dramatization by the patient of material that has eluded his memory ("the patient does not *remember* anything of what he has forgotten and repressed, but *acts* it out"). At this stage in his work, Freud is already aware of the danger "that the patient's actions outside the transference may do him temporary harm in his ordinary life," and for this reason attempts to secure the patient's "promise not to take any important decisions affecting his life during the time of his treatment . . . but to postpone all such plans until after his recovery." My colleague David Willbern directed me to this material, which is to be found in Sigmund Freud, *The Standard Edition of the Complete Psychological Works of Sigmund Freud* (London: The Hogarth Press, 1953–74) XII: 150–55. With regard to later elaborations of this notion, friends involved in clinical therapeutic work point me toward the ongoing serial publication, *The Psychoanalytic Study of the Child*, initiated, among others, by Anna Freud, as an important locus where the implications of acting out have been explored.

2. The edition I have used for Poe's "The Tell-Tale Heart" is *Poe's Tales of Mystery and Imagination*, Everyman's Library Edition, intro. Padraic Colum (New York: E. P. Dutton, 1968), 289–93.

3. English citations of Kafka in the present essay refer to Franz Kafka, *The Complete Stories*, ed. Nahum Glatzer (New York: Schocken, 1976), henceforth abbreviated "*CS.*" German introjections derive from Franz Kafka, *Sämtliche Erzählungen*, ed. Paul Raabe (Frankfurt: S. Fischer, 1972). Gregor gives away his own "cover" because in the second section of "The Metamorphosis" a cover is precisely the way in which he attempts to conceal himself. "One day he carried a sheet on his way back to the sofa (*das Leintuch auf das Kanapee*)—it cost him four hours' labor—and arranged it there in such a way as to hide him completely (*daß er nun gänzlich verdecht war*)," [*CS*, 114].

4. One of Conrad's most telling captions for his character Lord Jim, uttered by Marlowe, is "I only know that he is one of us," Joseph Conrad, *Lord Jim*, intro. Morton Dauwen Zabel (Boston: Houghton Mifflin, 1958), 161. Through this expression, Marlowe ironically refers to the duplicity of Jim's status and his claim: he is an absolutely mundane individual who would presume to a literary and extralegal plane. This paradox, as an instance of the status of fiction, must have been important to Conrad if he went on to name his subsequent epic, and its title-character, *Nostromo*, with its play on the first-person plural personal pronoun in Spanish, *nosotros*. Conrad is clearly fascinated and revolted by the juncture at which people and events assume (or claim) mythological (or imagistic) proportions.

PAIGE MATTHEY BYNUM

"Observe how healthily—how calmly I can tell you the whole story": Moral Insanity and Edgar Allan Poe's "The Tell-Tale Heart"

David R. Saliba has recently argued that Edgar Allan Poe's "structural omission of an objective viewpoint for the reader [in 'The Tell-Tale Heart'] forces the reader to experience the tale with no point of reference outside the framework of the story". "The reader", says Saliba, "is led through the story by the narrator with no sense of reality other than what the narrator has to say". This narrative technique forces the reader to identify with the narrator and to take the narrator's values as his own (pp. 142–43n). What Saliba fails to realize is that no one can read a text without an external sense of reality; all audiences bring to a work of literature some frame of reference that exists outside the text. And for Poe's audience in the 1840s, that frame of reference would have included a knowledge of a controversial new disease called 'moral insanity' and of the legal and philosophical dilemmas that surrounded its discovery. Poe's narrator in 'The Tell-Tale Heart' is a morally insane man, and Poe would have expected his readers to locate the symptoms of that condition in the language of his narration. Thus if we are to recover the meaning of the tale for Poe's audience, an audience that applauded 'The Tell-Tale Heart' at the same time that it shunned tales like 'Ligeia', 'William Wilson', and 'The Fall of the House of Usher'—indeed, if we are to assess the tale's significance for today's audience—we need to establish the medical history from which Poe drew.

From *Literature and Science as Modes of Expression*, edited by Frederick Amrine, pp. 141–152.
© 1989 by Kluwer Academic Publishers.

We begin, then, with the 'father of American psychiatry', Benjamin Rush. In 1787, Rush was placed in charge of the insane at the Pennsylvania Hospital, and his work in this institution culminated in the first book on psychiatry by a native American, *Medical Inquiries and Observations upon the Diseases of the Mind* (1812). In his introduction to two of the essays Rush included in *Diseases of the Mind*,[1] E. T. Carlson explains how Rush developed a new theory of insanity based on associationism and faculty psychology. Following the Scottish school of mental philosophy, Rush posited nine basic capacities or "faculties" in the human mind, grouping these nine faculties into three categories: the "passions" included the passions *per se*, the will, and faith or "the believing faculty"; the "intellectual faculties" encompassed the reason or understanding, imagination, and memory; and the "moral faculties" included the moral faculty itself, conscience, and a sense of deity (Carlson, p. ix).[2] Insanity had long been recognized as a disease affecting what Rush called the intellectual faculties. Where Rush broke with traditional psychiatric theory was in declaring that insanity did not necessarily involve a disorder of the intellect, that the moral faculties alone were capable of succumbing to disease (Carlson, p. x). Like Philippe Pinel in France, he realized that a form of insanity might occur which perverted the sense of moral responsibility necessary to deter crime. Thus in a normal individual, an innate moral sense could stave off the passions while the intellect calmly concluded the proper conduct. But if this moral sense, this power to distinguish between good and evil, were momentarily suspended, the opportunity for calm inquiry would be denied, and the individual's will would become committed to a criminal act before his reason could repudiate it (Rush, 1972, p. 1). He would then become the victim of an "irresistible impulse" forced upon the will "through the instrumentality of the passions" (Rush, 1830, pp. 262; 355–57). In modern terminology, he would be emotionally disturbed.

Startling as it was, Rush's theory of "moral derangement" received little attention in America before the 1830s. Then, in 1835, James Cowles Prichard published his classic discussion of the problem in *Treatise on Insanity and Other Disorders Affecting the Mind*. This work popularized the study of what Prichard termed "moral insanity", making it, in the words of one historian, the "focus of psychological studies and polemical arguments until the end of the century" (Carlson, p. xi). Following the leads of Pinel and Rush, Prichard restated and developed the body of theory which would eventually lead to the classification of psychopathic personalities. He posited a disease in which

> the intellectual faculties appear to have sustained little or no injury, while the disorder is manifested principally or alone, in the state

of the feelings, temper, or habits. In cases of this description the moral and active principles of the mind are strangely perverted and depraved; the power of self-government is lost or greatly impaired; and the individual is found to be incapable, not of talking or reasoning upon any subject proposed to him, for this he will often do with great shrewdness and volubility, but of conducting himself with decency and propriety.... His wishes and inclinations, his attachments, his likings and dislikings have all undergone a morbid change, and this change appears to be the originating cause, or to lie at the foundations of any disturbance which the understanding itself may seem to have sustained, and even in some instances to form throughout the sole manifestation of the disease (pp. 4–5).

A disturbance of the emotions could be both the cause and the "sole manifestation" of mental illness. The morally insane man might be rational, might realize that those around him would condemn his behavior, but he himself would not.

In the decade following the appearance of Prichard's study, the concept of moral insanity became the topic of political, social, and theological debate both at home and abroad. As Rush himself foresaw, any new theories which emphasized the power of man's emotions to determine his actions occasioned intense hostility when they conflicted with other, presumably more agreeable, Ideas about human nature. Such theories were opposed on the grounds that they degraded the quality of man's spiritual life, and for the more pragmatic reason that they reduced the incentives for good behavior. But nowhere were the new theories on moral insanity argued more strenuously that in the courts. Prior to the work of men like Rush and Prichard, if a person pleaded insanity in a court of law, he was presumed to be either an idiot or a raving maniac. A review of press releases concerning these trials, and of verbatim trial reports, shows that judges, counsel, witnesses, and observers tended to use three major criteria to establish insanity: the accused had to be unable to recognize right from wrong; he had to be illogical and virtually witless at all times; and he had to reveal a violent disposition before committing his offense ('Homicidal Insanity', p. 279; Wharton, I, 162–72). John Haslam's discussion of the jurisprudence of insanity in *Observations on Madness and Melancholy* (1810) reveals that madness was considered to be, in Haslam's words, as opposed to "reason and good sense as light is to darkness"; in order to exempt a man from criminal responsibility, the defense had to establish that he was "totally deprived of his understanding" and no more knew what he was doing "than an infant, than a brute, or a wild beast" (Haslam, 1975, p. 31; see also Coventry, p. 136). A man who, like Poe's narrator in 'The Black Cat', became unaccountably brutal, set fire to his home, and violently murdered his wife could not be judged insane if he appeared 'normal' to witnesses at the time of the trial.[3] And anyone who fled from the scene of a murder, or tried to hide the evidence, was legally sane because he was presumed to know right from wrong.

But the concept of moral insanity changed all this, and the legal dilemma posed by this new definition of madness was obvious. If God had so constituted men that their passions or impulses were not always governable by an intact reason, how could society punish them for indulging in these passions? As pleas of moral insanity became increasingly common, this question stymied a criminal court system established as an instrument of retribution rather than as an agency for determining mental health.[4] A reaction was inevitable and almost immediate. Judges found themselves asserting that moral insanity was, in Baron Rolfe's words, "an extreme moral depravity not only perfectly consistent with legal responsibility, but such as legal responsibility is expressly invented to restrain" ('Baron Rolfe's Charge to the Jury', p. 214). Some of America's leading pre–Civil War psychiatrists—men like Isaac Ray, Samuel B. Woodward, and Amariah Brigham—wrote numerous treatises and periodical articles delineating the characteristics and supporting the pleas of criminals claiming moral insanity, but they faced serious opposition within their own profession almost from the outset, and by the late 1840s even some distinguished asylum superintendents began denying the existence of a 'moral' insanity.

The views of these skeptical physicians were generally more in keeping with public sentiment, and those medical men who supported an accused murderer's claim of insanity came under increasingly sharp attacks in the periodical press. The average man tended to suspect deception in defense pleas of insanity, and newspapers often fanned these feelings. Thus by the time Poe wrote 'The Tell-Tale Heart', such trials were major events. When William Freeman was tried for the stabbing murders of the prominent Van Nest family in New York, the counsel included John Van Buren for the prosecution and ex-governor William H. Seward for the defense. Papers across the country kept track as seventy-two witnesses were called to testify as to his sanity, including a who's-who list of medical authorities, and Freeman himself, housed in a cage outside the courthouse, was the subject of "uncounted spectators" until he died of consumption in his cell almost eighteen months after his offense (*The Trial of William Freeman*, pp. 68–71, 79–80; Fosgate, pp. 409–14).[5]

Freeman and those like him were, to use the modern slang, "hot copy". The journals of the day devoted thousands of pages to analysis of them. Philosophical and literary societies debated the ethical and moral implications of decisions surrounding their cases. And writers like Poe—who was himself a trial reporter in the 1843 murder-by-reason-of-moral-insanity trial of James

Wood ('The Trial of James Wood', pp. 105–106)[6]—used them as models for some of their most disturbing creations.

One of these creations came to life in 'The Tell-Tale Heart'. Defendants in moral insanity trials were rarely allowed to speak in their own behalf, but Poe would let his character speak, and as he spoke, he would inadvertently let slip the very evidence which would establish him as morally insane.

The first thing we should notice about Poe's narrator is that his monologue is actually a long argument trying to establish not his innocence—he has already confessed to killing the old man—but rather his sanity. He builds this argument on the premise that insanity is irreconcilable with systematic action, and as evidence of his capacity for the latter, he explains how he has executed an atrocious crime with faultless precision. "This is the point", he tells us: "You fancy me mad. Madmen know nothing. But you should have seen *me*. You should have seen how wisely I proceeded—with what caution—with what foresight—with what dissimulation I went to work!" (Poe, 1978, p. 792). A madman, he implies, would be out of control, would be profoundly illogical and not even recognize the implications of his actions. His art in planning and coolness in executing his crime prove that he has the lucidity, control, and subtle reason which only a sane man could possess.

Poe's narrator is, of course, relying upon the old criteria used to establish insanity. But it would have been difficult for an audience reading his words in 1843 not to call to mind the medical publications and trial reports filling the popular press with a new theory of insanity. If they knew enough about this new theory, they might even have recognized Poe's narrator as a fair representation of Prichard's morally insane man. Like the patients in Prichard's study, he is capable of reasoning "with great shrewdness and volubility", but "his attachments . . . have undergone a morbid change" (Prichard, pp. 4–5).

This is not to say that Poe's narrator is always rational. He may be able to carry out his crime with a cool precision, but as he himself explains, his determination to murder his old friend stems from an irrational fear of his eye:

> Object, there was none. I loved the old man. He had never given me insult. For his gold I had no desire. I think it was his eye! yes it was this! One of his eyes resembled that of a vulture—a pale blue eye with a film over it. Whenever it fell upon me, my blood ran cold; and so by degrees—very gradually—I made up my mind to take the life of the old man, and thus rid myself of the eye forever. (1978, p. 792)

Poe skillfully refrains from divulging exactly what the narrator fears, and his readers have consistently picked up the gauntlet and put forth their own theories. Robert Shulman believes that the filmed-over eye suggests that the old man is cut off from "insight into the ideal and the beautiful" and that the narrator's fear thus represents man's "psychological dread that existence is meaningless", or more specifically, is a reflection of Poe's feelings toward the stepfather who "called into question the meaning of [his] life" (pp. 259–60). Arthur Robinson argues that the feared "Evil Eye" is actually the "Evil I", that the narrator "images himself as another and recoils from the vision" (pp. 101–2). And in his introduction to 'The Tell-Tale Heart', T. O. Mabbott concludes that the tale is founded on the "popular superstition" of the Evil Eye and points out that Poe may even be suggesting that it really *is* the old man's eye which drives the otherwise sane narrator mad (Poe, 1978, p. 789). However we feel about these interpretations, we should perhaps realize that much of Poe's audience, and certainly Poe himself, would have been familiar with Rush's theory (1830, p. 173) that the insane were "for the most part easily terrified, or composed, by the eye of a man who possesses his reason". They would have surmised that Poe's narrator is terrified by, in Rush's words, "the mild and steady eye" of a sane man.[7]

But it is not the eye alone which brings about the final decision to take the old man's life. Rather, it is a *peculiar sound*, and to understand the medical significance of this sound, we must go back to the beginning of the tale. The narrator opens his defense by declaring that although he is "very, very dreadfully nervous", he is not mad (1978, p. 792). Poe's readers probably would have recognized his nervousness as one of the common predisposing causes of moral insanity. Certainly most physicians writing at the time of Poe's tale would have agreed with Samuel B. Woodward (p. 288) that moral insanity, unlike mere depravity, was always preceded or accompanied by "some diseased function of the organs, more or less intimately connected with the nerves". Rush had maintained that "all those states of the body . . . which are accompanied with preternatural irritability . . . dispose to vice" (1972, p. 20). But even if the audience was uncertain about the significance of the narrator's dreadful nervousness, they certainly would not have been uncertain about the significance of his next statement. This nervousness, or "disease", had "sharpened [his] senses", he tells us, "not destroyed—not dulled them", and "above all was [his] sense of hearing acute" (1978, p. 792).

It would be difficult to think of a worse argument for sanity in 1843 than what Poe's narrator calls his "over acuteness of the senses" (1978, p. 795). Medical opinion at home and abroad had long held that "there is scarcely any symptom more frequently attendant upon maniacal . . . disorders than a defect, excess, or some kind of derangement in the faculty of hearing" (Reid, p. 190), and that it is frequently "noises in the ear, such as sounds made during the night in the chimney", and in particular, "the noises of clocks and of bells" (Sigmond, p. 589; 'On Impulsive Insanity', p. 620) which haunt the minds of these men.[8] We should not be surprised then to learn that, as he stands over his intended victim, Poe's narrator hears "a low, dull, quick sound, such as a watch makes when enveloped in cotton" (1978, p. 795). His assertion that "he knew *that* sound well, too" reminds us that he has also been hearing another sound—that of the death-watches in the wall. "Night after night" he had listened to their ticking, telling himself that "it is nothing but the wind in the chimney", until the night when, "excited to uncontrollable terror" by the noise, he stalks his victim (1978, p. 796).

After the murder, the ticking sound returns, and the fear, outrage and paranoia it inspires increase until the seemingly rational murderer must confess his crime to the unsuspecting police. Even this confession would have been considered strong evidence of moral insanity. In a typical case from 1832, a man on trial for the murder of his son was found insane because he had "slaughtered his unoffending son to whom he should have been attached", and then confessed. One reporter explains:

> The confession of the crime, I conceive, may be considered as an evidence of insanity of considerable weight. Not that every man who confesses a murder is to be considered insane, but, by this, taken along with other circumstances, as when the individual ... attempts to give reasons for the propriety of his conduct, we have a strong indication ... of the deranged condition of the intellect.... In short, it is so universal in such cases, that some very distinguished medical jurists consider this confession alone to be a significant test of insanity (Watson, 1832, p. 47).[9]

Observations such as this can be found throughout the trial reports of the 1830s and 40s, and while they may sound fairly obvious to today's readers, they contained new and fascinating information for Poe's. And this, of course, is the point. New medical theories were forcing upon Poe's audience questions of ethical moment and challenging their old ideas about the nature of man. It may even be that this audience, like most of the students I teach today, found the real terror in the story lay in identifying themselves not with the narrator, as Saliba suggests, but with the victim. It certainly would have been natural for Poe's 1843 readers to see themselves as the victims of the morally insane men discussed in the popular press, just as twentieth-century readers tend to associate themselves more with suffering families and felled presidents than with madmen who attack McDonald's and presidential assassins. In any case, Poe's narrator is maintaining a causal sequence—I can reason; therefore I am not insane—which

Poe's audience had just discovered was false, so that it is not only the experiences the narrator reports that are unusual and problematic, but the report itself. "Observe how healthily—how calmly I can tell you the whole story", he begins (1978, p. 792). But "calmly" could no longer be equated with "healthily". The narrator's explanation fails to coincide with his audience's knowledge, and the implication is that Poe intends to display this disagreement in order that the audience might experience and evaluate it. Far from being trapped inside the story, the audience would stand outside the narrative and use its knowledge of the current medical controversy to replace the speaker's version of events with a better one, or even to question the moral implications of such an argument.

The narrator tells them that he has suffocated an old man because of his eye. But to make such an argument is finally to flaunt your lack of motive, and indeed he begins his explanation by admitting that "object there was none" (1978, p. 792). Those readers who insist upon positing an external motive on the narrator's part, or an unconscious motive on Poe's, deny the story some of its power. Like the murder of the Van Nest family, this murder is all the more terrifying because it is gratuitous. The narrator's obsessions have no logical object in the manifest text, and the tension produced by his explaining at length something for which there is no satisfactory explanation took Poe's story to the heart of the vexing question of moral responsibility as it dramatized the increasingly problematic nature of the human personality.

For Poe's 1843 audience, the new medical science had done more than just drag Diana from her car; it had questioned the integrity of even the 'rational' mind. But what about today's audience? Clearly the medical sources Poe drew from are now outdated, and we no longer recognize Poe's medical allusions. But the deep-seated and not always clearly verbalized anxiety generated by the knowledge that men like Prichard and Rush imparted is still with us. What Poe's 1843 audience had learned—what his present audience is still struggling with—was that a murderous rage could be present in any man, could begin to manifest itself without motivation, and once manifest, could exert complete control. The will to do wrong was internally derived; it could no longer be referred to poisonous miasmatas, solipsism, alcohol, or intellectual indulgence. Even reason could provide no check on these murderous rages, since the most careful plans and meticulous arguments could be made to support the most vicious actions. This was, and is, the real terror of Poe's tale: that there is in man the potential for an inexplicable moral short-circuit that makes it impossible to find protection from the dangers that lay within our neighbors—and ourselves. It is to Poe's credit as an artist that he has given this terror an imaginative representation which has remained valid long after Prichard's theories have disappeared.

NOTES

1. Rush originally published these essays in 1786. They were reprinted in *Medical Inquiries and Observations upon the Diseases of the Mind* in 1812, where they went through five editions and numerous translations. In 1972, Brunner/Mazel reprinted them again as a separate volume, introduced by E. T. Carlson, entitled *Two Essays on the Mind*.

2. When combined with the notion that each faculty was connected to a particular area of the brain, Rush's theory gained widespread acceptance as phrenology. Poe was at one time an adherent to some of the ideas espoused by phrenology, but by the 1840s, his views were closer to the views of established medicine.

3. A case fitting this description actually exists. See 'John Ball's Case' (pp. 85–6). See also 'Ancient Case of Homicidal Insanity' (pp. 283–4), which gives the case of a man convicted for murdering his wife despite the fact that he felt she was one of the witches and wizards haunting him.

4. Thanks to the work of Pinel and the moral managers, public opinion regarding insanity was becoming more enlightened, and as public awareness increased, defense pleas of insanity became more common. There were only a few such cases before 1825, but by the late 1840s there were well over fifty.

5. For a good example of how newspapers reported on these trials, see the reports of the Freeman trial in the [*New York*] *Evening Post*, 19 March 1846, p. 1, col. 9, and the *New York Tribune*, 20 March 1846, p. 3, col. 1.

6. It is clear, however, that Poe knew something about moral insanity as early as 1837. In the first chapter of *The Narrative of Arthur Gordon Pym* (1837), Pym compares Augustus's intoxication to that state of madness which "frequently enables the victim to imitate the outward demeanor of one in perfect possession of his senses" (Poe, 1975, p. 50).

7. We should also remember that the fear-of-eyes theme runs throughout Poe's work of the 1830s and '40s and is not always associated with father-figures. Metzengerstein "turn[s] pale and [shrinks] away from the rapid and searching expression of his [horse's] earnest and human-looking eye" (Poe, 1978, p. 28). The narrator of 'Ligeia' is at first attracted to and then terrified of the black orbs of his first love. And of course, the narrator of 'The Black Cat' impulsively cuts out the searching eye of his pet.

8. Both Sigmond and the author of 'On Impulsive Insanity' are quoting from an essay by "Dr. Baillarger" which won an award from the French Academy of Medicine for the best dissertation on psychological medicine in 1844 (Sigmond, p. 585). See also Rush's discussion of "uncommonly acute" hearing in *Diseases of the Mind* (1830, p. 143). John E. Reilly (pp. 5–6) has also noticed that the increased acuteness of the senses was thought to be a sign of insanity in Poe's time, but he fails to note that the ticking and, later, ringing sounds heard by Poe's narrator were singled out by Poe's contemporaries as common hallucinations among the insane. He believes the narrator actually hears the noise made by death-watches in the wall, but resorts back to hallucination when he must explain why the ticking increases in tempo just before the murder.

9. Gunnar Bjurman points out (pp. 220ff) that one source for Poe's plot might have been Daniel Webster's 1830 pamphlet on the trial of John Francis Knapp. Webster describes a self-possessed murderer who, like Poe's narrator, "feels [his crime] beating at his heart, rising into his throat, and demanding disclosure" (XI, 52–54). There is evidence that Poe knew about Webster's pamphlet, but it should be remembered that

by 1843, Poe and his audience would have read many such pamphlets and reports. Between 1825 and 1838, the Philadelphia publishing house of Carey and Lea published almost twice as many medical books as those in any other category except fiction, and mental health was a staple concern in these works (Kaser, pp. 72, 119–23).

REFERENCES

'Ancient Case of Homicidal Insanity', *Connecticut Courant*, 15 November 1785, reprinted in *American Journal of Insanity* 3 (1847) pp. 283–4.

'Baron Rolfe's Charge to the Jury, in the case of the Boy Allnutt, who was tried at the Central Criminal Court, for the Murder of his Grandfather, on the 15th Dec, 1847', *Journal of Psychological Medicine and Mental Pathology* 1 (1848) pp. 193–216.

Bjurman, G.: *Edgar Allan Poe: En Litteraturhistorisk Studie*, Gleerup, Lund, 1916.

Carlson, E.: Introduction, B. Rush, *Two Essays on the Mind*, Brunner/Mazel, New York, 1972, pp. v–xii.

Coventry, C: 'Medical Jurisprudence of Insanity', *American Journal of Insanity* 1 (1844) pp. 134–44.

Fosgate, B.: 'Case of William Freeman, the Murderer of the Van Nest Family', *American Journal of the Medical Sciences* 28 (1847) pp. 409–14.

Haslam, J.: 'The Nature of Madness', in *Madness and Morals: Ideas on Insanity in the Nineteenth Century* (ed. by V. Skultans), Routledge and Kegan Paul, Boston, 1975, p. 31. (Excerpted from J. Haslam, *Observations on Madness and Melancholy*, Callow, London, 1810.)

'Homicidal Insanity, Case of Hadfield', *American Journal of Insanity* 3 (1847) pp. 277–82.

'John Ball's Case', *New York City-Hall Recorder* 2 (1817) pp. 85–6.

Kaser, D.: *Messrs. Carey & Lea of Philadelphia: A Study in the History of the Booktrade*, Univ. of Pennsylvania Press, Philadelphia, 1957.

'On Impulsive Insanity', *Journal of Psychological Medicine and Mental Pathology* 1 (1848) pp. 609–22.

Poe, E.: 'Metzengerstein', in *The Collected Works of Edgar Allan Poe* (ed. by T. O. Mabbott), Harvard Univ. Press, Cambridge, 1978, Vol. 2, pp. 15–31.

Poe, E.: *The Narrative of Arthur Gordon Pym* (ed. by H. Beaver), Penguin, Baltimore, 1975.

Poe, E.: 'The Tell-Tale Heart', in *The Collected Works of Edgar Allan Poe* (ed. by T. O. Mabbott), Harvard Univ. Press, Cambridge, 1978, Vol. 3, pp. 789–99.

Prichard, J.: *A Treatise on Insanity and Other Disorders Affecting the Mind*, Sherwood, Gilbert, and Piper, London, 1835.

Reid, J.: *Essays on Hypochondriasis and Other Nervous Affections*, Longman, Hurst, Rees, Orme, and Brown, London, 1823.

Reilly, J.: 'The Lesser Death-Watch and "The Tell-Tale Heart"', *American Transcendental Quarterly* 2 (1969) pp. 3–9.

Robinson, A.: 'Poe's "The Tell-Tale Heart"', in *Twentieth Century Interpretations of Poe's Tales* (ed. by W. Howarth), Prentice-Hall, Englewood Cliffs, 1971, pp. 94–102.

Rush, B.: 'An Enquiry into The Influence of Physical Causes upon the Moral Faculty', in *Two Essays on the Mind*, Brunner/Mazel, New York, 1972, pp. 1–40.

Rush, B.: *Medical Inquiries and Observations upon Diseases of the Mind*, 4th edn., John Grigg, Philadelphia, 1830.

Saliba, D.: *A Psychology of Fear: The Nightmare Formula of Edgar Allan Poe*, Univ. Press of America, Lanham, 1980.

Shulman, R.: 'Poe and the Powers of the Mind', *ELH* 37 (1970) pp. 245–62.

Sigmond, G.: 'On Hallucinations', *Journal of Psychological Medicine and Mental Pathology* 1 (1848) pp. 585–608.

'The Trial of James Wood', *Proceedings of the American Antiquarian Society* 52 (1843) pp. 105–6.

The Trial of William Freeman, for the Murder of John G. Van Nest, including the Evidence and the Arguments of Counsel, with the Decision of the Supreme Court Granting a New Trial, and an Account of the Death of the Prisoner, and of the Post-Mortem Examination of His Body by Amariah Brigham, M.D., and Others (reported by B. Hall), Derby, Miller & Co., Auburn, 1848.

Watson, A.: 'Three Medico-legal Cases of Homicide, in which Insanity was pleaded in Exculpation', *Edinburgh Medical and Surgical Journal* 38 (1832) pp. 45–58.

Webster, D.: *Writings and Speeches*, National Edition, 18 vols., Little Brown and Co., Boston, 1903.

Wharton, F.: *A Treatise on Mental Unsoundness Embracing a General View of Psychological Law*, 2 vols., Kay & Brother, Philadelphia, 1873.

Woodward, S.: 'Moral Insanity', *Boston Medical and Surgical Journal* 30 (1844) pp. 323–36.

SHAWN ROSENHEIM

Detective Fiction, Psychoanalysis, and the Analytic Sublime

"We have gone so far as to combine the ideas of an agility astounding, a strength superhuman, a ferocity brutal, a butchery without motive, a grotesquerie in horror absolutely alien from humanity, and a voice foreign in tone to the ears of men of many nations, and devoid of all distinct or intelligible syllabification.... What impression have I made upon your fancy?" I felt a creeping of the flesh as Dupin asked me the question. "A madman," I said, "has done this deed—some raving maniac escaped from a neighboring Maison de Santé."
—Edgar Allan Poe, "The Murders in the Rue Morgue"

I

Though "The Murders in the Rue Morgue" may be said to have initiated the genre of detective fiction, many twentieth-century fans have been put off by what seems like Poe's capricious violation of an implicit narrative convention. The ape, it is alleged, represents an instance of bad faith, since no reader could reasonably be expected to include animals in a list of potential murderers. More generally, we may take Poe's ape story as an index of a deeper bad faith on the part of the whole genre, in its frequent imbalance between the detective story's protracted narrative setup and its often unsatisfying denouement. There is often an embarrassing sense on the part of readers of detective fiction that its typically Gothic revelations

From *The American Face of Edgar Allan Poe*, edited by Shawn Rosenheim and Stephen Rachman. ©1995 by The Johns Hopkins University Press.

81

are incommensurate with the moral weight suggested by the genre's narrative form. In this sense, too, Poe's orangutan is an emblem of readers, who—their attention solicited by an unworthy narrative dilemma—find that the real crime has been practiced on their own sensibility. In the words of Geoffrey Hartman:

> The trouble with the detective novel is not that it is moral but that it is moralistic; not that it is popular but that it is stylized; not that it lacks realism but that it picks up the latest realism and exploits it. A voracious formalism dooms it to seem unreal, however "real" the world it describes.... The form trusts too much in reason; its very success opens to us the glimpse of a mechanized world, whether controlled by God or Dr. No or the Angel of the Odd. (Hartman 1975, 225)

Though well taken, Hartman's caution is hardly original: already in the first detective story, Poe recognized the problem. As Poe indicated in a letter to Phillip Cooke, he was aware that the promise of detective fiction to unriddle the world was ultimately tautological: "Where is the ingenuity of unravelling a web which you yourself have woven for the express purpose of unravelling? These tales of ratiocination owe most of their popularity to being something in a new key. I do not mean to say that they are not ingenious—but people think they are more ingenious than they are—on account of the method and air of method" (Poe 1966, 2:328).

Poe's comment interests me because, while he demystifies the detective story, insisting that the narrator's solution to the crime is, in fact, no "solution" at all, but a *coup de théâtre* staged by the author from behind the scenes, he also recognizes the willingness of readers to be deceived by the story's "method and air of method." Such an air of method might also be described as the genre's penchant for analysis, a term that recurs throughout the Dupin stories.[1] "Rue Morgue" begins with a discussion of "analysis," and in a letter describing "Marie Rogêt," Poe emphasizes the same term: "under the pretense of showing how Dupin . . . unravelled the mystery of Marie's assassination, I, in fact, enter into a very rigorous analysis of the real tragedy in New York" (Poe 1969–78, 3:718). Though it may at first seem curious that the literary genre most vocally devoted to the powers of the ratiocinative mind should vex those powers on the mindless acts of Poe's orangutan, on consideration, Poe's use of the ape in "Rue Morgue" emerges as something more than a simple narrative miscalculation or mere sideshow. In brief, the ape permits Poe to elaborate a cryptographic argument about language and human identity, in which the extreme contrast between the ape's physicality and Dupin's inhuman reason tells us something about the constitutive oppositions of the genre. And since detective fiction in general, and Poe's more particularly, has enjoyed a long and privileged relation to psychoanalytic reading, Poe's experiments with the monkey may tell us something about how we, as readers, are ourselves made to ape his ape.

"Analysis" in several senses has been a key to the theoretical ubiquity of "The Purloined Letter." But while that story is unquestionably a great achievement, Poe purchases the analytic force of his narrative only by purging the text of any attempt at realist representation (Limon 1990, 103). Hence, Barbara Johnson's too-familiar claim that Minister D—'s letter is "not hidden in a geometrical space, where the police are looking for it . . . but is instead located 'in' a *symbolic* structure" is correct only because of Poe's refusal to engage the difficult project of representing the texture of social experience (Johnson 1980). In sharp contrast to the outdoor settings of "Marie Rogêt," or even to the street scenes in "Rue Morgue," "The Purloined Letter" retreats from the boulevards, parks, and waterways of the teeming city, with their social and sexual ambiguities, into the enclosed and private spaces of Minister D—'s chambers. Hence, the remarkable success of "The Purloined Letter" as a locus for literary and psychoanalytic theory—indeed, as one of *the* venues by which French theory has translated itself into America—begins to seem the consequence of playing cards with a stacked deck. The tale's theoretical richness derives from the fact that Lacan, Derrida, Johnson, and the others who have written in their wake have chosen a text that is already supremely two-dimensional, already overtly concerned with allegorizing the operations of the signifier.

In fact, the semiotic purity of "The Purloined Letter" is an exception in Poe's detective fiction, which focuses more generally on the tension between representations of three-dimensional bodies and language, which is either two-dimensional in its printed form or, as speech, proves uncannily disembodied and invisible. The dominant form of the genre is far closer to "Rue Morgue" or, in its true-crime mode, to "The Mystery of Marie Rogêt," in which Poe is less concerned with the "itinerary of the signifier" narrowly conceived than he is with the problems posed by the difficult intersection between the human capacity for language and the brute fact of incarnation. Poe's obsession with corpses, especially prominent in the late fiction, reveals his continuing anxiety over the body's refusal to suffer complete encipherment into language. Significantly enough, Poe's deaths are almost invariably associated with injuries to the organs of speech. The horror of Valdemar's mesmeric dissolution in "The Facts in the Case of M. Valdemar" stems from the grotesque contrast between his putrefying body and his "wonderfully, thrillingly distinct—syllabification" (Poe 1984b, 839–40), as "ejaculations of 'dead! dead!'" burst "from the tongue and not the lips of the sufferer" (ibid., 842). In "Rue Morgue" the strangled Camille L'Espanaye's tongue is "bitten partially through" (ibid., 410). Marie Rogêt bears "bruises and impressions of fingers" about her throat, and "a piece of lace was found tied so tightly around the neck as to be hidden from sight; it was completely buried in the flesh, and was fastened by a knot which lay just under the left ear" (ibid., 513). And in "Thou Art the Man," often considered Poe's fourth detective story, the narrator ("Mr. P.") exposes and destroys the murderer Charley Goodfellow by confronting him with the speaking corpse of his victim, who bursts out of a wine cask with impressive consequences:

> There sprang up into a sitting position, directly facing the host, the bruised, bloody and nearly putrid corpse of the murdered Mr. Shuttleworthy himself. It gazed for a few moments ... with its decaying and lack-lustre eyes ... uttered slowly, but clearly and impressively the words, "Thou art the man!" and then, falling over the side of the chest as if thoroughly satisfied, stretched out its limbs quiveringly. (Ibid., 740)[2]

Such obsessive instances of mutilated language suggest that for Poe the disjunction between linguistic and physical identity was always traumatic. As in so much detective fiction, the violence attendant on social relations in "Rue Morgue" results from the represented encounter between two-dimensional signs and three-dimensional bodies, and might properly be described as cryptonymic. I borrow the term from Nicholas Abraham and Maria Torok, who in their reinterpretation of Freud's case study hypothesize that the Wolf Man's physical symptoms stem from a punning, multilingual "verbarium" of key (or code) words, which indirectly name the principal traumas of his life. The words are "encrypted" in the self to avoid analysis by the self, for whom they pose insoluble psychic double binds. In consequence, it becomes an essential but impossible task to say whether the words name a real event or whether in themselves they produce the symptoms they are meant to explain.[3] Derrida describes the Wolf Man in language equally well suited to the involutions of psychic space manifested in, say, Roderick Usher: he had "edified a crypt within him: an artifact, an artificial unconscious in the Self, an interior enclave, partitions, hidden passages, zigzags, occult and difficult traffic" (Abraham and Torok 1986, xliv); the only passage through this Gothic architecture of the mind is through the magic words of the verbarium, coded translingually across English, Russian, and German, to keep the crypt, that "monument of a catastrophe," impermeable (ibid., xlv). As the comparison to Usher suggests, cryptonymy involves an unambiguously Gothic understanding of language. Not only Derrida's diction but the case study's corresponding themes of paralysis, violation, and unspeakability are common property of the Gothic novel and of nineteenth-century hysteria.

As I have noted elsewhere (Rosenheim 1989), to an extraordinary degree cryptography provides secret organizing principles for Poe's trilogy of detective stories. The cryptograph reflects on the level of the sign what Dupin embodies on the level of character, and what the form of detective fiction implies on the level of narrative: the fantasy of an absolutely legible world. As it is encountered in Poe's essays on secret writing, cryptography is the utopian inverse of cryptonymy, since in it reader and writer are fully present to one another within their two-dimensional cipher. Conceptually, analysis is closely associated with cryptography. Both depend on the "separating or breaking up of any whole into its parts so as to find out their nature, proportion, function, relationship, etc.,"[4] and both emphasize the abstract, symbolic force of mind over matter, which provides a form of mental leverage over the world. But already in the moment of creating the genre of detective fiction, Poe suggests that the only "analysis" it can offer may itself be a fiction. While cryptography seems to propose a detour around the Gothic aspects of cryptonymy—a way of avoiding its disturbing physicality—cryptography takes on disturbing cryptonymy features whenever Poe attempts to represent actual bodies. The problem is that cryptography provides an *alternative body* in conflict with one's corporeal investment; since even in cryptography language is never truly free of the material shell of the signifier, this linguistic self finds itself in tension with one's embodied identity.

Despite the story's promise of legibility, "Rue Morgue" intimates that the triumph of the detective's analytics cannot be clearly distinguished from the effects of the analytics on the reader's body. To the degree that the reader invests his belief in this formal drive toward legibility, he becomes Poe's dupe, for should the reader attempt to imitate Dupin, he quickly finds that his analysis devolves into mere repetition.[5] And yet, to that same degree, these stories threaten to become meaningful: if the uncanny anticipation of the story's own interpretation is at all significant, it is so because the text discloses in the reader's body the nature of the interpretive desires that initiate one's reading. Like the purloined letter, the lesson of "Rue Morgue" is hidden in plain sight, announced in the story's first lines: "The mental features discoursed of as the analytical are, in themselves, but little susceptible of analysis. We appreciate them only in their effects" (Poe 1984b, 397). While our readings certainly produce "effects," the desire to discover the right relation of analysis to literature is ultimately doomed by the impossibility of establishing a metalanguage uncontaminated by the materiality of signification. In this respect, the narrator's attempt in "Rue Morgue" to keep his analytic discourse free from the corporeal opacity of his subject resembles Freud's procedure in his case studies. If detective fiction is notoriously susceptible to psychoanalytic interpretation, this is only because psychoanalysis, too, has often seemed to presume the separation of its analytical procedures from the materiality of its objects—a separation between language and the body that "Rue Morgue" both constructs and, finally, destroys.

II

Following Richard Wilbur, critics have long recognized speech in "Rue Morgue" as a symbolic expression of identification, noting that Dupin's use of a high and a low register links him with the high and low voices of the sailor and the ape (Wilbur 1967). But Poe is finally less interested in pitch than in syllabification, which runs on a continuum from the orangutan's grunts to Dupin's "rich tenor," with its "deliberateness and entire distinctness" of enunciation (Poe 1984b, 410–12). Hence Poe's own deliberation in staging the ape's crime within earshot of such a polyglot group of auditors, each of whom hears in the orangutan's voice someone speaking an unfamiliar language. Henri Duval: "The shrill voice, this witness thinks, was that of an Italian. . . . Was not acquainted with the Italian language." William Bird: the voice "appeared to be that of a German. . . . Does not understand German." Alfonzo Garcia: "The shrill voice was that of an Englishman—is sure of this. Does not understand the English language, but judges by intonation" (Poe 1984b, 409–10). Similarly, Isidore Muset, "—Odenheimer," and Alberto Montani, respectively attribute the voice to Spanish, French, and Russian speakers. Poe even has Dupin supplement his references to the "five great divisions of Europe" with mention of "Asiatics" and "Africans," in what amounts to a Cook's Tour of the varieties of human speech:

> Now, how strangely unusual must that voice have really been, about which such testimony as this *could* have been elicited!—in whose *tones*, even, denizens of the five great divisions of Europe could recognize nothing familiar! You will say that it might have been the voice of an Asiatic—of an African. . . . Without denying the inference, I will now merely call your attention to [the fact that] . . . no words—no sounds resembling words—were by any witness mentioned as distinguishable. (Ibid., 416)

What is at stake in this inventory? As with the case studies of deaf-mutes and feral children that appeared toward the end of the eighteenth century, the orangutan offered Enlightenment thinkers a liminal figure of the human at a time when language was crucially involved in the definition of humanity. By the 1840s, however, the ape had been reduced to a comic or grotesque image. But given Poe's insistence on the syllabic nature of speech, it is also important to recognize the orangutan's affiliation with a tradition of philosophical inquiry.[6] The most comprehensive discussion of the orangutan's relation to language is given in *The Origin and Progress of Language*, by James Burnet, Lord Monboddo, who devotes sixty pages to this question in order to understand "the origin of an art so admirable and so useful as language," a subject "necessarily connected with an inquiry into the original nature of man, and that primitive state in which he was, before language was invented" (Burnet 1974, 1:267). Monboddo hypothesizes that the orangutan is actually a species of humankind, being "a barbarous nation, which has not yet learned the use of speech" (ibid., 270). The taxonomic name of the orangutan, *Homo sylvestris*, is merely a translation of the Malay "Ourang-Outang," which, according to the naturalist Buffon, "signifies, in their language, a wild man" (ibid., 272). According to Monboddo, orangutans use tools, grow melancholy when separated from their tribes, and are capable of conjugal attachment and even shame. Monboddo cites an explorer who saw a female orangutan that "shewed signs of modesty . . . wept and groaned, and performed other human actions: So that nothing human seemed to be wanting in her, except speech" (ibid., 272–73).

By enlisting orangutans in the same species as humans, Monboddo intends to demonstrate that what separates the two is less biology than culture, epitomized by the possession of language. For Buffon, this lack of speech discredits the orangutan's evolutionary pretensions. Monboddo ridicules Buffon, however, for making "the faculty of speech" part of the essence of humanity, and for suggesting that "the state of pure nature, in which man had not the use of speech, is a state altogether ideal and imaginary" (ibid., 293). Buffon thus anticipates the current association of language and human origins. For Poe as for Buffon, the "state of pure nature" is "altogether ideal" and precisely "imaginary," since, ontogenetically if not phylogenetically, human consciousness is a function of the subject's mirroring in language.

This tradition provides a context for understanding the dramatic process by which the narrator discovers the identity of the killer. From the start, Poe has planted clues: the crime is "brutal," "inhuman," "at odds with the ordinary notions of human conduct." Now Dupin remarks on the crime's strange combination of features:

> "We have gone so far as to combine the ideas of an agility astounding, a strength superhuman, a ferocity brutal, a butchery without motive, a *grotesquerie* in horror absolutely alien from humanity, and a voice foreign in tone to the ears of men of many nations, and devoid of all distinct or intelligible syllabification. . . . What impression have I made upon your fancy?"

I felt a creeping of the flesh as Dupin asked me the question.
"A madman," I said, "has done this deed—some raving maniac
escaped from a neighboring *Maison de Santé*." (Poe 1984b, 423)

The narrator's suggestion is close, but "the voices of madmen, even in their
wildest paroxysms . . . have always the coherence of syllabification" (ibid.,
558). Identification of the criminal depends, again, on Dupin's understanding of language; in fact, the testimony of the crime's auditors constitutes an
aural cryptogram. The origin of this moment goes back to "A Few Words
on Secret Writing," in which Poe remarked that of the hundred ciphers he
received, "there was only one which we did not immediately succeed in solv-
ing. This one we *demonstrated* to be an imposition—that is to say, we fully
proved it a jargon of random characters, having no meaning whatsoever."
Poe's ability to interpret signs requires him to recognize when a set of signs
violates the "universal" rules of linguistic formation. The claim to cryptographic mastery depends on the logically prior ability to recognize when a
set of characters is not even language. By having the solution to the crime in
"Rue Morgue" turn on the aural cryptogram, Poe simultaneously dramatizes
both the power of human analysis and his fear of what life without language
might be like.

After its recapture the orangutan is lodged in the *Jardin des Plantes*.
Until his death in 1832, the *Jardin* was Georges Cuvier's center of research;
as the repeated juxtaposition of Cuvier and Dupin indicates, Poe finds in
the zoologist's mode of analysis an analogue to his own technique of detection.[7] Cuvier was famous for his ability to reconstruct an animal's anatomy
from fragmentary paleontological remains, through systematic structural
comparison. As a contemporary of Poe's wrote: "Cuvier astonished the world
by the announcement that the law of relation which existed between the
various parts of animals applied not only to entire systems, but even to parts
of a system; so that, given an extremity, the whole skeleton might be known
. . . and even the habits of the animal could be indicated" (*Review* 1851).[8]
Like Cuvier's bones, and in implicit analogy with them, syllables are for
Poe linguistic universals, basic morphological units that form the necessary
substrate to thought. Individual words possess meaning for the linguist only
through their participation in a global system: "the word is no longer attached
to a representation except insofar as it is previously a part of the grammatical
organization by means of which the language defines and guarantees its own
coherence" (Foucault 1973, 280–81).

Cuvier seems to provide a methodological justification for Poe's
cryptographic reading of the world. But if this is so, what should we make of
Cuvier's key role in revealing the true nature of the murderer? Having teased
the reader's narrative appetite with oblique clues concerning the killer's
nature, Dupin introduces the text of Cuvier with a theatrical flourish, sure

that his revelation will produce its intended effect: "It was a minute anatomical and generally descriptive account of the large fulvous Ourang-Outang of the East Indian Islands. The gigantic stature, the prodigious strength and activity, the wild ferocity, and the imitative propensities of these mammalia are sufficiently well known to all. I understood the full horrors of the murder at once" (Poe 1984b, 424). This is a curious passage, not least because in Poe's version, the description of the orangutan virtually reverses Cuvier's actual claims. Not content to note that the orangutan is "a mild and gentle animal, easily rendered tame and affectionate," Cuvier disparages "the exaggerated descriptions of some authors respecting this resemblance" to humans (Cuvier 1832, 54–55); he at once deflates both the ape's anthropic pretensions and its wildness. That Poe knew this text seems almost certain: M'Murtrie, who translated Cuvier's book, seven years later published with Poe and Thomas Wyatt *The Conchologist's First Book*, with "Animals according to Cuvier." Yet evidently Poe's intellectual allegiance to Cuvier was subservient to his need to magnify the melodramatic and Gothic aspects of the murders. In the final analysis, it is not the crime but the solution that produces the reader's uncanny shiver, not the violence but the minute and clinical attention that Dupin requires of the narrator. To understand why the killer's simian origins produce "the full horrors" of which the narrator speaks, we need first to examine the effects of the revelation that Poe's narrative produces.

III

Throughout the Dupin stories, Poe offers models for the nature of analysis, including games of odd and even, theories of mental identification, and the elaborate comparison of the respective merits of chess and whist. Yet as we discover in "Rue Morgue," analysis itself must remain disappointingly invisible to the reader, except through its intensely pleasing effects:

> We know of them, among other things, that they are always to their possessor, when inordinately possessed, a source of the liveliest enjoyment. As the strong man exults in his physical ability, delighting in such exercises as call his muscles into action, so glories the analyst in that moral activity which *disentangles*. He derives pleasure from even the most trivial occupations bringing his talent into play. He is fond of enigmas, of conundrums, of hieroglyphics. (Poe 1984b, 397)

In its basic narrative structure, "Rue Morgue" is itself an enigma whose effects, according to its own logic, should clarify the nature of analysis. But the opening discussion reverses the ordinary process of interpretation: the crime and its solution "will appear to the reader somewhat in the light of a commentary upon the [analytic] propositions just advanced" (ibid., 400), rather than the other way around. Nor is it clear exactly why we should experience "the liveliest enjoyment" from the ensuing tale of violence. Might we understand the tale as an allegory of the superiority of brain to brawn, in which Dupin handily defeats both the sailor's evasions and the ape's brute difference? Certainly; but the pleasure of such a reading is not itself analytical, and hence brings us no closer to understanding the properties that the narrative so ostentatiously foregrounds. Since the narrator has compared analytic pleasure to that enjoyed by the strong man, we ought perhaps to consider the two "strong men" of the tale as guides. The first of these is the orangutan (*Homo sylvestris*), possessed of "superhuman" strength; the second is its owner, "a tall, stout, and muscular-looking person" who comes equipped, as in a fairy tale, with "a huge oaken cudgel" (ibid., 426). But these figures seem to exercise their powers only in violence: the elder L'Espanaye's head is "nearly severed" "with one determined sweep" of the ape's "muscular arm" (ibid., 430), and though the sailor seems amicable by comparison, even he spends his energy whipping the ape into submission, and his muscles tense at the thought of killing Dupin ("The sailor's face flushed. . . . He started to his feet and grasped his cudgel" [ibid., 427]). In practice, while the pleasures of the analyst seem only figurally related to those of his muscular counterpart ("As the strong man exults . . . so glories the analyst"), the narrative that follows demonstrates that the relation between the two is causal: the analyst's skills are called for because of the strong man's exertion, as Dupin pits his thought against the unwitting power of the ape and the sailor's potential for violence.

According to Peter Brooks, any given story has a central metaphor that, however dissolved into the thread of the narrative, articulates the story's primary relationships. And since all narrative can be mapped rhetorically as a relation between the poles of metaphor and metonymy, we can describe the narrative's duration as a metonymy "acting out of the implications of metaphor," which at once reveals the meaning of the impacted initial metaphor and transforms it through its narrative embodiment (Brooks 1985, 13).

Citing the example of Conan Doyle's "Musgrave Ritual," Brooks shows that the obscure and apparently meaningless ritual practiced by the Musgraves is actually a metaphor that condenses and shapes the action of the story. Regardless of whether Brooks is right to contend that the relation between initial metaphor and narrative metonymy holds for all stories, it is undeniably true of detective fiction in general, and of its founding text as well. The first rhetorical figure encountered in "Rue Morgue"—the analogy between the pleasures of analysis and those of strength—provides the story's structuring metaphor; in fact, the tale has everything to do with the proper way of understanding the relationship between the physical and the mental, and the pleasures associated with each.

Take as an emblem of this disjunction the difficulty that the Mmes L'Espanaye find in keeping head and body together: Camille L'Espanaye is strangled; her mother's throat is "so entirely cut that upon an attempt to raise her, the head fell off" (Poe 1984b, 411, 406). "Rue Morgue" repeatedly stages the violent separation of heads and bodies, literal and figurative, and while Dupin and the orangutan are the most visibly polarized emblems of this split, the form of the tale repeats this pattern, joining its analytic head to the fictive body through the most insecure of narrative ligatures: "The narrative to follow will appear to the reader somewhat in the light of a commentary upon the propositions just advanced" (ibid., 400). However one wishes to allegorize this relation of heads to bodies—as an opposition between spirit and matter, analysis and effects, or ego and id—it is the distinguishing structural feature of the text at every level. But though "Rue Morgue" formally repeats the opposition between body and head in the relationship of narrative and commentary, we can identify Brooks's initial metaphor only in retrospect, since Poe's text conceals its metaphors as metonymies until the narrative's climactic revelation, by which time we as readers have been thoroughly implicated in a scene at which we imagined ourselves only spectators.

Generically, this implication has already been built into the text through its combination of the Gothic with what I call the analytic sublime. Besides its extravagant setting in a "time-eaten and grotesque mansion, long deserted through superstitions into which we did not inquire, and tottering to its fall" (ibid., 400–401), "Rue Morgue" reveals its generic debt in the sensational violence of the killings, the segmentation of space into barely permeable vesicles, and the uncanniness of the crime's resolution. Although Eve Sedgwick argues compellingly that as a genre the Gothic is preeminently concerned with male homosocial desire, Poe's detective stories find their activating tension less in the closeting of sexual difference than in the closeting of consciousness within the body. Despite its overt disavowal of the Gothic ("let it not be supposed," the narrator reminds us, "that I am detailing any mystery, or penning any romance" [ibid., 402]), Poe employs an aura of analytical reason only to intensify the reader's experience of violence and disorder.

In the Gothic's implicit spatial model, Sedgwick suggests, an "individual fictional 'self'" is often "massively blocked off from something to which it ought normally to have access": air, personal history, a loved one. Regardless of the specific lack, it is the unspeakability of this occlusion that is generically distinctive: "The important privation is the privation exactly of language, as though language were a sort of safety valve between the inside and the outside which being closed off, all knowledge, even when held in common, becomes solitary, furtive, and explosive" (Sedgwick 1986, 17).[9] Thus although the detective story, with its long retrospective reconstructions, seems par excellence the genre in which language is adequate to its task of description, in the end, the apparent rationality of the detective is a device used to create Sedgwick's Gothic division. Far from offering a safety valve between inner and outer, language itself separates the analyst from the object, thereby creating the pressure differential between self and world that language is pressed to describe. The impalpable tissue separating inside and outside is consciousness itself, which can never be identical either with itself or with the body. The more intensely Poe thematizes disembodied reason (the analytic sublime), the more powerfully Gothic will be the moment in which our identification with the body of the ape is revealed.

This use of reason against itself appears with particular clarity in the episode in which Dupin discovers the exit by which the killer escaped from the quarters of the Mmes L'Espanaye. In this first instance of the locked-room mystery, the doors to the L'Espanaye home are locked; there are no secret passages or "preternatural events"; and the condition of the bodies rules out suicide. The two windows are shut, each fastened by "a very stout nail" pushed into a gimlet hole drilled through frame and casement. Yet on visiting the house, Dupin displays absolute confidence in his logical powers: "The impossibility of egress, by means already stated, being thus absolute, we are reduced to the windows. It is only left for us to prove that these apparent 'impossibilities' are, in reality, not such." Reasoning that "the murderers *did* escape from one of these windows," Dupin decides that the sashes

> *must*, then, have the power of fastening themselves. There was no escape from this conclusion. I had traced the secret to its ultimate result—and that result *was the nail*. It had, I say, in every respect, the appearance of its fellow in the other window, but this fact was an absolute nullity (conclusive as it might seem to be) when compared with the consideration that here, at this point, terminated the clew. "There *must* be something wrong," I said, "about the nail." I touched it; and the head, with about a quarter of the shank, came off in my fingers. The rest of the shank was in the gimlet-hole, where it had been broken off. (Poe 1984b, 419)

This is what Freud called the "omnipotence-of-consciousness" with a vengeance: the evidence of the senses is "an absolute nullity" against the locked room of Dupin's logic ("There was no escape from this conclusion"). As predicted, and in apparent confirmation of his hypothesis, the nail-head pops off at Dupin's touch, as if his analysis was a type of narrative thaumaturgy, able to bring about changes in the world through mere enunciation ("'There must be something wrong,' I said, 'about the nail'"). Such confusion of causes and effects is a version of the tale's split between analysis and action, an indication that Poe's analytical sublime contains the seeds of its own undoing. The abstract introduction to a tale of horror (also familiar from "The Imp of the Perverse") intensifies the shock of the narrative by increasing the contrast between the narrative's ratiocinative calm and the brutality to follow. And since excessive contrast is itself a Gothic convention, "Rue Morgue" stages the relation between the story's introduction and its main body as another instance of the Gothic. Indeed, the nail itself anticipates my conclusion: its status as a token of the power of reason is immediately undermined by Dupin's recognition that the nail itself is fractured. Like everything else in "Rue Morgue," the nail—an apparent integer—splits into head and body.

IV

This constant recurrence of heads and bodies is structurally parallel to the separation in detective fiction of the metonymy and metaphoric poles of language. Working with clues associated with the narrative's originating crime, the detective's analytical method is primarily a form of metonymy, which is, in turn, associated with the frame narrative of the detective's analysis, and with its origins in cryptography. Conversely, the core narrative of most detective stories obsessively concerns itself with bodies, most commonly with their violation and murder. Metonymy, Lacan suggests, is evidence of the displacement of desire for the mother onto the signifying chain itself. As the law of the signifier, the law of the father separates the infant from the mother at the moment when Oedipal injunctions manifest themselves in, and as, the child's newly acquired language. The child attempts to recapture its original plenitude through the use of language, but this displaced search turns into an identification of suspended desire with the process of signification itself:

> And the enigmas that desire seems to pose for a "natural philosophy"—its frenzy mocking the abyss of the infinite, the secret collusion with which it envelops the pleasure of knowing and of dominating with a jouissance, these amount to no other derangement of instinct than that of being caught in the rails— eternally stretching forth towards the *desire for something else*—of metonymy. (Lacan 1977, 166–67)

In place of the child's imaginary, there are only the "rails" of metonymic linkage, which, far from leading back to the mother, constitute the bars separating one from her being. But this "desire for something else" is not without compensatory pleasures, chief among which is the "jouissance" of employing language to structure the observable world, investing it with the sense of an almost tangible approach to the object of desire. The rails teeter constantly along the edge of remembrance, "at the very suspension-point of the signifying chain" (ibid.).

In its concern with evidence, the detective's search is a variation on the metonymic suspension displayed by the narrator of the Gothic romances, who tends "to muse, for long unwearied hours, with [his] attention riveted to some frivolous device on the margin or in the typography of a book" (Poe 1984b, 227). This obsessive attention is a defense mechanism designed to turn the mind away from something that must seem to be repressed, but which, in fact, hovers teasingly close to consciousness:

> There is no point, among the many incomprehensible anomalies of the science of mind, more thrillingly exciting than the fact . . . that in our endeavors to recall to memory something long forgotten, we often find ourselves *upon the very verge* of remembrance, without being able, in the end, to remember. And thus how frequently, in my intense scrutiny of Ligeia's eyes, have I felt approaching the full knowledge of their expression—felt it approaching—yet not quite be mine—and so at length entirely depart! (Ibid., 264–65)

Compare this to the narrator's reaction to Dupin's description of the strength, ferocity, and "harsh and unequal voice" possessed by the orangutan: "At these words a vague and half-formed conception of the meaning of Dupin flitted over my mind. I seemed to be upon the verge of comprehension, without power to comprehend—as men, at times, find themselves upon the brink of remembrance without being able, in the end, to remember" (ibid., 421). In both cases, the quality of this near-memory, and the habits of both excessively attentive narrators, correspond to Lacan's metonymic subject "perversely" fixated "at the very suspension-point of the signifying chain, where the memory-screen is immobilized and the fascinating image of the fetish is petrified" (Lacan 1977, 167).

Lacan's rhetorical analysis permits us to see how completely the metonymic frame narrative of the tale disembodies both analyst and reader, even as the Gothic narrative core of the detective story foregrounds metaphors of the body.[10] This metaphoric pull toward embodiment is crystallized in the basic scenario of "Rue Morgue," which, as Marie Bonaparte noted long ago, is a particularly nasty Oedipal triangle. For Bonaparte, the orangutan represents the infant, whose obsession with the question of the mother's sexual difference is only settled through the symbolic castration involved in Mme L'Espanaye's decapitation. Bonaparte's reading depends on a style of anatomical literalization now out of fashion, discredited in an era in which psychoanalytic critics rightfully prefer textual and rhetorical criticism to readings that, as Brooks notes, mistakenly choose as their objects of analysis "the author, the reader, or the fictive persons of the text" (Brooks 1987, 2). The problem is that "Rue Morgue" continually solicits what can only be described as bad Freudian readings. Bonaparte's biographical interpretation of Poe's fiction is, in the main, enjoyably unconvincing, but her monomaniacal inventory of sexual symbols (of, for instance, the L'Espanayes' chamber as a gigantic projection of the interior female anatomy) is difficult to dismiss. From the rending of the double doors of the L'Espanaye home ("a double or folding gate . . . bolted neither at bottom nor top" forced "open, at length, with a bayonet"), to the ape's futile ransacking of Mme L'Espanaye's private drawers ("the drawers of a *bureau* . . . were open, and had been, apparently, rifled, although many articles still remained in them" [Poe 1984b, 421]), to the identification of the broken and the whole nail, the story overcodes its anatomical symbols. Discovered in its crimes, the orangutan's "wild glances" fall on "the head of the bed, over which the face of its master, rigid with horror, was just discernible." The ape stuffs Camille "head-down" in the chimney; the L'Espanayes live in a room "at the head of the passage"; the nail in the window behind the bed is fixed "nearly to the head"; Dupin looks over "the head-board minutely"; the other nail too is "driven in nearly up to the head." The ape flees from its master's bed to the L'Espanayes, where it swings itself through the window "directly upon the headboard of the bed." "Head" is used twenty times, "bed," "bedstead," or "bedroom" seventeen times; as well as rhyming aurally, "head" and "bed" continually chime through their contiguity in the text, inviting the reader to link them through metaphor. Even the fractured window-nail can represent the mother's phallus: "Il y a le mystère du clou mutilé d'une des fenêtres, sans doute symbole, sur le mode 'mobilier,' de la castration de la mère." Dupin's inductions about the broken nail constitute a *fort-da* game in which he resolves the question of the maternal phallus by both denying its presence ("'There *must* be something wrong,' I said, 'about the nail.' I touched it; and the head . . . came off in my fingers") and affirming it ("I now carefully replaced this head portion and . . . the fissure was invisible"). Such an explanation helps clarify why the analysis of the nail musters such weird intensity: "There *must* . . . be something wrong with the nail" (Bonaparte 1949, 439).

My claim is not that such anatomical allegorizing substantiates psychoanalytic criticism, but that Freudian readers have long been attracted to detective fiction just because the genre's structure and themes so often echo central psychoanalytic scenarios. What looks like Poe's eerie anticipation of psychoanalytic motifs may say as much about generic as about psychic structure. Certainly, the literary interest of Freud's case studies depends in no small part on an essentially cryptographic sense of power over the body. Despite Freud's frequent attempts to distance himself from writers of fiction, his early conception of psychoanalysis as "the task of making conscious the most hidden recesses of the mind" (Freud 1963a, 96), of rendering the body transparent to language, is driven by the same themes of cryptographic interiority at play in Poe's detective fiction. And Dupin's boast that "most men, in respect to himself, wore windows in their bosoms" (Poe 1984b, 401) is actually a more modest version of Freud's famous declaration in his study of Dora: "He that has eyes to see and ears to hear may convince himself that no mortal can keep a secret. If his lips are silent, he chatters with his finger-tips; betrayal oozes out of him at every pore" (Freud 1963a, 96).

Although critics have remarked on the embarrassing frequency with which detective stories draw on stock psychoanalytic imagery, no one has yet called attention to how thoroughly "Rue Morgue" seems to gloss the analytic process itself. Freud describes the "essence of the psychoanalytic situation" as follows:

> The analyst enters into an alliance with the ego of the patient to subdue certain uncontrolled parts of his id, i.e., to include them in a synthesis of the ego. . . . [If] the ego learns to adopt a defensive attitude towards its own id and to treat the instinctual demands of the latter like external dangers, this is at any rate partly because it understands that the satisfaction of instinct would lead to conflicts with the external world. (Under the influence of its upbringing, the child's ego accustoms itself to shift the scene of the battle from outside to inside and to master the *inner* danger before it becomes external.) (Freud 1963b, 253)

Freud's clinical observations would serve almost equally well to describe the sailor's visit to Dupin, with Dupin standing in for the analyst, the sailor for the analysand, and the orangutan as a figure for the remembered "primal scene." In *Dora*, Freud notes that "the patients' inability to give an ordered history of their life insofar as it coincides with the story of their illness is not merely characteristic of the neurosis," but is, in fact, a defining feature of mental illness; and Freud's essential test for recovery simply is the patient's newfound ability to narrate his or her life, to "remove all possible symptoms and to replace them by conscious thoughts" (Freud 1963a, 31, 32). In this case, the sailor must recount under duress the story of the crime, which is formally parallel to the dreams that provide the analytic material for Freud's case studies. His wish to hide his knowledge makes sense in terms of the plot, but it is less easy to explain away Dupin's insistence, at once solicitous and stern, that the sailor narrate what he knows. Dupin, one might say, enters into an alliance with the sailor in order that he might "subdue certain uncontrolled parts of his id," unmistakably represented by the ape. As a corollary, Dupin repeatedly insists that the sailor acknowledge the beast as his own: "Of course you are prepared to identify the property?" (Poe 1984b, 427), even as he declares that the sailor is both innocent and complicit: "You have nothing to conceal. You have no reason for concealment. On the other hand, you are bound by every principle of honor to confess all" (ibid., 428). Pressed to take a reward for ostensibly recovering the ape, Dupin continues the same theme: "You shall give me all the information in your power about these murders in the Rue Morgue" (ibid., 427).

Forced at gunpoint to answer, the sailor responds first by losing the ability to articulate ("The sailor's face flushed up, as if he were struggling with suffocation. . . . He spoke not a word" [Poe 1984b, 427]), and then by threatening compensatory violence ("He started to his feet and grasped his cudgel" [ibid.]), as the story of the ape homeopathically reproduces itself in the sailor's telling. The stress of confession threatens to produce a repetition of the original crime, but Dupin's mixture of firmness and kindness ("I perfectly well know that you are innocent of the atrocities in the Rue Morgue. It will not do, however, to deny that you are in some measure implicated in them" [ibid., 427]) permits him to redirect his symptomatic repetition into narrative—precisely the result of a successful analytic intervention predicted by Freud. The sailor explains how, having brought the ape from Borneo to Paris in order to sell it for profit, he returned one night to find that the orangutan had escaped into his bedroom,

> into which it had broken from a closet adjoining, where it had been, as was thought, securely confined. Razor in hand, and fully lathered, it was sitting before a looking-glass, attempting the operation of shaving, in which it had no doubt previously watched its master through the key-hole of the closet. Terrified at the sight of so dangerous a weapon in the possession of an animal so ferocious, and so well able to use it, the man, for some moments, was at a loss what to do. He had been accustomed, however, to quiet the creature, even in its fiercest moods, by the use of a whip, and to this he now resorted. Upon sight of it, the Ourang-Outang sprang at once through the door of the chamber, down the stairs, and thence, through a window, unfortunately open, into the street. (Ibid., 428–29)

Having only heard up to this point about the animal's "intractable ferocity,"
this image of the orangutan is rather touching; even when the ape imitates
"the motions of a barber" with the Mmes L'Espanaye, its purposes, we are
told, are "probably pacific" (ibid., 430). Poe offers us a Darwinian revision
of Freud, a primate scene in which the ape—still "in the closet," forced to
peep through a keyhole—sees its master shaving, and tries to imitate him.
Shaving codes the body as a part of culture, not nature; and as in David
Humphreys's contemporary poem "The Monkey" (printed in Duyckinck
and Duyckinck 1875, 1:392), the ape takes up the razor out of a wish to be
human.[11] But without language, the developmental scenario implied by the
ape's mimicry stalls: whatever its "imitative propensities," as a mute, the ape
cannot readily make its intentions known. The ape's frustrated turn from
gesture to violence reveals the abject inadequacy of mimesis in comparison
with speech. Unable to manipulate abstract symbols, the ape takes out its
rage on the flesh; and while the story's focus on injured mouths and throats
may be an instance of displacement upward, it is also a direct attack on the
organs of speech. The orangutan represents both Bonaparte's murderous
infant, poised at the moment of discovering sexual difference, and a limin-
ally human, highly evocative image of the body's resistance to signification.
These elements are synthesized in a Lacanian revision of the primal scene
as the entry into signification. Poe's use of the orangutan serves as his own
myth of human origins, which condenses within itself both individual and
evolutionary history, both linguistic and sexual desire.

Thanks to Dupin's narrative therapy, the sailor is afforded the opportunity to break the cycle of repetition through the type of analytic transference that, in Brooks's words, "succeeds in making the past and its scenarios
of desire relive through signs with such vivid reality that the reconstructions it proposes achieve the *effect of* the real" (Brooks 1987, 13). Although
it is meaningless to speak of curing a fictional character, this protoanalytic
scene is one way in which Poe stages the reader's textual cathexis, though
such a proleptic parody may suggest that, like "Rue Morgue" itself, the
psychoanalyst's function is to manufacture a narrative rather than to reveal
one. The sailor's mistake has been to assume that once he had succeeded
in lodging the ape at his own residence, the danger that it posed was over.
The sailor has yet to learn to "treat the instinctual demands of the [id] like
external dangers." Hence, the captive ape escapes from the sailor, forcing him to face the violent consequences of its acting-out. The process of
admitting his possession of the ape is a precondition for its taming, which
requires that the sailor objectify and confront as an external danger ("no
mean enemy") the fact of the bodily unconscious. The recapture of the
erstwhile brute (a story Poe does not even bother to recount) represents
the sailor's psychic reintegration. As Freud writes: "The struggle between

physician and patient, between intellect and the forces of instinct, between recognition and the striving for discharge, is fought out almost entirely on the ground of transference-manifestations. This is the ground on which the victory must be won, the final expression of which is lasting recovery from the neurosis. . . . in the last resort no one can be slain *in absentia* or *in effigie*" (Freud 1963b, 114–15). By implication, literature might be said to stage *in effigie* just such ego-training sessions, teaching the reader "to shift the scene of the battle from outside to inside": from behaviors to an internalized encounter with the text.

Once the sailor confesses, and thereby owns up to his implication in the killings, the story is finished; the narrator has "scarcely anything to add," and hastily concludes by noting that the ape "was subsequently caught by the owner himself, who obtained for it a very large sum at the *Jardin des Plantes*. Le Bon was instantly released, upon our narration of the circumstances (with some comments from Dupin) at the *bureau* of the Prefect of Police" (Poe 1984b, 431). Since the real story of "Rue Morgue" concerns the production of uncanny effects in the reader, Poe has no qualms about violating the principles of narrative construction. Instead, the extreme brevity of the denouement, and the untidiness of the story's conclusion, remind us that Poe's characters are merely puppets, technical apparatuses deployed in the attempt to intensify our affective transference onto his tales. Although the allegorical reading sketched here could be elaborated further, the parallels between Freud's method in the case studies and Poe's narrative are clear. The elaborate sexual symbolism, the fetishization of analysis, the literalization of the "talking cure," and, above all, the story's peculiar staging of metaphor and metonymy are coordinated devices through which Poe enhances the reader's identification.

Thus far, the reader has had little incentive to identify with anyone except Dupin. But though Dupin's cryptographic power is specifically predicated on his linguistic prowess, the resolution of this case is not a matter of language alone. Instead, Dupin now finds himself confronting the tangible world, carefully measuring the "impression" made by the orangutan's fingers on Camille L'Espanaye's neck against the span and pattern of a human hand, only to find that the prints on the strangled woman are not even approximately the same ("'This' I said, 'is the mark of no human hand'" [ibid., 423]). Dupin continues his physical investigation: "Besides, the hair of a madman is not such as I now hold in my hand. I disentangled this little tuft from the rigidly clutched fingers of Madam L'Espanaye. Tell me what you can make of it: 'Dupin!' I said, completely unnerved, 'this hair is most unusual—this is no *human* hair'" (ibid.). Recall that in the opening paragraph of the story, the analyst is said to glory "in that moral activity which *disentangles*": just the word Dupin uses to describe the process of physically extracting his tuft of hair from the "rigidly clutched" hand of the corpse. For all the text's insistence on the separation between the pleasures of the strong man and those of the analyst, the solution of the Rue Morgue murders requires that Dupin make forceful, even violent, contact with the traces of the ape.

After producing his assembled physical evidence, Dupin asks the narrator: "What impression have I made upon your fancy?" repeating as a metaphor the word used to refer to the uncanny and inhuman marks left on the dead woman's neck. Prior to the moment in which Dupin histrionically reveals the orangutan as the culprit, the reader's body has been anesthetized by Dupin's disembodied analytics (an anesthetization also evident in Dupin, who in moments of excitement becomes "frigid and abstract," his eyes "vacant in expression" [ibid., 401, 415]). In the "creeping of the flesh" that follows (ibid., 423), the narrator's body identifies with the ape through Dupin's recreation of the crime, revealing that he, too, through his direct somatic response, is implicated in the narrative to which he listens. "A symptom," writes Lacan, is "a metaphor in which flesh or function is taken as a signifying element" (Lacan 1977, 166); and in the moment when the reader's skin shivers in sympathy with the narrator, we witness the overthrow of the metonymic order. In the shift to the metaphoric, in the symptomatic reproduction within the reader's body of a sensational response, the reader reveals his collaboration with the ape. Through the creation of this response, Poe circumvents Freud's complaint that in analysis "the patient hears what we say but it rouses no response in his mind" (Freud 1963b, 251). To rouse the mind, a text must also arouse the body: only through the symptomatic commitment of the reader's flesh can the text realize its transferential effects.

Appropriately, it is the knowledge of his own embodiment that permits Dupin to solve the mystery of the L'Espanayes' deaths. This is the implication of Dupin's final comments on the Prefect, in which he takes pains to emphasize the futility of the latter's "bodiless" wisdom: "In his wisdom is no *stamen*. It is all head and no body, like the pictures of the Goddess Laverna—or, at best, all head and shoulders, like a codfish. But he is a good creature after all. I like him especially for one master stroke of cant, by which he has attained his reputation for ingenuity. I mean the way he has *'de nier ce qui est, et d'expliquer ce qui n'est pas'*" (Poe 1984b, 431). Though figured as a "creature," it is just the Prefect's failure to negotiate between head and body that prevents him from imagining the animal nature of the killer. As a kind of walking bust, all head and shoulders, the Prefect, not Dupin, is an emblem for excessive rationality, unable to accommodate the ape's physical presence. By contrast, Dupin twice notes his admiration for the animal. "I almost envy you the possession of him," he admits to the sailor (Poe 1984b, 431); and we may suppose that Dupin longs for the animal's intense physicality, even as he revels in the physical effects, the "creeping of the flesh," he produces in his listeners. (Once more, Dupin appears as a stand-in for Poe, who also relies for his very bread and butter on the ability to conjure identification.) "Where is the ingenuity of unravelling a web which you yourself have woven for the express purpose of unravelling?" Poe asked of Cooke; we may now be able to answer that it lies in having in the meantime caught something in that web. In the present case, Dupin's greatest exertions are not to catch the monkey, but its owner, lured in by the text placed in the newspaper. Just so with the story's readers: drawn in by another piece of paper, by another thread or web, we find ourselves trapped within its self-dissolving structure, as any assumptions about the nature of analysis are undone by our own somatic performance.

As "The Murders in the Rue Morgue" concludes, the divergent senses of the word "stamen" crystallize its irreconcilable oppositions:

> "stamen, n.; pl. stamens rare stamina, [L., a warp in an upright loom, a thread; lit., that which stands up, from *stare*, to stand.] 1. a warp thread, especially in the ancient upright loom at which the weaver stood upright instead of sitting. [Obs.] 2. in botany, the male reproductive organ in flowers, formed principally of cellular tissue.[12]

Insofar as "stamen" refers to the male generative organ of a flower, it marks the (male) reader addressed by the text; call this the Freudian reading, in which to have a male body seems inseparable from complicity in the orangutan's gendered violence. But the first meaning, now obsolete, indicates the warp thread in a loom; and through familiar paths (loom, weaving, text), we arrive at the stamen as the narrative thread running throughout Poe's text. The story's overdetermined treatment of heads and bodies, words and things, analysis and its effects, implies the close association of the origins of narrative with the discovery of sexual difference, though it is impossible to tell which came first. Instead of reinforcing an evolutionary hierarchy that would separate us from our simian relations, the cryptographic narrative structure of "Rue Morgue" acts to remind us of our corporeal investment: through the story's enacted rhetoric, the reader lives out the distance between the tale's opening metaphor and its closing one—between the simile comparing analysis and the strong man's pleasure, which safely separates its terms even as it joins them, and the metaphor of the stamen, which reveals the degree to which the reader, too, finds himself hopelessly entangled.

NOTES

1. It is a cliché of detective-fiction criticism that its most avid readers are professionals distinguished for their own analytic abilities—doctors, lawyers, and the like.

W. H. Auden, one remembers, was a compulsive reader of detective fiction, as is failed Supreme Court nominee Judge Robert Bork, who consumes at least one a day.

2. The deception is accomplished by thrusting "a stiff piece of whalebone" down the throat of the corpse and doubling it over in the wine cask, so that it springs up when released. As for Mr. Shuttleworthy's impressive accusation, the narrator "confidently depended upon [his] ventriloquial abilities" (Poe 1984b, 742).

3. "It is not a situation *comprising* words that becomes repressed; the words are not dragged into repression by a situation. Rather, *the words themselves, expressing desire, are deemed to be generators of a situation that must be avoided and voided retroactively*" (Abraham and Torok 1986, 20). For hints of a cryptonymic reading of Poe's writing, see Riddel 1979.

4. *Webster's New Twentieth-Century Dictionary*, s.v. "analysis."

5. I use the male pronoun as a way of recognizing how extremely "The Murders in the Rue Morgue" genders its readers. While it would be profitable to investigate how the female reader locates herself in Poe's text, I am concerned here to elucidate the dominant assumptions of the genre, which begins with this story.

6. For a collection of eighteenth-century treatments of feral children, see Malson 1972, which includes Jean Itard's famous treatment of the Wild Boy of Aveyron. Shattuck 1980 offers a detailed but dull interpretation of Itard's work. The idea of a criminal orangutan was not original to Poe: Peithman records that Poe "very likely saw an article, 'New Mode of Thieving,' in the *Annual Register for 1834* . . . which tells of an 'extraordinary burglary' in which a woman entering her bedroom is attacked by a 'Monkey (or a Ribbed-face Baboon) which threw her down, and placing his feet upon her breast, held her pinned firmly to the ground.'" The animal, it turns out, belonged to "itinerant showmen" from whom it had "been let loose for the sake of plundering" (Poe 1981a, 196–97).

7. Cuvier actually boasted about the superiority of his method to that of the detective: "This single track therefore tells the observer about the kind of teeth; the kind of jaws, the haunches, the shoulder, and the pelvis of the animal which has passed: it is more certain evidence than all of Zadig's clues" (Coleman 1964, 102). Voltaire's novel is typically cited as the source for the detective's method, in the inferential reasoning by which three brothers perfectly describe a horse they have not seen, relying only on the circumstantial traces that remained.

8. Foucault suggests the intellectual ties between Dupin and Cuvier by using a quotation from Schlegel: "the structure or comparative grammar of languages furnishes as certain a key of their genealogy as the study of comparative anatomy has done to the loftiest branch of natural science" (Foucault 1973, 280).

9. Sedgwick's emphasis on male homosocial desire initially seems like a promising way of reading Poe's detective stories, which manifest many of the gendered conventions—including the doubling of criminal and detective, the detective's social and physical alienation, and the violence directed against female bodies—that have long characterized crime fiction. Yet Poe's homosocial pairs keep turning into repetitions of a single self (Dupin and the narrator, Dupin and Minister D—, D— and his imagined brother), without the triangulation of difference needed to set sexual desire in play. On the Gothic and male homosociality, see Sedgwick 1985, 83–117.

10. Reacting against this type of tropic determination, Geoffrey Hartman warns critics not to move too quickly from rhetorical analysis to narrative significance: "The detective story structure—strong beginnings and endings and a

deceptively rich, counterfeit, 'excludable' middle—resembles almost too much that of symbol or trope. Yet the recent temptation of linguistic theorists to collapse narrative structure into this or that kind of metaphoricity becomes counterproductive if it remains blind to the writer's very struggle to outwit the epileptic Word" (Hartman 1975, 214). Hartman's caution is well taken, but the meaning of the detective story's rhetorical form lies primarily in its somatic effects on the reader, and not in its unsustainable claims to revelation.

11. Attempting to imitate its master, Humphreys's animal accidentally cuts its own throat (Poe 1981a, 197). Poe habitually associates hair, the sexualized body, and violence. The first thing discovered at the crime scene are "thick tresses—very thick tresses—of grey human hair . . . torn out by the roots," "perhaps half a million of hairs at a time" (Poe 1984b, 422); and Marie Rogêt's jilted paramour identifies her body by stroking her arms to see if they have her characteristically luxuriant hair.

12. *Webster's New Twentieth-Century Dictionary*, s.v. "stamen."

JOHANN PILLAI

Death and Its Moments:
The End of the Reader in History

On its own account, historiography takes for granted the fact that it has become impossible to believe in this presence of the dead that has organized (or organizes) the experience of entire civilizations; and the fact too that it is nonetheless impossible "to get over it," to accept the loss of a living solidarity with what is gone, or to confirm an irreducible limit.
—Michel de Certeau[1]

All history, moreover, must more or less blindly encounter the problem of a transferential relation to the past whereby the processes at work in the object of study acquire their displaced analogues in the historian's account.
—Dominick LaCapra[2]

A historiographical paradox leads me, in what follows, to perform a reading of a "tale," a narrative which declares as such its fictiveness, in its relation to history, which it purports to transcend or slide past.[3] It is not my intention here simply to identify or reconstruct the historical conditions under which the tale was produced, nor to relate it to the various times of its reception, nor again to describe its putative extratextual referents.[4] My concern is rather with the temporal mode of "modernity"—by which I mean the *contemporary readability*, the presentness—of a text which has left

From *MLN* 112, no. 5 (December 1997): 836–875. © 1997 by The Johns Hopkins University Press.

its moment of origin and floats before a reader in any age, apparently with no strings attached; that is, with the historiographical relation between the narration of a fictional tale and the critical performance of reading it.[5]

This relation, in its most general terms, has two fundamental aspects. First, the understanding that a tale is a narration of events—real, ideal or imagined—and hence establishes, within its own temporality, logical, causal, figurative, and other kinds of relations between signs of objects, subjects, and events. The tale thus functions in itself as a story or history of "what it is about."[6] A second aspect concerns the act of reading the tale, an act which simultaneously constitutes the tale as a history, and (in doing so) establishes itself in a metahistorical relation to the tale. The performance of reading thus takes as its point of origination the text of the tale which it has itself constituted as origin. The circularity of this relationship is the abyssal ground of what is commonly articulated as a battle between literary theory and literary history, or simply as *crisis*.[7]

To read the tale critically is to read in the mode of crisis, to participate in a hearing without a sentence being pronounced: for the tale demands that its reader recognize from the outset its status as fiction—and accordingly *suspend*, while reading, the arbitrarily established conventions by which we are accustomed to distinguish between the conventions of reference, the levels of understanding termed "literal" and "figurative." It is precisely this elision of difference which enables both the mythopoeic distancing of the events referred to in the tale from a past "historical reality" and the historical realization of these events in the experiential time of the reader. The historical conditions of the tale, in short, are located in the present of its being told and heard—in its lived presentness to a reader in any age.[8] And it is the hermeneutic relation of the narrative voice of the tale to the narrative voice of criticism that determines this paradoxical temporality; its articulation requires the reading, not only of a tale—Poe's "The Tell-Tale Heart" will serve as example—but also, in the space before and after the tale, the full and expressive silence which precedes the beginning and succeeds the end, of reading.

I

"The Tell-Tale Heart"—the title—is first of all, and by convention, an index, pointing to what the tale will be about. Simultaneously, however—it is here initially that the literal/figurative distinction must be suspended—it labels or names, confers an identity on the text it signifies[9], and thus this text which confronts the reader can be, *is*, nothing but the heart itself, palpable and red—not read as a representation of a heart, but the very bodily organ responsible for circulation, the seat of emotion, of passion, of the affections. It is the organ which sustains life—and yet, paradoxically, a heart on its own seems to imply its own extraction from a body; it may produce no circulation, may or may not beat. Beyond what it *is*, too, lies the question of what it *does*, for this is a heart which tells a tale—a "tell-tale" heart; and by the same token an informing heart, a give-away, a tattler; a warning, betrayer, traitor. The tale it will tell is also—for such is also the function of a title to indicate—*about* the tell-tale heart; it is an organ which tells the story of itself. The narrative voice which tells the tale is no less the voice *of* the tale, both the subject and the object of its own narration.

This circular, abyssal self-mirroring—by which the tale names itself as an organ without a body,[10] a fragment which tells a tale about a fragment which tells a tale—might appear on the surface to close it off from any attempt to situate it within an external historicity. The first word of the text, however—"True!"—indicates otherwise; it situates what follows within the factual context of a (granted) past history:[11]

> nervous—very, very dreadfully nervous I had been and am; but
> why *will* you say that I am mad? The disease had sharpened my
> senses—not destroyed—not dulled them. Above all was the sense
> of hearing acute. I heard all things in the heaven and in the earth.
> I heard many things in hell. How, then, am I mad?[12]

The apostrophe—and certainly the entire narration is an extended apostrophe—prosopopoeically gives face to its addressee, locates the time of narration in the present of the reader. Or rather, in the present of an implied reader, an invisible addressee who might, or who has already, diagnosed the narrator—"why *will* you say . . .?" The dread and anxiety of the narrator reflect his (her?) being ill at ease, the victim of a dis-ease.[13] But the question is taken up again: "How, then, am I mad?" How, indeed, are we to read this question? What reader could conclude at this point that the narrator is mad? These apostrophic questions, their implicit answers, serve to close the text off from the actual reader in another sense by insisting, counterproductively, that the narrator is not mad but has been, or will be, categorized as such regardless; the narrator's rationalizations attempt to breach—while simultaneously his denials reinforce—the virtual barrier of the disciplinary separation[14] by which the *reader* maintains a sense of security (sane, empirical) in relation to the text, is able to demarcate the limits of the text as fiction. Thus, paradoxically, the typical reader of this text on the one hand takes the narrator at his word, believes that the tale describes the commission of a murder; while on the other hand is convinced of the insanity of the narrator, refusing to believe the latter's arguments in his own defense.[15] To consider the narrative as "*true!*" in both respects—the rationalizations and the denials—would be to breach the demarcation between the perceived criminality and insanity of the events related in the fictional text, and the culturally constructed sanity and morality of the historical reality which the reader is living.

This typical, automatic response—which believes the narrator's description of events, but refuses to believe his evaluation of them—not only reflects a culturally determined delimitation of a madness/sanity boundary but also indicates a confusion of fiction and reality on the part of a reader who, missing altogether the nature of the tale's fictionality—which necessitates a suspension of these differences—arbitrarily reads some parts of the text literally, and treats others as metaphorical.[16] To read the tale *as* a tale means to take its internal logic as simultaneously, and at all times, both literal and figurative, historical (in the sense of the perceptual, experiential reality it provides in the present of the reader) and fictional. Thus, for example, in reply to his own apostrophe, and as if to refute the purported diagnosis of madness, the narrator claims that the dis-ease "had sharpened my senses . . . not dulled them." By *senses*, initially, one assumes a reference to wits, *mental* faculties: he is mentally alert (sharp) and hence not mad. But the further qualification regarding his sense of hearing suggests that the narrator's claim to sanity is based on a certain *sensory* acuteness; a moment later, this is carried to the point of being *supersensory*: he hears all things in heaven and earth, and many in hell. There are no grounds for privileging these qualifications one over the other in terms of credibility; taken together in the *res gestae* they show state of mind, while simultaneously warning the reader not to mistake an extraordinary sense of hearing for madness—that is, not to misjudge the narrator.

For this is also a judicial or diagnostic hearing, at which the narrator makes his apology, and where the reader is instructed to hear fairly, to "*Hearken!* and observe how healthily—how calmly I can tell you the whole story." The reader is invited to sharpen his or her senses, to hear what the narrator hears in heaven, earth and hell; in short, to become like the narrator on levels mental, sensory and supersensory, cross the boundary between history and fiction.[17]

In what follows, the nature of this boundary begins to be defined. The narrator establishes initially that the events under consideration have no identifiable motive—no cause or origin:

> It is impossible to say how first the idea entered my brain; but once conceived, it haunted me day and night. Object there was none. Passion there was none. I loved the old man. He had never wronged me. He had never given me insult. For his gold I had no desire.

The "idea," which arises spontaneously, is ghostly and persistent, and of obscure purpose ("object") as well as origin. At its heart there is not passion, but love—the two assertions cancel each other out. Neither revenge nor desire is the motive, and yet there is one consistent characterization of the narrator's state of mind: he is "very, very *dreadfully* nervous." The fear, the dread of the narrator is projected, embodied, finds its expression, and is figured forth, in the image of the old man's eye:

> I think it was his eye! yes, it was this! One of his eyes resembled that of a vulture—a pale blue eye, with a film over it. Whenever it fell upon me, my blood ran cold; and so by degrees—very gradually—I made up my mind to take the life of the old man, and thus rid myself of the eye for ever.

These two consecutive passages reveal the predicament of presentness, the temporal mode of modernity which characterizes the tale, in that they stage the twofold and paradigmatic founding gesture of historiography—*and then its negation*: first, the positing of an (absence of) origin for the narrative which will follow, and the figuration of that archic absence as an alterity—"*his* eye," the eye of the other—which legitimates the narrated events; secondly, the eschatological projection, into the future, of the figured origin as the end and purpose of the narration, as an *eschaton* which legitimates it in retrospect; and finally, the proposed negation of this twofold gesture by the elimination of the eye, the very figure which defines and determines the historiographical operation of the narrator. "The Tell-Tale Heart" thus both affirms and denies its status as a narrative of historical events, and in this gesture establishes its modernity as a textual space both within and without history.[18]

The consequences of such a temporal paradox can only be unsettling for the act of reading, if we hearken to the complex relation betokened by the homophonic and homonymic play on *eye/I*, between the narrative I and the eye/I of the other, the old man.[19] It is this singular eye/I which is simultaneously the narrating subject, the object of the narrative, and the origin and telic end of the narration. At stake in the death which is to come—on the level of sound, on the crucial level of *hearing*—is the (self-)elimination of the very "I" which speaks, of the narrative voice itself—and, by extension, since the reader is implicated in this eye/I persona in the act of reading and writing which retells the tale, in the act of hearing which replicates the narrator's disease: what is at stake is precisely the critical relation between fiction and history—the *end* of the reader.

The narrator's dread is hypostatized prosopopoeically in the eye: its resemblance to the eye of a carrion-eating bird suggests that death is imminent; its association with the gaze of the old man, that the death awaited is that of the narrative voice. Here too, perhaps, we have the first sign of the absent body of which the tell-tale heart posits itself as an organ and a metonymy—and yet, curiously, is not—that film which veils the pale blue eye of the old man: is it not the very film of death, the dimming vision of dying eyes? The narrator's blood runs cold, in a turn of phrase which both expresses his fear and dread, and foreshadows a killing in cold blood. It also suggests the cold temperature of a corpse and hence the consanguinity of the narrator and the old man. The narrative I decides "to rid *myself*" of the eye of the other, for paronomastically that eye/I is his own; we shall see (for we are not only to "hearken," but to "observe") that the stakes are indeed high in exchanging glances with his, for it is our own eye/I which is implicated in the narrator's apostrophe:

> Now this is the point. You fancy me mad. Madmen know nothing. But you should have *seen* me. You should have seen how wisely I proceeded—with what caution—with what foresight—with what dissimulation I went to work! I was never kinder to the old man than during the whole week before I killed him.

In the first place, the narrator's initial apostrophe—"why *will* you say . . ."—is now qualified: "You fancy me mad." If this fancy is deluded, then the contemptuous "madmen know nothing" is a thrust at the reader ("you") as well as the narrator ("I"), for determining the limits of madness depends on the gaze of the reader, on *our* ability to see; twice we are told: "you should have *seen*. . . ." The reader's judicial gaze becomes a critical factor in the middle term of the convoluted enthymeme which governs the tale, and of which the major premise is that madmen know nothing. What will dispel the fancy of madness is our seeing now not only "how healthily—how calmly" the tale is told, but "how wisely" its events take place, and with what *foresight*—the ability to provide for, but also *see* into, the future. Indeed, the very nature of the event described as the murder of the old man by the narrator (". . . I killed him") is thrown into question by the playful linguistic exchange between eye and I which establishes a scopic reciprocity between the two: the narrator's phrase "to take the life of the old man" suggests not simply killing, but substitution and resemblance—*taking on* his life.

It is this exchange which is revealed in the thanatoptic premeditation that follows:

> And every night, about midnight, I turned the latch of his door and opened it—oh, so gently! And then, when I had made an opening sufficient for my head, I put in a dark lantern, all closed, closed, so that no light shone out, and then I thrust in my head. Oh, you would have laughed to see how cunningly I thrust it in! I moved it

slowly, very slowly, so that I might not disturb the old man's sleep. It took me an hour to place my whole head within the opening so far that I could see him as he lay upon his bed. Ha!—would a madman have been so wise as this? And then, when my head was well in the room, I undid the lantern cautiously—oh, so cautiously—cautiously (for the hinges creaked)—I undid it just so much that a single thin ray fell upon the vulture eye. And this I did for seven long nights—every night, just at midnight—but I found the eye always closed; and so it was impossible to do the work; for it was not the old man who vexed me, but his Evil Eye. And every morning, when the day broke, I went boldly into the chamber, and spoke courageously to him, calling him by name in a hearty tone, and inquiring how he had passed the night. So you see, he would have been a very profound old man, indeed, to suspect that every night, just at twelve, I looked in upon him while he slept.

Here several structures of repetition combine. There is, first, a temporal movement, which becomes increasingly more precise, and also more measured: "every night, about midnight . . . every night, just at midnight . . . every night, just at twelve. . . ." The duration of events staged in the narrator's description of his movements—"oh, so gently! . . . slowly—very, very slowly . . . cautiously—oh, so cautiously . . ."—takes up the pace of his decision to kill the old man "by degrees—very gradually," his proceeding "with what caution." The metrical style of the narration is itself an indication of "how healthily—how calmly" the narrator can tell the whole story.

But there is another kind of repetition here, to which this temporal movement lends its measure. The narrator "opened" the door, "made an opening," put in a lantern "all closed, closed." He placed his head within the opening, and then "undid the lantern"—that is, *opened* it. For seven days, he could proceed no further, because he found "the eye always *closed*." There is also a contrapuntal movement of physical penetration and withdrawal here which echoes the mental penetration of the narrator when "the idea entered my brain",[20] as the idea haunts the narrator, so he, by day and night, haunts the old man: "I put *in* a dark lantern . . . no light shone *out* . . . I thrust *in* my head . . . I thrust it *in*. . . ." What, then, is the nature of the space—of the inside and outside—of these events? What is implied by the measure of the narrator's words, by the opening and closing they describe?

These characterizations establish, first, the interchangeability of head, lantern and chamber—even the apparently insignificant reference to creaking hinges connotes, by association, both the panel of the lantern and the door of the chamber—since knowledge of and in each is determined by optical perception; it is light which enables the narrator to see. The events described take place in a chamber, but the space of the chamber is coextensive with the space of the narrator's head, for these events are recounted in the light of his memory—perhaps his hallucination, perhaps his dream. This space is also coeval with the space of the text of the narration, and the physical space of the pages into which we, as readers, are looking—both through the narrator's eyes and as critical observers of the narrator. The optical thresholds—the door, the panel of the lantern—which mark the difference between inside and outside mark, no less, the separation between the eye/I of the reader and the eye/I of the narrator.

"His door," "the room," "the chamber," are architectural commonplaces, but a "chamber" is also the cameral seat of a judge conducting a hearing out of court. And chambers define the brain, the eye—and the heart: the upper cavities, or auricles, derive their name from the Latin word *auris*, or ear. We return, then, to the narrator's—and the judicious reader's—extraordinary sense of hearing: in the opening and closing, the in/out movement of the narrator's actions there must be heard a pulsing, systolic and diastolic: the textual heartbeat of a system of circulation.

The nature of this circulation does not appear to be bodily; indeed luxation from all physical contexts, or the positing of the body as absent, appears to be the very premise of the tale's title, and apart from a few *disjecta membra*—the narrator's hand which opens the door, his thumb which in a moment will slip on the metal fastening of the lantern—no physical features are given in the tale which would permit the identification of its narrator or characters. The two organs whose senses circumfuse the economy of the text are the ear (the sense of hearing) and the eye (the sense of sight). What circulates in the economy of the tell-tale heart and its reading—through the valvular opening and closing of doors and panels, through the ebb and flow of the narrator's movement and vision—is *light*, which enables the scopic exchange of the gaze, the eye; and conterminously—through the caesurae and hiatuses of the narrative voice, through the space between narrator and reader—its homologue, *sound*: the specular exchange of the subject, the I.

Thus are implicated, in the thin ray of light released by the narrator to enable vision, three gazes: not only the narrator's, and that of the old man,[21] but the apostrophized reader's as well: "So *you see*, he would have been a very profound old man, indeed, to *suspect* that every night, just at twelve, I *looked* in upon him while he slept."[22] It is in following the injunction to "*Hearken! and observe*," in the critical acts of hearing and seeing, that the reciprocal nature of the relation between narrator and reader is realized; indeed, the very laugh he attributes to the *reader*—"you would have laughed . . ."—is expressed by the narrator himself in a singular exclamation: "Ha!" And when he asks, not altogether rhetorically, "would a madman have been so wise as this?" it must be remembered that one of the measures of wisdom is fore*sight*.

Now presumably, taking the life of the old man, if we assume the traditional interpretation of this event as a murder, could be achieved easily enough while the old man is unconscious: we are told of the "old man's sleep:" that "he lay upon his bed," that the narrator "found the eye always closed," that "I looked in upon him while he slept." But the act which the narrator contemplates is not, *cannot* be murder, and it is precisely for this reason that when the eye is closed he finds it "impossible to do the work"—which will "rid myself of the *eye*/[I] for ever"—which entails a blinding and self-negating act of narrative and historiographical suicide.

What is in fact required for the narrator to proceed is the penetration by light of the old man's eye: it is necessary, for "death" to occur, that the *old man's* eye be open, able to see. It is this eye which vexes the narrator, afflicts him like a disease; for it is indeed a dis-ease, ultimately, by which the narrator is vexed: not a sickness as such, but the dread of a specular subject which refuses to die, an EVIL EYE/I, which, mirrored back in the gaze of the narrator, always declares: "I/EYE LIVE!"

These observations are all prefatory to the night of the central event of the tale, when the narrator makes his move:

> Upon the eighth night I was more than usually cautious in opening the door. A watch's minute hand moves more quickly than did mine. Never before that night had I *felt* the extent of my own powers—of my sagacity. I could scarcely contain my feelings of triumph. To think that there I was, opening the door, little by little, and he not even to dream of my secret deeds or thoughts. I fairly chuckled at the idea; and perhaps he heard me; for he moved on the bed suddenly, as if startled. Now you may think that I drew back— but no. His room was as black as pitch with the thick darkness (for the shutters were close fastened, through fear of robbers), and so I knew that he could not see the opening of the door, and I kept pushing it on steadily, steadily.
>
> I had my head in, and was about to open the lantern, when my thumb slipped upon the tin fastening, and the old man sprang up in the bed, crying out—"Who's there?"

In this controlled slowness of movement[23] the narrator feels his powers, his *sagacity*—the wisdom of foresight—but his estimation of the old man is thrown into question when he assumes the latter will "not even . . . dream of my secret deeds or thoughts." Like a suspicion, a dream is—if not an intangible thought—a vision, a sight, a *seeing* during sleep; and at this very moment, the old man "moved on the bed suddenly, as if—"—as if, indeed, he is aware of the other's thoughts. Although the narrator tries to explain this in terms of his chuckle—"perhaps he *heard* me" (and let us not forget the narrator's own extraordinary sense of hearing)—he is able to know, remarkably, what the old man is dreaming. And whence that attribution of fear to the old man—"as if startled"? No sound, in fact, is made by the narrator; he merely chuckles "at heart," "fairly." Similarly, in a room with shutters "close fastened" like his lantern,[24] the narrator is able to attribute "fear of robbers" to the old man, a fear which recalls his own dreadful nervousness. He also *knows* what the old man can see: "I knew that he could not see the opening of the door." As the "idea" enters the narrator's brain and he the room, as he knows the mind of the old man, so, now, his own "secret deeds or thoughts" appear to enter the old man's. The relation between the two is indeed puzzling, and the pressing question, the central problematic of the text, is that of the narrator's identity, which is posed suddenly, fearfully, by the old man: "Who's there?"

To this critical question the narrator makes no reply, but in what follows, the relation between narrator and old man is elaborated with surprising sympathy:

> I kept quite still and said nothing. For a whole hour I did not move a muscle, and in the meantime I did not hear him lie down. He was still sitting up in the bed listening;—just as I have done, night after night, hearkening to the death watches in the wall.
>
> Presently I heard a slight groan, and I knew it was the groan of mortal terror. It was not a groan of pain or of grief—oh, no!—it was the low stifled sound that arises from the bottom of the soul when overcharged with awe. I knew the sound well. Many a night, just at midnight, when all the world slept, it has welled up from my own bosom, deepening, with its dreadful echo, the terrors that distracted me. I say I knew it well. I knew what the old man felt, and pitied him, although I chuckled at heart. I knew that he had been lying awake ever since the first slight noise, when he had turned in the bed. His fears had been ever since growing upon him. He had been trying to fancy them causeless, but could not. He had been saying to himself—"It is nothing but the wind in the chimney—it is only a mouse crossing the floor," or "it is merely a cricket which has made a single chirp." Yes, he has been trying to comfort himself with these suppositions; but he had found all in vain.

The narrator keeps silent; and so must the old man, for despite the former's acute sense of hearing, he does not hear him lie down. And he *knows* that the old man is still sitting up, doing what he himself is best at: *listening*, "just as I have done." In this dreadful silence, punctuated by the ticking of death watches,[25] a sound is heard; and the narrator identifies it with absolute certainty: "I knew it was the groan . . . I knew the sound well . . . I knew what the old man felt." And the reason (dreadfully nervous) he is able to identify this sound of "mortal terror" and "awe" is that at the same time that it emanates from the old man, *just at midnight*, it wells up "from my own bosom." The voice of the old man is thus doubled, in a "dreadful echo," in the narrator's own voice.[26]

The groan is "stifled"; it is no longer clear from which soul it emanates. The effect of this loss of breath, this unspeakable suffocation, is to increase "the terrors that distracted me"—and here the narrator's *dis-traction* suggests not merely lack of concentration, but a pulling asunder, a physical dismemberment; it also characterizes a mind torn in different directions, whence mental derangement, madness.[27] Since as readers we too—even though no sound is actually uttered—have been privy to the singular laugh ("Ha!") of the narrator, we must take this matter under advisement; if and indeed the old man hears the narrator chuckle "at heart," then must his own hearing be likewise extraordinary.

We are told that, like the narrator's, the old man's fears have been "growing upon him." Like the narrator, the old man has been "trying to fancy them causeless . . ."[28] and, simultaneously, in a repetition of the narrator's figuration of origin, fancying their causes: the wind, a mouse, a cricket. These fancies are not altogether aleatory—the "wind" carries in its connotations the breath of the narrator and of life; "mouse" is etymologically related to the "muscle" which the narrator does not move;[29] and the sound made by the hinges of the lantern, that *creak*, not only means, in an archaic sense, to utter a vulturine croak, but also describes the strident sound of insects, the creak of crickets and refers, by extension, to a death watch—but, we are told, futile to indulge:

> *All in vain*; because Death, in approaching him, had stalked with his black shadow before him, and enveloped the victim. And it was the mournful influence of the unperceived shadow that caused him to feel—although he neither saw nor heard—to *feel* the presence of my head within the room.
>
> When I had waited a long time, very patiently, without hearing him lie down, I resolved to open a little—a very, very little crevice in the lantern. So I opened it—you cannot imagine how stealthily, stealthily—until, at length, a single, dim ray like the thread of the spider, shot from out the crevice and full upon the vulture eye.

The old man's attempts—to "fancy [his fears] causeless," and then to name and figure the origin of his fears—are to no avail because of the impending moment which will, in theory, negate cause and origin—the moment of Death. This is a moment neither seen nor heard, only felt—for Death stands without the narrative economy of light and sound marked by eye and ear, as its legitimating ground, as its origin and end; and within that economy, as an enveloping influence, a *shadow* which—unlike an optical shadow, a visible figure cast by the form of a body, interrupting light—must therefore appear *unperceived*, a figure personified. Death is thus behind and foregrounds every move of the narrative voice: as the narrator stalks the old man, so Death; as the narrator is preceded by a dark lantern, so Death, "his black shadow before him."

In the confusion of this approach, the antecedents of "his," "him" and the "victim" cannot be differentiated—for whose is the shadow? To whom does it appear? And who the victim? Indeed, as Death, old man and narrator become for a moment indistinguishable, the focus of the narration shifts—from the narrator's feelings to those of the old man as they are known and felt by the narrator. The Old Testament psalmist's dauntlessness in the valley of the shadow of death[30] is ironically both gainsaid—in the awe and fear shadowing both narrator and old man—and affirmed, for if, as they dreadfully echo each other's voices, old man and narrator shadow each other, then Death is both the subject and object of the narrative action, both slayer and victim. The outcome of such a self-negation of death can only be a new subject within and without history, a subject which, in spite of itself—and terrifyingly to the reader whose commentary must in its execution echo and shadow the voice of the tale—declares, "I live!"

The narrator waits, "without hearing" and unable to see—as the old man, "neither saw nor heard"—and a crack is opened in the lantern. The crevice releases light; the narrator's eye opens; by this light he will see. His furtiveness—"stealthily, stealthily"—is transparent, for *stealth* refers to the practice of stealing, and the chamber is in darkness, the shutters drawn, *through fear of robbers*: as the narrator's fears are figured in the eye/I of the old man, so the latter's are answered in the eye/I of the narrator. As the lantern opens, enabling the narrator's vision, a ray of light is released like a spider's thread—the thread of Arachne, by which suicide is aborted into life.[31] The gaze is a predatory act, light the medium of predation; and the vision of the gazing I is reciprocated by the sudden sight of the vulture eye:

> It was open—wide, wide open—and I grew furious as I gazed
> upon it. I saw it with perfect distinctness—all a dull blue, with a
> hideous veil over it that chilled the very marrow in my bones; but

> I could see nothing else of the old man's face or person: for I had
> directed the ray as if by instinct precisely upon the damned spot.

Light enters the eye of the old man, but it is the *narrator's* gaze which is
described. By neither madness nor passion is he seized, but dread of the veil
videlicet, that hideous surface which marks the coincidence and refraction
of his and the old man's gaze.[32] The old man's "face or person" is invisible,
for the focus, instinctive and inevitable, is on the subjectivity represented by
the eye/I, the damned spot[33] which marks the state and position—moral,
mental, topographical, temporal—of the narrative I/eye relative to (across
the disciplinary boundaries between the historical and the fictional, the
literal and the figurative) the listener and observer; marks, in short, the
beginning and the end of the tale, the critical state of the eye/I which is the
very *subject* of the tale.

Two gazes hang in suspense on a thread of light; now, and in this long
moment, the narrator becomes conscious of a sound, a rhythmic beat which
has hitherto remained subliminal:

> And now have I not told you that what you mistake for madness
> is but over-acuteness of the senses?—now, I say, there came to
> my ears, a low, dull, quick sound such as a watch makes when
> enveloped in cotton. I knew *that* sound well too. It was the beating
> of the old man's heart. It increased my fury, as the beating of a drum
> stimulates the soldier into courage.

As eye confronts eye, the tell-tale heart is heard *within* "The Tell-Tale
Heart": it is a sound described and figured within—as an abyssal echo
of—the sound of the narrator's own voice. And indeed, the narrator "knew
that sound well too;" he admits a familiarity with the old man's heartbeat
which one would have only with one's own.[34]

The effect of "the beating of the old man's heart" is thus that it—elid-
ing the differences between the narrator's self and the other's—"increased
my fury"; the heartbeat can only be compared to "the beating of a drum,"[35]
for what increases the narrator's fury is the resonance of the extraordinarily
sensitive barrier responsible for his acuteness of hearing: a tympanic mem-
brane stretched across the abyss between the voice of the tell-tale heart and
its echo; an *eardrum* which reverberates in time to the measure of the heart's
low/dull/quick sound.[36] As the narrator's fury increases, the measure of tale-
telling builds: less calm, more repetitive; less healthy, more strident.

> But even yet I refrained and kept still. I scarcely breathed. I tried
> how steadily I could maintain the ray upon the eye. Meantime the

hellish tattoo of the heart increased. It grew quicker and quicker, and louder and louder every instant. The old man's terror *must* have been extreme! It grew louder, I say, louder every moment!—do you mark me well? I have told you that I am nervous: so I am. And now at the dead hour of the night, amid the dreadful silence of that old house, so strange a noise as this excited me to uncontrollable terror. Yet, for some minutes longer I refrained and stood still. But the beating grew louder, louder! I thought the heart must burst. And now a new anxiety seized me—the sound would be heard by a neighbour!

The narrator *refrains*,[37] both movement and breath stifled. His gaze wavers; he attempts to keep the light steady; the palpitations increase. The ominous beating sound—one of many the narrator hears "in hell"—is also audible to the reader[38]—as the rhythmic repetition, "quicker and quicker, and louder and louder," of the tell-tale heart. And now, at the moment when their identities appear to have merged, a subtle distance is introduced in the reciprocal vision of the narrator and old man. Rather than declare his knowledge that "the old man's terror" *was* extreme, the narrator conjectures—the italics stress this—that it "*must* have been extreme." As the sound grows louder, he demands, "do you mark me well"?[39] To mark is to hear, to hearken; it is also to delimit a boundary, *differentiate*: we are asked, in short, to recognize the "me" which speaks, to answer the old man's question, "Who's there?" And indeed, the "dreadful silence" recalls the "dreadful echo" of the shared groan—but the heartbeat, which the narrator "knew . . . well" a moment ago, has now become *so strange*. This sound, which but an instant past was likened to the soldier's stimulus to courage, now ironically causes "uncontrollable terror"; there is an emphatic shift from the old man's terror to the narrator's own, and a "new anxiety" seizes the narrator ("me").

Not that he may be heard by the old man, but that his preternatural sense of hearing may be shared by a neighbor. It is the possibility of a social intrusion, the intrusion of a third party in the narrator's private and specular vision[40] that precipitates him into action:

The old man's hour had come! With a loud yell, I threw open the lantern and leaped into the room. He shrieked once—once only. In an instant I dragged him to the floor, and pulled the heavy bed over him. I then smiled gaily, to find the deed so far done. But, for many minutes, the heart beat on with a muffled sound. This, however, did not vex me; it would not be heard through the wall. At length it ceased. The old man was dead. I removed the bed and examined the corpse. Yes, he was stone, stone dead. I placed my hand upon the heart and held it there many minutes. There was no pulsation. He was stone dead. His eye would trouble me no more.

What occurs here has a striking symmetry: both narrator and old man utter a cry—there is a *yell*, and also a *shriek*. The narrator underscores the singularity of the old man's shriek by doubling it in his repetition: "once—once only." And instead of throwing open the door, he throws open the *lantern*: coinciding with the yell and the shriek is a flash of light, a blinding moment of sight. There is, however, no detailed description of a murder, no sudden moment of death[41]—the crucial act of physical violence is glaringly and conspicuously omitted.

Eventually, as the narrator becomes calmer, the danger of the heart's being audible to a neighbor of extraordinary hearing decreases—until finally, after "many minutes," the heartbeat stops. The heavy bed—burden of sleep and dreams—is "removed" with no apparent effort, its plane a plane of reflection between the narrator and the old man—or metempsychosis—whose thoughts, dreams, and even pulses, seem to synchronize. The old man, we are told no less than thrice, is dead;[42] the owner of the vulture eye has himself become carrion. Or so it would appear. For in the uncanny light of resemblance between narrator and old man, what certainty is there that "the heart" upon which he places his hand is not the narrator's own? that the "muffled sound" has not been the subsiding of his own heartbeat quickened by "uncontrollable terror"? And if from the narrator's own heart "no pulsation" can be felt, then who has died? whose voice speaks? what dread voice narrates the tale?

For if the narrator has, as he claims, rid himself of the eye/I forever—"His eye/[I] would trouble me no more"—one would expect the narrative to end here. Yet (for reasons which will soon become clear) it does not, proceeding immediately to an explicit scene of physical dismemberment:

> If you still think me mad, you will think so no longer when I describe the wise precautions I took for the concealment of the body. The night waned, and I worked hastily, but in silence. First of all I dismembered the corpse. I cut off the head and the arms and the legs.
>
> I then took up three planks from the flooring of the chamber, and deposited all between the scantlings. I then replaced the boards so cleverly, so cunningly, that no human eye—not even *his*—could have detected anything wrong. There was nothing to wash out—no stain of any kind—no bloodspot whatever. I had been too wary for that. A tub had caught all—ha! ha!

The narrator has built part of his defense against the accusation of madness on his sagacity, and one of its measures is his ability to dissimulate. The body—a disarticulated head, arms and legs—is introduced briefly as *corpus delicti* before being concealed from human detection.[43] No mention is made of the heart or its beat; and there is "no stain . . . no bloodspot," for suddenly humanized in death, the damned spot of the vulture eye can no longer be seen; the subjectivity represented by the old man's I has been incarnated, killed, dismembered and interred. It would seem that the narrator has put an end to "the terrors that distracted me"—and yet an acute sensibility might notice, *sotto voce*, an ominous doubling of that singular chuckle we heard earlier into almost an ironic laugh: "ha! ha!"

Some four hours have passed in dissimulation—"the night [has] waned"[44]—since midnight, when the groan of mortal terror was heard, and a knock at the door signals the neighbor's intrusion that the narrator had anxiously and fearfully anticipated:

> When I had made an end of these labors, it was four o'clock— still dark as midnight. As the bell sounded the hour, there came a knocking at the street door. I went down to open it with a light heart,—for what had I *now* to fear?
>
> There entered three men, who introduced themselves, with perfect suavity, as officers of the police. A shriek had been heard by a neighbour during the night; suspicion of foul play had been aroused; information had been lodged at the police office, and they (the officers) had been deputed to search the premises.

The appearance of the three policemen—identical in number, significantly, to the "three planks" under which the corpse is concealed—marks a sudden expansion of the events described by the narrator into a volume of social space. The focus on the old man's chamber has broadened to place it in perspective in "that old house"; the possibility of a neighbor, and now the "street door" and "police office," suggest encounters and sights in an organized world beyond darkness and closed shutters.[45] The reason for this societal intervention in the narrator's world is that a sound has been overheard by a neighbor: not the heartbeat the narrator feared, but "a shriek"—and thus, curiously, not the voice of the narrator, who gave a "loud yell," but the voice of the old man:

> I smiled,—for *what* had I to fear? I bade the gentlemen welcome. The shriek, I said, was my own in a dream. The old man, I mentioned, was absent in the country. I took my visitors all over the house. I bade them search—search *well*. I led them, at length,

to *his* chamber. I showed them his treasures, secure, undisturbed. In the enthusiasm of my confidence, I brought chairs into the room, and desired them *here* to rest from their fatigues, while I myself, in the wild audacity of my perfect triumph, placed my own seat upon the very spot beneath which reposed the corpse of the victim.

The narrator welcomes and disarms the officers with comparable suavity: with the old man absent in the country, only he himself could have been overheard.[46] Confirming our suspicions, he claims the old man's shriek as his own; in the same breath he suggests that all that has occurred has occurred in a dream—a text produced in his own sleep. He then displays a surprising familiarity with the old man's treasures, confidently inviting the policemen to rest in the latter's own chamber, where his corpse is encrypted.[47] And now, in an extraordinary moment, the narrator faces his inquisitors upon the very spot below which the body has been concealed, a scene which brings together simultaneously the entire series of reflections and refractions which have structured the text: narrator | old man; narrator | reader; eye | eye; I | I; self | other; sleep | waking; yell | shriek; inside | outside; presence | absence; dissimulation | truth; fiction | fact; figurative | literal; sanity | insanity; nervous | mad.

The bar ("|") which here represents the fold between these possibilities is in some cases a physical barrier—as when it stands for the heavy bed, with the narrator on top and the old man pressed below; or for the three planks of the floor, with the narrator seated above, and the old man dismembered below. It may be architectural or mechanical: the chamber or street door between inside and outside space, the window shutters or lantern panel on the hesitant threshold of darkness and light; physiological: the veil over the eye, the tympanum of the ear; psychological or philosophical: the line between dreams and consciousness, or truth and falsehood, fact and fiction, self and other. It may stand for rhetorical difference, such as that between a shriek and a yell; for an ideological or societal barrier between legitimate action and crime, or what is accepted as truth and what as metaphor; for historical distance, such as the hermeneutic space between the reader and the text; or for a limit of systematic thought, as in the case of disciplinary barriers drawn by the clinical or legal professions to separate health from sickness, or sanity from madness.

The number of policemen corresponds to the number of floorboards below the narrator because they have the same function: although they are portrayed sitting and talking with the narrator, the three men are not physical characters; rather, they are figures of society, of the *internalized law which separates the narrator from himself,* separates what is superficial from what is latent, what exists within the limits of systematic thought from what is unthought, the social and historical self from absolute alterity. The three floorboards and the three men thus do not react; they simply mark a limit, social and psychological, the bar ("|") between self and other:

> The officers were satisfied. My *manner* had convinced them. I was singularly at ease. They sat, and while I answered cheerily, they chatted familiar things. But, ere long, I felt myself getting pale and wished them gone. My head ached, and I fancied a ringing in my ears: but still they sat and still chatted. The ringing became more distinct:—it continued and became more distinct: I talked more freely to get rid of the feeling: but it continued and gained definitiveness—until, at length, I found that the noise was *not* within my ears.

The narrator's *singularity* continues to draw attention to the absence of the old man, and his paleness and headache reveal his internal tension,[48] which manifests itself psychologically and physiologically as a fancied "ringing in my ears." The sound becomes more distinct and yet more distant, as it is casually, almost accidentally, revealed to be a *feeling* whose source is, in fact, *outside* his ears; the effect of this tympanic tension between inside and outside is to stimulate the narrator to speak:

> No doubt I now grew *very* pale—but I talked more fluently, and with a heightened voice. Yet the sound increased—and what could I do? It was *a low, dull, quick sound—much such a sound as a watch makes when enveloped in cotton*. I gasped for breath—and yet the officers heard it not. I talked more quickly—more vehemently; but the noise steadily increased. I arose and argued about trifles, in a high key and with violent gesticulations, but the noise steadily increased. Why *would* they not be gone? I paced the floor to and fro with heavy strides, as if excited to fury by the observation of the men—but the noise steadily increased. Oh God! what *could I* do? I foamed—I raved—I swore! I swung the chair upon which I had been sitting, and grated it upon the boards, but the noise arose over all and continually increased.

As the sound from within and without the narrator's ears increases, it is echoed and reflected in the increasing fluency, pitch, speed and intensity of his own narration. This voice—the voice of "The Tell-Tale Heart"—now describes its own collapse as the narrator is rapidly disarticulated into three uncontrollable, twitching fragments: first, his speech, which proceeds from his *head*: fluent, heightened, quick, vehement, high-pitched, foaming, raving, swearing. Second, his *arms*: gesticulating violently, swinging the chair. Finally, his *legs*: arising, furiously and excitedly "pac[ing] the floor to and fro with heavy strides." This disarticulation, this dis-traction (preceded by a gasp for breath), is an experience on the level of narrative voice, of what has been described by that voice and enacted as the physical dismemberment of the old man: "First of all I dismembered the corpse. I cut off the head and the arms and the legs."

Previously at pains to establish that it was not the voice of madness, the narrator's voice is now *vehement*,[49] and the "I" paces the floor, foaming and raving. All that separates the dissevered parts of the narrative voice from the severed limbs of the old man is the thin bar ("|") of three floorboards—the bar which marks the limit between speech and silence; the bar at which the narrator must be heard:

> It grew louder—louder—*louder*! And still the men chatted pleasantly, and smiled. Was it possible they heard not? Almighty God!—no, no! They heard!—they suspected—they *knew*! they were making a mockery of my horror!—this I thought, and this I think. But any thing was better than this agony! Any thing was more tolerable than this derision! I could bear those hypocritical smiles no longer! I felt that I must scream or die!—and now—again!—hark! louder! louder! louder! *louder*!—

The three men smile, as the narrator smiled a moment ago, and their smiles are *hypocritical*—grinning thespian masks.[50] The narrator's despair—"Oh God! . . . Almighty God!—no, no!"—and agony come from the fear that what is concealed may be made known, that the three men's demeanor re-presents and mirrors, mocking and deriding, his own dissimulation. It is his suppression of knowledge of the old man which threatens to burst through; and silence would seem to be the wisest course. Yet, paradoxically, the narrator feels that there are only two options: "I must scream or die." This feeling seems inexplicable—the narrator has confessed no guilt, no remorse has been admitted, and the entire narration has been based on a justification of the sanity of his actions—until one recalls the moment of "death," when the narrator leaped into the room and confronted the old man. The reason for the policemen's visit soon afterwards was that "[a] shriek had been heard by a neighbour during the night"; there no mention is made of the narrator's "loud yell," and here no conclusion can be drawn but this: that the yell and the shriek sound as one voice. And that the narrator is closer to the truth than he admits when he claims that the shriek was his own in a dream.

The moment when the narrator must "scream or die" is now suspended on the brink of identity or difference: it is a moment of uncertainty suspended on the bar between narrator and old man, a wavering between the presence and absence of the old man's voice within the narrator's voice. The moment is resolved dramatically in the crisis of the narrator's final words, where a complex network of relationships is suddenly unravelled: the narrator ironically accuses the policemen of his own act of dissimulation, confesses his own commission of the deed, and calls for an unveiling or unmasking—a removal of the floorboards which will reveal the old man's presence. In the same punning breath, he calls on his listeners to hearken—"hear, hear!"—and distances himself from his own narration, from the voice of the "Tell-Tale Heart," by referring to it in the third person—"his heart." All of this happens without warning, in a sudden, bone-chilling, singular *shriek*—by which the yell of the narrative voice becomes possessed by its other, comes to its end in the I of the old man:

> "Villains!" I shrieked, "dissemble no more! I admit the deed!—tear up the planks!—here, here!—it is the beating of his hideous heart!"

II

Forgiven be the reader whose reason is stretched, whose blood runs cold, on hearing these last words. The end of the tale, the climactic shriek, plunges and recedes in a sudden void before the critical eye. A murder is committed; the killer possessed; a dead voice speaks through a living mouth. A death has occurred—a suicide; a disembodied voice speaks from beyond the grave. No murder may have taken place, no death—or else it may be a corpse's voice which shrieks at the end of the tale. The narrator has taken the old man's life; the narrator has disappeared; only the old man remains. Narrator and old man are the same—or are not the same at all. There neither is, nor ever was, an old man. Nothing has happened in the tale; or if it has, it was only a dream, the old man's or the narrator's. A second reading must recognize the voice of the narrator as that of the old man. What judgment can be passed, now that it is no longer clear that a crime has been committed, that any event within the space of narration has not been a hallucination, and no longer certain from the close of the tale what can be said of it when it began? What has happened in the tale, and what, in its reading, must be the end?

The narrator's shriek confronts the reader with a synesthetic image in light and sound. Striking our eye, impinging on our eardrums, is the homophonic imperative to "hear, hear!"—which is also a deixis, a pointing out in space—both *here* and *here*!—of the hideous site of the tell-tale heart.

Visually, unspeakably, the image is the sight of a heart cut out from a body, and soul: beating, living, palpitating, red. The space of the end unfolds before us in mingled horror and vertiginous fascination, a moment not adequated by speech.[51] Here, and in this space, reader and narrator share a present, for the latter's cries have brought the events of the narrative's past into the time of its reading: *"and now—again!—hark! louder! louder! louder! louder!"* The tale thus ends in the past of its narration and simultaneously in the present of its reading: now the reader must construct the sequel to the tale; now its consequences must by implication follow. These events, projecting forward beyond the end—on a literal level the charge of madness; arrest, questioning and confinement, perhaps—must then become the past, *precede the tale's beginning*, for the end of the tale has placed the reader in its narration's past, facing a future which is already a figment of the narrator's memory.

As the critical "I" stands on the brink of this temporal vortex, drawn inexorably down into the maelstrom's eye of narrative time, ghostly echoes and fleeting associations suggest a momentary diversion, a respite, in two of Poe's other tales. The narrator of "The Black Cat" speaks from a "felon's cell . . . for tomorrow I die and today I would unburden my soul"; it is in order to provide "a cause for my wearing these fetters and for tenanting this cell of the condemned" that the speaker in "The Imp of the Perverse" narrates.[52] The incarceration of the "Tell-Tale Heart"'s narrator is implicit in the denials of his own madness and in his final confession to officers of the law. In all three cases, the narration is an act of speech—suspended on the threshold between life and its radical other. Thus the "Cat" narrator is "consigned . . . to the hangman"; the "Imp" ends with a rhetorical question: "To-day I wear these chains, and am *here!* To-morrow I shall be fetterless!—*but where?*" Between the here of today and the where of tomorrow—when presumably the narrator will be damned, executed, or found to be mad—the difference is both spatial and temporal, marked by the physical and conceptual boundaries of the cell which both contains and compels the act of narration.

The "I" of "The Black Cat" confronts its other in the eye of a black cat: "I took from my waistcoat-pocket a penknife, opened it, grasped the poor beast by the throat, and deliberately cut one of its eyes from the socket. I blush, I burn, I shudder, while I pen the damnable atrocity. . . ." Here two acts conjoin as one—the act of telling or penning the tale and the act of penknifing the eye/I of the other, (self-)mutilation or *ommacide*—in the atrocious performative of narration. The deed is consummated in a "death scene" where the cat is hanged, executed by the suspension of breath and speech; damnation physical and symbolic is then visited upon the narrator, in the form of flames which consume his worldly wealth and leave, at the head of his bed, a gigantic image in bas-relief of a hanged cat. A second, identical, one-eyed cat appears thereafter to vex him, marked in white fur upon its

chest the gallows, a symbol of death and resurrection.[53] When the narrator
finally strikes, the blow of his axe is displaced from the cat (which vanishes)
to his wife, whose corpse he walls up in the cellar. He is calm when the law
arrives—"I scarcely knew what I uttered at all"—but as the officers are about
to leave, the narrator raps on the wall with a cane, precisely on the spot where
his wife is immured:

> I was answered by a voice from within the tomb!—by a cry, at
> first muffled and broken, like the sobbing of a child, and then
> quickly swelling into one long, loud, and continuous scream,
> utterly anomalous and inhuman—a howl, a wailing shriek, half
> of horror and half of triumph, such as might have arisen only out
> of hell, conjointly from the throats of the damned in their agony
> and of the demons that exult in the damnation. . . . Swooning, I
> staggered to the opposite wall. . . . In the next [instant] a dozen
> stout arms were toiling at the wall. It fell bodily. The corpse,
> already greatly decayed and clotted with gore, stood erect before
> the eyes of the spectators. Upon its head, with red extended
> mouth and solitary eye of fire, sat the hideous beast whose craft
> had seduced me into murder, and whose informing voice had
> consigned me to the hangman.

The tale ends with the shriek of the narrator's alter ego—figured as
the black cat and represented metonymically by a single I/eye and a mouth
whose words are red and read. The voice which finally betrays the narrator
of "The Black Cat" is his own, but in it a difference, a strangeness, has been
introduced, "anomalous and inhuman," and in which the narrator cannot
recognize himself. It is for this reason that the voice of the cat is described
as at the same time the voice of the damned and the voice which exults in
damning. Just as the "Tell-Tale Heart" ends in the old man's shriek, here the
narrator will become the other, take on the life of the hanged black cat and
in his turn be hanged.

In the premeditated murder of "The Imp of the Perverse," the relation
of stalker to stalked is explicit, and not simply a relation of perpetrator to
victim—"I am one of the many uncounted victims of the Imp of the Perverse," the narrator declares—but a complex of exchanges involved in the act
of reading. Both the narrator and his victim read, prefiguring and implicat-
ing—"I need not vex you with impertinent details"—our own narrative. The
brief "murder scene" thus describes not an act of violence, but the substitution of the narrator's light for the reader's, a pharmaceutical replacement of
the air in the victim's ill-ventilated apartment by air of the narrator's own
making:[54]

At length, in reading some French memoirs, I found an account of a nearly fatal illness that occurred to Madame Pilau, through the agency of a candle accidentally poisoned. I knew my victim's habit of reading in bed. I knew, too, that his apartment was narrow and ill-ventilated. But I need not vex you with impertinent details. I need not describe the easy artifices by which I substituted, in his bed-room candle-stand, a wax-light of my own making for the one which I there found. The next morning he was discovered dead in his bed. . . .

Unsuspected, the narrator inherits his victim's estate and enjoys years of "absolute security"—until, at length, he comes to be haunted by a thought "like the ringing in our ears," a temptation to confess: "And now my own casual self-suggestion, that I might possibly be fool enough to confess the murder of which I had been guilty, confronted me, as if the very ghost of him whom I had murdered—and beckoned me on to death." The narration ends with the narrator's betrayal by his *own* voice, which breaks into social space out of a confinement here revealed to be psychological. The limits of containment are breached, and a shortage of breath, a gasp, a swoon, preludes the end:

I walked vigorously—faster—still faster—at length I ran. I felt a maddening desire to shriek aloud. . . . I still quickened my pace. I bounded like a madman. . . . At length the populace took the alarm, and pursued me. I felt *then* the consummation of my fate. Could I have torn out my tongue, I would have done it—but a rough voice resounded in my ears—a rougher grasp seized me by the shoulder. I turned—I gasped for breath. For a moment I experienced all the pangs of suffocation; I became blind, and deaf, and giddy; and then some invisible fiend, I thought, struck me with his broad palm upon the back. The long-imprisoned secret burst forth from my soul. They say I spoke with a distinct enunciation, but with marked emphasis and passionate hurry, as if in dread of interruption. . . . Having related all that was necessary for the fullest judicial conviction, I fell prostrate in a swoon. . . .

The three tales taken together, "Imp," "Cat" and "Heart," present a composite narrative pattern in its several dimensions. On the simplest level, each tale is told by an unnamed narrator ("I"), and features a second character who is the narrator's figurative double or alter ego: the old man, the black cat, the victim who reads. The narrator's voice speaks to an implied reader (or engages in an internal monologue) initially in a self justifying mode of confession, and describes a "murder" of the narrator's other. The dead other is then interred—under floorboards, behind a wall, as a "long-imprisoned secret" in the narrator's mind. Eventually, in a social space—policemen, the crowd in the street—the narrator is driven by an irrepressible urge to betray himself, and does so by a second narration within the tale, the other's voice: the cry of the black cat, the shriek and heartbeat of the old man, the narrator's own voice unknown to him—"they say I spoke with a distinct enunciation . . ."—in confession.[55]

Each narrative places in relief its own voice, as a radical alterity within this compelling moment of speech; the moment staged as a death scene is thus revealed to be a scene of recognition in which the subject and object of narration confront each other, exchange identities, and yield to difference. The relation enacted in each tale—between subject and object, or the act of narration and the acts described by narration—is grounded, strangely and irreducibly, in a quality, tendency, feeling or character, which the "Cat" narrator identifies as "the spirit of PERVERSENESS," and the "Imp" as "a paradoxical something:"

> . . . one of the primitive impulses of the human heart—one of the indivisible primary faculties or sentiments, which give direction to the character of Man[;] . . . a perpetual inclination, in the teeth of our best judgment, to violate that which is *Law*, merely because we understand it to be such[;] . . . [an] unfathomable longing of the soul *to vex itself*—to offer violence to its own nature. . . . ("Cat," 225)

> . . . an innate and primitive principle of human action, . . . a *mobile* without motive, a motive not *motiviert*. Through its promptings we act without comprehensible object; . . . through its promptings we act, for the reason that we should *not*. . . . ("Imp," 281)

These characterizations locate perversity, in its role as the founding and self-undermining ground of the tales' telling, within the compass of the fundamental trope of irony:[56] the relation between narrator and old man appears in this context as a doubling within the sign "I" of the narrating subject—I = (self | other)—where the bar or veil separating self from other is a plane of infinite reflection between the subject and its self-perception as object, a crevice or space marking the disjunction between an I and an I which do not altogether see eye to eye.

This relation finds its paradigmatic moment in death; it is the play of irony in the narration of death which is staged in these three tales. The "death scene" in the "Tell-Tale Heart" should be the end of the narration, a moment where difference is erased and beyond which there is no further possibility of language. The moment appears, however, as a staging *within* the language of narration, of the end of narration—a staging in language of the impossibility of language. An irreducible difference is thus introduced—the veil which prevents recognition, the fine line between a shriek and a yell—even in Death, which becomes a sign. Death—where the bar of difference must disappear, and self and other become one—is prevented at the moment it occurs from being itself; it is recovered, absorbed, circumscribed by language and folded back on itself in the ironic doubling—(shriek | yell)—of the narrative voice.

The dissolution of language which must follow the moment of death is then enacted both *in* and *as* the language of narration: *within* the narration as a description of the dismemberment of the old man, and—doubling and repeating this dismemberment—*as* the narrator's voice, which itself becomes disarticulated in the act of narration. Even as it asserts its singularity, the narrator's voice doubles and folds in upon itself: the "corpse," the "body" described *in* the text is at the same time doubled as the body *of* the text; it coincides physically with the textual space of its narration. What confronts the reader is the *corpus* of the old man: a textual avatar or embodiment of the old man's (dead, absent) voice as a presence in the narrator's, the sound of the tell-tale heart in the sound of "The Tell-Tale Heart."

It is a sound always *stifled*, like the beat of a watch muffled in cotton, because the temporality of the narrative voice—its yell—is caught on the threshold of an absolute moment of language, between screaming and dying, between narration and its impossibility. The space of the narrative, its duration, is doubled back upon itself and negated as the narrating subject collapses into its own object; as the "I" falls back from death into the abyssal voice of the other. The return of the dead occurs as a necessary event, of and in the language of the tale, for Death cannot signify itself without being other than itself, and it is this—the appearance of the end of language in the middle of language—which is reflected—"I live!"—in the gaze of the old man's evil eye.

This apparition, like a burst of dark laughter, confronts the reader across the chasm which falls between literature and criticism. The act of reading abolishes chance, for it draws the reader into an inevitable hermeneutic relation with alterity within the sign of Death: the recognition scene of narrator and old man is ultimately enacted between the I/eye of the narrator and the I/eye of the reader, as the transferential relation of the narrative voice of the tale to the narrative voice of criticism. The narrative I's gestures are doubled—perversely, allegorically[57]—by the critical I: in our act of quotation, which foregrounds the voice of the narrator; in the cutting, pasting and articulation of the "Tell-Tale Heart" within a narrative of criticism, which

echoes the narrator's dismemberment of the old man; in the (deictic, exemplary) introduction of evidence to sustain the argument of criticism, which
repeats the narrator's gesture of "hear, here!" Death—its sign—envelops the
act of reading, wherein narrative I and critical I exchange glances across a bar
which now appears as the space—linguistic, cultural, historical—between
reader and text.

Between the text and the reader's eye, this space is physical; semioti-
cally, it also represents a temporal distance within the sign of Death: the
natural belatedness of criticism with respect to literature. The narrator of
the "Tell-Tale Heart" decides to rid "[him]self" of the eye/I of the old man,
which is figured as the origin and eschatological end of the narrative: thus
Death—the confrontation/recognition/murder/suicide of the narrator's other's I/eye—becomes present in the middle of narrative time as a sign whose
full meaning would be the end of narrative time. The sign of Death is then
ironically emptied of its meaning and folded back on itself in a fell resurrection, betraying itself in the duplicitous shriek of the old man. This fold,
eliminating origin and end, precludes the possibility of narrative time, of
plot and of the narrative's functioning as a history of what it is about. The text
of the tale thus appears without history and floats before the reader in history—hermetic, masqued, closed in on itself; a disembodied voice, a veiled I.
That it is cast adrift from its time of origin and present to a reader in any age
accords it the temporal status of myth;[58] the tale is paradigmatically modern,
for it shares a present with any and every reader. As "primary text" the tale
becomes the mythic point of origin which legitimates the historiographical
operation of "secondary literature"—the figure of origin for the critical I.

The eye of the reader must then inevitably take up the gaze of the narrative I, perversely continue the life of the narrative in the strange voice of
criticism, its afterlife.[59] The act of reading "The Tell-Tale Heart" stages a
doubling of the reading subject across the bar of history—I (literature | criti-
cism). Not because it describes the horror of historical events is it a tale of
dread, but because it threatens the reader from across the chasm—threatens
to breach the boundary between the I of fiction and the I of criticism. For if
the text is an internal monologue, the critical eye penetrates into the mind of
the narrator when reading; the act of reading is also a process by which the
narrator's secret deeds or thoughts enter the mind of the reader.[60] And if,
again, the voice of the tale speaks from beyond the grave, its address throws
into question the spatial and temporal location of the reader in relation to the
"here!" from which it can be heard. What case can now be made for reading—betrayed, indicted, arraigned by its own voice?

Two lines of argument appear for the critical subject. The first is
a "historicization" of the tale, where the frames of reference would be its
conditions of production and reception. A recognition that the conditions

of a text's production in the past, even as they shape the present of its reading, are reconstructed and themselves shaped by that reading, compels an understanding of the tale's present conditions of reception as prejudicial in reconstructing its past.[61] From this perspective, the relation of the tale to the present centers not on its author or implied author, but on the occasional identities of the narrative I and its implied reader as they are determined for the space of a reading by the social and ideological contexts imposed by the actual reader on the subject positions they represent: homosexual, heterosexual, oedipal, biographical, feminist, marxist, postcolonial, etc.[62] Armed with contemporary social and linguistic codes, preconceptions about madness, conventions of interpretation; and imposing and intruding ideologically on the tale, the reader—in the role of policeman or arbiter of social law—patrols its neighborhood, marking the borders or limits of its closure. Thus both the tale and its criticism are tethered to the specificity of the historical moment of reading: localized, politicized, historicized, *explained*.

The alternative critical path—precarious, partaking of the tale's paradoxical temporality—affirms the modernity of criticism as the mode of being of the tale in its afterlife. Here, in this dread undertaking, the imperative of criticism is to extend the life of literature beyond its natural end by sharing its present and generalizing it beyond the specificity of its own historical moment. A criticism founded on the primary myth of literature as its object must itself be granted the temporality of myth: the critical I takes the life of the narrative I, becomes both the subject and the object of its own narration. The primary mythopoeic gesture of modernity is thus given by the "death of the author" and the "disappearance of the subject"; a *modern* criticism acquires the ontological status of literature,[63] and the reader—agent of history and historical agent—two apparently incompatible roles: critically demythologizing the tale by demonstrating the relevance of its myth to the present, and at the same time preserving the myth in the afterlife of the tale by refusing the present of criticism. This double gesture of literary theory, perverse in the extreme, is fundamental to history and its writing; it does not oppose itself to anything that would properly be called "literary history." The I of criticism, indeed, has no choice but to speak, gazing unblinkingly from a tale of history condemned always to be present, to be *here*—literature.

NOTES

1. de Certeau, *The Writing of History*, 5.
2. LaCapra, *History & Criticism*, 11.
3. The tale, by its very formulation in a formal, fictional genre, appears to sidestep the epistemological question of what "reality" it refers to. I consider the determination of the tale's frame of reference to be a function of the performance of

reading, following Jan Mukarovsky: "The change which the material relationship of the work—the sign—has undergone is thus simultaneously its weakening and strengthening. It is weakened in the sense that the work does not refer to the reality which it directly depicts, and strengthened in that the work of art as a sign acquires an indirect (figurative) tie with realities which are vitally important to the perceiver" (Mukarovsky, 74–90; Newton, 36). From this perspective, the language of the tale constructs and refers to a fictional world which assumes a certain reality for the reader in the present; the "realness" this fictional world appears to have will depend on the various factors which constitute the hermeneutic space between reader and text: social, cultural, linguistic, psychological, and so on.

4. On the internal and heuristic coherence of fictions, see Vaihinger, *The Philosophy of As If*. Necessary heuristic fictions, critical or readerly, include the assumptions that a text reflects the life of an author, a psychological state, or a social reality at the time it was written. These approaches tacitly imply that fiction in a pure state is impossible, since it requires the mediation of non-fiction; or that the language of fiction can only be understood if it is grounded in the (supposedly extratextual) ordinary language of non-fiction; in short, that fiction is always contaminated by something to which it is radically different, and yet on which it depends, and which appears in various formulations as "non-fiction," "ordinary language," "common sense," "truth," or "reality" More explicitly constructed are approaches to literature which read into a text from the past the moral or sociological concerns of "today," and which claim therefore to have demonstrated its universal, eternal, intrinsic or literary value—when what has in fact been demonstrated is its susceptibility to critical appropriation and ideological manipulation.

5. I use "modernity" here in the very specific sense that "[i]t designates more generally the problematical possibility of all literature's existing in the present, of being considered, or read, from a point of view that claims to share with it its own sense of a temporal present" (de Man, "Lyric and Modernity," 166). LaCapra's formulation of a "transferential relation to the past," which appears in the epigraph to this paper, is essentially a re-articulation in Freudian terms of one of the paradigmatic gestures of deconstruction: the repetition and continuation, within criticism, of the mode of being of its object, literature. LaCapra's sense of "displaced analogues" appears to correspond to de Man's concept of "allegories of reading." (See the latter's "Semiology and Rhetoric" and "Literary History and Literary Modernity.")

6. This is a broad interpretation of what M. H. Abrams terms the *universe* of a work of art: ". . . the work is taken to have a subject which, directly or deviously, is derived from existing things—to be about, or signify, or reflect something which either is, or bears some relation to, an objective state of affairs" (Abrams, 6). The notion that a text can be history or the converse trivializes neither term; the factors which establish a text's status as a narration of fact or fiction are not intrinsic to it; rather, they are the ideological, conventional limits placed on its possibilities of interpretation by the community of its interpreters. For a selection of views on the ethical and pragmatic necessities and consequences of limiting interpretive possibilities, see Levinson and Mailloux, *Interpreting Law and Literature*.

7. For broad-ranging studies of the constitutive aspects of metahistorical discourses, see de Certeau, *The Writing of History*, LaCapra, *History & Criticism*, Rancière, *The Names of History*, and White, *Metahistory*. Suggestive engagements in the long tradition of the theory-history debate are Jauss, "Literary History as a Challenge . . ." and de Man, "The Resistance to Theory." A detailed study of the

concept of crisis can be found in de Man's "Criticism and Crisis," where he argues that "all true criticism occurs in the mode of crisis" (8).

8. Thus de Certeau: "On the one hand, writing plays the role of a burial rite, in the ethnological and quasi-religious meaning of the term; it exorcises death by inserting it into discourse. On the other hand, it possesses a symbolizing function; it allows a society to situate itself by giving itself a past through language, and it thus opens to the present a space of its own" (*The Writing of History*, 100).

9. See Valdes and Miller, *Identity of the Literary Text*, for a collection of diverse and thoughtful essays on the nature of textual identity. An overview of some of the assumptions involved in relatively broad definitions of textuality is provided by various authors in Veeser, *The New Historicism*, and the editor's closing essay in *Reader-Response Criticism* (Tompkins, 201–32).

10. On the need to "imaginatively construct the body," see Ortega y Gasset, "The Difficulty of Reading." The social implications of the organ without a body are explored in Deleuze and Guattari's *Anti-Oedipus*.

11. Our identification of the genre of the text has already constituted a judgment of its truth-value; this prejudice must be bracketed momentarily, for the space of our reading, if we are to reserve judgment on the narrator and examine the narration on its own terms.

12. The story is quoted in its entirety in this essay from Poe, *Collected Works*.

13. This is an archaic sense of the word, etymologically derived from Latin *dis-* (privative) + *esse*, to be. (The derivations here and throughout this paper are taken from *The Compact Oxford English Dictionary* and *Webster's Deluxe Unabridged Dictionary*, hereafter denoted *OED/WUD*.) My use of etymology here and elsewhere in this essay calls for some comment. The question of whether or not the author, Poe, intended the meanings which I attribute to his words is bracketed in this reading because my focus is on the relationship between the text and the reader in the present. This philological approach neither affirms nor denies the author's intention; it concerns itself rather with opening and enriching the possibilities of interpretation in the tale by following the echoes and resonances of its language. The role of the reader becomes more complex in consequence: the narrator's apostrophe may address a character who does not appear in the tale; or he may be talking to himself—in which case the reader overhears a mental conversation or internal monologue. To encompass these and other possibilities, I use the term "the reader" to refer to the subject position occupied by the narrator's listener, the position with which the actual reader enters into a (negative, positive or neutral) relation.

14. The modes of classification and principles of exclusion by which systematic thought—legal/penal, medical, and psychiatric—marks its own limit of separation from what it cannot think, are explored "archeologically" in Michel Foucault's *Discipline & Punish*, *The Birth of the Clinic*, and *Madness and Civilization*.

15. Most readers of this tale assume that the narrator describes an actual murder; see, for instance, Frank, on the Gothic "I" in "Neighbourhood Gothic . . ."; Witherington on the reader as voyeur in "The Accomplice . . ."; and the various readings derived from psychoanalytic theory: Davis, "Lacan, Poe, and Narrative Repression"; Rajan, "A Feminist Rereading . . ."; Sussman, "A Note on the Public and the Private. . . ."

16. I use the word "arbitrary" here in Saussure's sense, to suggest not randomness or anarchy, but determination by (social) convention (*Course in General Linguistics*, 68–69, 73.) Most readers of "The Tell-Tale Heart," for example, assume

that the narrative voice is male, although the narrator's gender is never specifically identified (see note 62 below). This assumption may be conditioned by a number of factors: knowledge of the author's sex, or of that of typical narrators in his oeuvre; the traditional, patriarchal treatment of narrators as male; or the attribution of an active role to a masculine protagonist. A recognition that such prejudices are conventions of reading reveals the strategies of closure employed by past generations of readers of the tale.

17. Here it is not simply a matter of empathizing with the narrator; listening to the voice of the text on its own terms involves a self-consciously critical act, the recognition that, as Hayden White remarks in a commentary on New Historicism, "one's philosophy of history is a function as much of the way one construes one's own special object of scholarly interest as it is of one's knowledge of 'history' itself" (White, "New Historicism," 302).

18. For still classic surveys of eschatological models of history, see Bultmann, *History and Eschatology*; Kermode, *The Sense of an Ending*; and Löwith, *Meaning in History*.

19. The I/eye homophony is discussed in terms of its relationship to inter-subjectivity and the concept of the double in Halliburton's excellent book, *Edgar Allan Poe: A Phenomenological View*. Other related studies can be found in Hamel, "Un texte à deux voix"; and Williams, *A World of Words*. A detailed treatment of the I/eye subject in general can be found in Lombardo's *Edgar Poe et la Modernité* (esp. 7–69).

20. Joan Dayan, in two passing references to this tale, acknowledges that the heart which will beat under the floorboards "is of course the narrator's own" (144), and recognizes the "language of penetration" used here. She fails, however, to reconcile this with her assertion that "Poe turns the protracted attempt to look into the old man's bedroom in order to kill him into a most secret and transgressive act of love" (*Fables of Mind*, 225).

21. Etymologically, "suspicion" connotes mistrust, the act of looking askance; Latin *suspicere*: *sub*, up from under, + *spicere*, to look at (*OED/WUD*).

22. In similar fashion, the narrator's voice at daybreak becomes indistinguishable from the sound of the tell-tale heart—with its "hearty" tone and "courageousness" (Latin *cor*, heart [*OED/WUD*])—which speaks first to the old man, but ultimately to the reader.

23. The comparison of the narrator's hand to the minute hand of a watch does not merely or simply convey inordinate slowness of movement; it suggests, as well, the personification of time in and as the figure of the narrator. In this comparison converge, too, the ticking of the watch and the beating of the tell-tale heart with the temporality of the events described in the text and of the voice of narration, for metaleptically the "hand" is both that which writes and, by extension, the voice in which that hand narrates. The echo of a familiar expression also resonates in the text's title: a *tell-tale* is a mechanical device used for recording or indicating temporal measure; the *tell-tale clock*, for example, is a clock "with an attachment of some kind requiring attention at certain intervals, by which the vigilance of a watchman may be checked" (*OED/WUD*).

24. The narrator's "thin ray" of light cuts through the "thick darkness," evoking traditional metaphorical associations: optical perception (to *see* meaning to *perceive* or to understand) set against blindness or obscurity (incomprehension); or a transition from ignorance to knowledge.

25. The "death watches in the wall" point, on the one (minute) hand, to the narrator's association with time; and, on the other hand, to the relation of this temporality to death, a relation to ending which will find its articulation in the end of the tale. A death watch is also, however, a vigil kept by the dead or the dying or those who attend them; and both narrator and old man, by their wakefulness "night after night," are implicated in this act of seeing. On a third level—the most immediate sense of the word—a death watch is an insect which makes a sound like the ticking of a watch, and is considered superstitiously to be an omen of death.

26. Similarly, both narrator and old man share their vigil—"I knew that he had been lying awake"—and echo each other's dissimulation—"lying." And since a wake is a vigil or a death watch, it may be, in this dissimulation, that no death will occur—nor has, in the past which the tale describes.

27. Latin *distrahere*, to pull apart (*OED/WUD*).

28. The shifting tenses here—"Yes, he *has* been trying to comfort himself with these suppositions; but he *had* found all in vain"—indicate the temporal dilemma of the narrative voice, fluctuating between the past of the old man and the present of the narration, in which a third voice—the I/eye of the reader—is implicated, and where the old man yet lives.

29. The word "muscle" is derived from the Latin *musculus*, "little mouse," from the shape of certain muscles (*OED/WUD*).

30. The reference is to *Psalms* 23:4. The "shadow" may also be seen here as a Jungian, archetypal projection of the unknown self.

31. According to classical mythological accounts, the Lydian princess Arachne competed with the goddess Athena in a weaving contest, and proved herself superior. Made to feel guilt and shame for her pride, Arachne attempted to hang herself, but Athena prevented the suicide by turning her into a spider and the rope into a cobweb. Thus the moment when Arachne should cease to weave is transformed into a textual eternity where arachnids unceasingly (and to our knowledge, unknowingly) fabricate webs which are allegorical narrations of the original myth. For various versions of this myth, see Bulfinch, 91–93, and Graves, 98–99. Ovid's account is presented in prose and poetry respectively in *Metamorphoses*, trans. Innes, 134–38; and *The Metamorphoses*, trans. Gregory, VI. v. I. 145, 163–167.

32. Certainly the narrator grows "furious," a characterization which—ironizing his earlier denials—seems to indicate passion, madness, and the raging of a disease whose symptom is a fearful chill; but these indications are occasional rather than causal at this moment; and even the vexatious "dull blue" of the old man's eye serves here only to throw into relief the "sharpened" senses resulting from the narrator's disease.

33. This "spot," medically speaking, suggests a speck on the eye symptomatic of a disease; its damning implies judicial condemnation as well as, theologically, a consignment to hell—where the narrator hears many things. But telling, too, is the evocation of a moment when the somnambulous Lady Macbeth is able "to receive at once the benefit of sleep and do the effects of watching"—symptomatic, Shakespeare's Doctor of Physic admits, of a "disease beyond my practice." Indeed, the narrator's sympathy with the old man suggests the entire narration may be a somniloquy. That the narrative assumes the textuality of a dream envisioned by the narrator and pleads conversely, reciprocally—since the old man may indeed be dreaming of his secret deeds and thoughts—that the narrator himself is figured in the cycle of the old man's dream. In this context, it is doubtful whether knowledge—of

secret deeds and thoughts, disclosed to the reader in the confidence of reading—can remain material in calling the narrator's power to account. Nor is it simply a matter of extenuating circumstances or diminished responsibility, for the "damned spot" here is not merely a physical object or location but a conceptual, alephic mark which signifies bloodstain, consanguinity, moral stain, state of mind, self-consciousness of guilt or fear—in short, the entire shifting network of relationships which surrounds and informs the eye/I.

Curiously, the intertextual relationship between "The Tell-Tale Heart" and *Macbeth* has not received any critical attention, although each text sheds some light on the other: thus, Poe's allusion to Act V, Scene I of the play suggests, among other things, a female protagonist, sleepwalking, accountability and guilt, the blood of a murder victim ("the old man") which spreads metaphorically into a stain on the conscience, and a complex relation between power and knowledge; or again, taking structural elements as an example, Lady Macbeth's taper is transformed into the "Heart" narrator's lantern, and the knocking she hears at the gate into the knocking he hears at the door when the policemen arrive (Shakespeare, *The Tragedy of Macbeth*, 115–18).

34. The narrator's refutation of his reader's judgment is here more pointed, having progressed from "you say . . ." to "you fancy . . ." to "you mistake . . ."; and while in the same glossing breath his sensibility is subtly characterized as *over*acute, this admission of excess also has a different ironic effect: to indicate that what is sensed and heard is of the order of the supersensory. The sound, both familiar and unfamiliar, which comes to the narrator's ears is *dull*, like the color of the old man's eye; and also *quick*, in contrast to the slowness of the narrator's actions. It is akin to the *low stifled sound* heard earlier—the groan of terror which arises from both the old man's and the narrator's bosom. Death has indeed "enveloped the victim," and here it is the *watch*—which figures not only the heartbeat, the life of the old man, but also the very temporality of the narrative voice, the historical life of the narrator whose hand moves slower than a minute hand—which is enveloped, stifled. The narrator's relation to the old man, simultaneously close and murderously distant, may be considered from a variety of perspectives, the most obvious being the homoerotic and the Oedipal.

35. The soldier's "courage" here recalls the bold and hearty tone in which the narrator addresses the old man at daybreak (cf. n.22).

36. Some depths of the eardrum are sounded in Jacques Derrida's "Tympan." Derridean "difference" and its variations suggest numerous critical frames within which the relation between narrator and old man may be situated. One such frame, which is not discussed here except by implication, is that which circumscribes the relation between an author—in this case, Poe—and his or her literary persona (the narrative "I"); some explorations of this frame are provided in Derrida, *The Ear of the Other*.

37. Etymologically, to "refrain" connotes the reining in of a (soldier's) horse: Latin *refrenare*, to bridle, from *frenum*, bridle (*OED/WUD*). This is one of several latent allusions to soldiering (cf. n.35, n.39, n.48; for their possible significance, see n. 45).

38. The "tattoo" must be understood here not simply as a beat; it is also a stained inscription marking the surface, or outer limits of the (still absent) body.

39. This question also inserts itself into a continuing chain of associations: in addition to drawing attention to the "me" of the voice, *mark* evokes both "spot" and

"tattoo"—as well as the quotidian connotation of marking the time, and the soldier's of marking time.

40. For a discussion of the broader implications of this intrusion, see Sussman, "A Note on the Public and the Private. . . ."

41. It is, in fact, only by implication, by the suggestiveness of the word "heavy," that the critical tradition has assumed the old man is being pressed or held down by the bed. The narrator, in fact, smiles (as he earlier chuckled, and as we would have laughed to see), that the deed is *so far done*; it is not yet completed, and the heart actually continues to beat "for many minutes." Its sound is muffled, like that of the "watch . . . enveloped in cotton" and the "stifled sound" of the shared groan, suggesting—but only *suggesting*—that what is taking place is a suffocation, a press-ing of the old man (so that, like the narrator, he can scarcely breathe) to death. For both narrator and old man have been likened to a timepiece: the former's hand to a minute-hand, the latter's heartbeat to a watch.

42. The narrator's turn of phrase—"I examined the corpse"—is clinical and unemotional in its detachment, reminding us for a moment of how lucidly, "how healthily—how calmly" he can tell his story.

43. Latin *de* (privative) + *tegere*; uncover (*OED/WUD*). Thus a "detective" is one who uncovers.

44. The narrator remarks that "the night waned," but there is no indication of any more light in the chamber than is provided by the lantern, for the shutters are, as always, "close fastened." Even at four in the morning it is as *dark* as at midnight—but when the narrator opens the door a few moments from now, he will do so with a "light" heart. The playful, contrasting juxtaposition of light and dark in this pas-sage suggests that "darkness" and "night" can be understood in context not simply as physical phenomena, but as metaphors of truth (against the *light*heartedness of the narrator's dissimulation) or of the burden of conscience (made light of by his concealment of the corpse). On another level, the narrator's "light" heart ironically reflects the heaviness of the bed which he pulled over the old man.

45. The three men at the door are suave—their urbanity suggests a breadth of social experience—and as *police* they represent the force of order in the *polis* or city, a trinity of civil law. This legal intervention indicates one of many subtexts in the tale: its underlying interrogation of the efficacy of law. As the reference to the Old Testament (n.30), and later, the narrator's exclamations—"Oh God! [. . .] Almighty God!"—refer obliquely to divine law, so the scattered references to soldiers (see n.37) point to the possibility of martial law, one alternative when civil law has broken down.

46. The old man's absence "in the country" implies the narrator's presence in the city or *polis*.

47. The narrator's characterizations of his state of mind, however, seem to belie his confidence: *enthusiasm*, connoting daemonic possession; *triumph*, evoking Bacchic frenzy; and *wild audacity*—passion uncontrollable, madness, and distrac-tion. Similarly, he projects his own tiredness onto the officers, inviting them to "rest from their fatigues," when in fact it is he who has been engaged in "labors" through the night.

48. The narrator is "at ease," a phrase which at first suggests relaxation, but then recalls his dis-ease—and the military drill command which describes a state less relaxed than standing "easy." His *singularity* continues to draw attention to the absence of the old man, and his pallor evokes the latter's "pale blue eye." He *fancies*

hearing a sound (as we fancied him mad, and as the old man tried to fancy his fears causeless), a reminder of that "dreadful echo" resonating through the tale, and of the bell which "sounded the hour," coinciding with the policemen's knocking on the door and a hint that what the narrator is hearing may be imaginary.

49. The word *vehement* today means intense or severe, but derives from roots (Latin *vehere*, to carry, + *mens*, mind) meaning "carried out of one's mind" (*OED/WUD*).

50. Greek *hupokrites*, actor; from *hupokrinein*, to play a part (*OED/WUD*).

51. The narrative's play on the auditory imperative "hear" and the visual deixis "here" may be seen as the staging of a hiatus or disjunction between the mediation of representation and the immediacy of experience, or the sign and its referent. This moment marks an apocalyptic transition from the end of narrative time to the time of the reader, and finds its rhetorical and psychoanalytic analogues in the idea of the "sublime" and "ekphrasis." For expositions of these concepts, see Fry, "Longinus at Colonus"; Weiskel, "The Logic of Terror"; and Mitchell, "Ekphrasis and the Other."

52. Passages quoted here of "The Black Cat" and "The Imp of the Perverse" are taken from Poe, *The Complete Illustrated Stories and Poems*, 235–43 and 439–45, respectively.

53. The word "gallows" is derived from the Middle English *galwe*, cross or apparatus for hanging, from the Old English *gealga* (*OED/WUD*).

54. This substitution may be seen as a narrative parricide which constitutes and supplements the "structurality" of the narration. The various permutations and configurations of narrative pharmacology are explored in minute detail in Derrida's *Dissemination*.

55. The relation suggested here between the individual and society perhaps calls for a socio-historical analysis of the narrator in terms of what Michel Foucault calls the *soul*—"which, unlike the soul represented by Christian theology, is not born in sin and subject to punishment, but is born rather out of the methods of punishment, supervision and constraint. This real, non-corporal soul is not a substance; it is the element in which are articulated the effects of a certain type of power and the reference of a certain type of knowledge, the machinery by which the power relations give rise to a possible corpus of knowledge, and knowledge extends and reinforces the effects of this power" (*Discipline and Punish*, 29).

56. Hayden White characterizes the dialectical dilemma of historiographical irony as follows: "In Irony, figurative language folds back on itself and brings its own potentialities for distorting perception under question. . . . The trope of Irony . . . provides a linguistic paradigm of a mode of thought which is radically self-critical with respect not only to a given characterization of the world of experience but also to the very effort to capture adequately the truth of things in language. It is, in short, a model of the linguistic protocol in which skepticism in thought and relativism in ethics are conventionally expressed" (*Metahistory*, 37–38). In a similar vein, Paul de Man, following Friedrich Schlegel, comments: "Irony divides the flow of temporal existence into a past that is pure mystification and a future that remains harassed forever by a relapse within the inauthentic. It can know this inauthenticity but can never overcome it. It can only restate and repeat it on an increasingly conscious level, but it remains endlessly caught in the impossibility of making this knowledge applicable to the empirical world. It dissolves in the narrowing spiral of a linguistic sign that becomes more and more remote from its meaning, and it can find no escape from this spiral" ("The Rhetoric of Temporality" 222).

57. I use "allegory" here in de Man's sense: "The meaning constituted by the allegorical sign can . . . consist only in the *repetition* (in the Kierkegaardian sense of the term) of a previous sign with which it can never coincide, since it is of the essence of this previous sign to be pure anteriority. . . . Allegory designates primarily a distance in relation to its own origin, and, renouncing the nostalgia and the desire to coincide, it establishes its language in the void of this temporal difference. In so doing, it prevents the self from an illusory identification with the non-self, which is now fully, though painfully, recognized as a non-self" ("The Rhetoric of Temporality" 207).

58. Here I am referring to Lévi-Strauss's general characterization of the time-frame of myth: ". . . a myth always refers to events alleged to have taken place in time. . . . But what gives the myth an operative value is that the specific pattern described is everlasting: it explains the present and the past as well as the future [. . .] Whatever our ignorance of the language and the culture of the people where it originated, a myth is still felt as a myth by any reader throughout the world" ("The Structural Study of Myth," 84–86).

59. I take the supplementary relation between literature and criticism to be analogous to that quality of a text which Walter Benjamin calls "translatability"—by which the original text calls for translation as its mode of being in its afterlife. Thus "the language of a translation can—in fact, must—let itself go, so that it gives voice to the *intentio* of the original not as reproduction but as harmony, as a supplement to the language in which it expresses itself, as its own kind of *intentio*" ("The Task of the Translator," 79).

60. A general paradigm for a phenomenological approach to this relation between reader and text is outlined in Georges Poulet's analysis of "interior objects": "I am someone who happens to have as objects of his own thought, thoughts which are part of a book I am reading, and which are therefore the cogitations of another. They are the thoughts of another, and yet it is I who am their subject . . . Whenever I read, I mentally pronounce an *I*, and yet the *I* which I pronounce is not myself. This is true even when the hero of a novel is presented in the third person, and even when there is no hero and nothing but reflections or propositions: for as soon as something is presented as *thought*, there has to be a thinking subject with whom, at least for the time being, I identify, forgetting myself, alienated from myself . . . Reading, then, is the act in which the subjective principle which I call *I*, is modified in such a way that I no longer have the right, strictly speaking, to consider it as my *I*. I am on loan to another, and this other thinks, feels, suffers, and acts within me" ("Criticism and the Experience of Interiority" 59–60).

61. This would be a pragmatic approach to criticism, prioritizing either the past or the present as the determining field of meaning and ignoring or refusing to engage the hermeneutical situation. Against this, Hans-Georg Gadamer suggests that "[t]he real meaning of a text as it addresses the interpreter does not just depend on the occasional factors which characterize the author and his original public. For it is also always co-determined by the historical situation of the interpreter and thus by the whole of the objective course of history. . . . The meaning of a text surpasses its author not occasionally, but always. Thus understanding is not a reproductive procedure, but rather always a productive one. . . . It suffices to say that one understands *differently when one understands at all*" (280). Similarly the present can only afford occasional closures, because it too is only a moment in the flow of history: "Indeed, it is even a question whether the special contemporaneity of the work of art

does not consist precisely in this: that it stands open in a limitless way for ever new integrations. It may be that the creator of a work intends the particular public of his time, but the real being of a work is what it is able to say, and that stretches fundamentally out beyond every historical limitation" (*Warheit und Methode*, 96, translated and quoted in the "Editor's Introduction" to Gadamer, *Philosophical Hermeneutics*, xxv and xxvi, respectively).

62. I regretfully employ these terms here in their most general (and perhaps unfashionable) senses and usages, acknowledging that each implies a wealth of diverse "isms" and approaches to texts which are outside the limited framework of this essay. Gita Rajan has remarked, to take one example, that the narrator's gender is never explicitly identified in the text; this could, of course, be the case even when the narrator asks, "would a mad*man* have been so wise as this?" She then goes on to declare, in the absence of gender markings, "that the narrator is indeed female . . . I propose to dislodge the earlier, patriarchal notion of a male narrator for the story. I argue, instead, that a gender-marked *rereading* of this tale reveals the narrator's exploration of her female situation in a particular feminist discourse" (Rajan, "A Feminist Rereading. . . ," 284). Predictably, Rajan, now occupying the subject position of the narrator, prepares to "take the life of the old man"—in this case, a "masculinist" reading of the tale by Robert Con Davis; and her reading of the tale becomes a somewhat formulaic allegory of the relation between her own feminist criticism and the tradition of masculinist criticism—an allegory which regretfully does not question its own status as such, or the tale as its own myth of origin.

63. This is a point of departure for studying the implications of Paul de Man's question: "Could we conceive of a literary history that would not truncate literature by putting us misleadingly *into* or *outside* it, that would be able to maintain the literary aporia throughout, account at the same time for the truth and the falsehood of the knowledge literature conveys about itself, distinguish rigorously between metaphorical and historical language, and account for literary modernity as well as for its historicity? Clearly, such a conception would imply a revision of the notion of history and, beyond that, of the notion of time on which our idea of history is based" ("Literary History and Literary Modernity," 164).

WORKS CITED

Abrams, M. H. *The Mirror and the Lamp*. New York: Oxford University Press, 1953.

Benjamin, Walter. "The Task of the Translator," *Illuminations*. Trans. Harry Zohn. Ed. Hannah Arendt. New York: Schocken Books, 1969, pp. 69–82.

Bulfinch, Thomas. *Mythology. A Modern Abridgment by Edmund Fuller*. New York: Dell Publishing, 1959, reprint 1979.

Bultmann, Rudolf. *History and Eschatology: The Presence of Eternity*. New York: Harper Torchbooks, 1962.

The Compact Oxford English Dictionary, Second Edition. Oxford: Clarendon Press, 1992.

Davis, Robert Con. "Lacan, Poe, and Narrative Repression," *Lacan and Narration: The Psychoanalytic Difference in Narrative Theory*. Baltimore: The Johns Hopkins University Press, 1984.

Dayan, Joan. *Fables of Mind: An Inquiry into Poe's Fiction*. New York: Oxford University Press, 1987.

de Certeau, Michel. *The Writing of History*. Trans. Tom Conley. New York: Columbia University Press, 1988.

Deleuze, Gilles and Felix Guattari. *Anti-Oedipus.* Trans. Robert Hurley et al. Minneapolis: University of Minnesota Press, 1983.

de Man, Paul. *Blindness and Insight.* Minneapolis: University of Minnesota Press, 1983.

————. "Criticism and Crisis," *Blindness and Insight,* pp. 3–19.

————. "Literary History and Literary Modernity," *Blindness and Insight,* pp. 142–65.

————. "Lyric and Modernity," *Blindness and Insight,* pp. 166–86.

————. "The Resistance to Theory," *The Resistance to Theory.* Minneapolis: University of Minnesota Press, 1986, pp. 3–20.

————. "The Rhetoric of Temporality," *Blindness and Insight,* pp. 187–228.

————. "Semiology and Rhetoric," *Allegories of Reading.* New Haven: Yale University Press, 1979, pp. 3–19.

Derrida, Jacques. *Dissemination.* Trans. Barbara Johnson. Chicago: University of Chicago Press, 1981.

————. *The Ear of the Other: Otobiography, Transference, Translation.* Ed. Christie McDonald. Lincoln: University of Nebraska Press [Schocken Books], 1985.

————. "Tympan," *Margins of Philosophy.* Trans. Alan Bass. Chicago: University of Chicago Press, 1982, pp. ix–xxix.

Foucault, Michel. *Discipline & Punish.* Trans. Alan Sheridan. New York: Vintage Books/ Random House, 1977.

————. *The Birth of the Clinic.* Trans. A. M. Sheridan Smith. New York: Pantheon Books/ Random House, 1973.

————. *Madness and Civilization.* Trans. Richard Howard. New York: Vintage Books/Random House, 1965.

Frank, F. S. "Neighbourhood Gothic: Poe's Tell-Tale Heart," *The Sphinx* 1981 v.3 [4]: 53–60.

Fry, Paul H. "Longinus at Colonus." *The Reach of Criticism: Method and Perception in Literary Theory.* New Haven: Yale University Press, 1983, pp. 47–86.

Gadamer, Hans-Georg. *Warheit und Methode: Grundzüge einer philosophischen Hermeneutik.* Tübingen: Mohr, 1960. Excerpts translated and quoted in "Editor's Introduction," *Philosophical Hermeneutics.* Trans. and Ed. David E. Linge. Berkeley: University of California Press, 1976, pp. xi–lviii.

Graves, Robert. *The Greek Myths: 1.* Middlesex, England: Penguin, 1960.

Halliburton, David. *Edgar Allan Poe. A Phenomenological View.* Princeton: Princeton University Press, 1973.

Hamel, Bernard. "Un texte à deux voix." *Textes et Langages* 5 (1982): 6–18.

Jauss, Hans Robert. "Literary History as a Challenge to Literary Theory," *Toward an Aesthetic of Reception.* Minneapolis: University of Minnesota Press, 1982, pp. 3–45.

Kermode, Frank. *The Sense of an Ending: Studies in the Theory of Fiction.* New York: Oxford University Press, 1967.

LaCapra, Dominick. *History & Criticism.* Ithaca: Cornell University Press, 1985.

Levinson, Sanford and Steven Mailloux, eds. *Interpreting Law and Literature: A Hermeneutic Reader.* Evanston: Northwestern University Press, 1988.

Lévi-Strauss, Claude. "The Structural Study of Myth," *Myth: a Symposium.* Ed. Thomas A. Sebeok. Bloomington: Indiana University Press, 1965, pp. 81–106.

Lombardo, Patrizia. *Edgar Poe et la Modernité: Breton, Barthes, Derrida, Blanchot.* Birmingham, Alabama: Summa, 1985.

Löwith, Karl. *Meaning in History.* Chicago: University of Chicago Press, 1949.

Macksey, Richard and Eugenio Donato. *The Structuralist Controversy: The Languages of Criticism & the Sciences of Man.* Baltimore: The Johns Hopkins University Press, 1972.

Mitchell, W. J. T. "Ekphrasis and the Other," *Picture Theory: Essays on Verbal and Visual Representation*. Chicago: University of Chicago Press, 1994, pp. 151–81.

Mukarovsky, Jan. *Aesthetic Function, Norm, and Value as Social Facts*. Trans. M. E. Suino. Ann Arbor, 1979. Reprinted in *Twentieth-Century Literary Theory: A Reader*. Ed. K. M. Newton. New York: St. Martin's Press, 1988.

Newton, K. M., ed. *Twentieth-Century Literary Theory: A Reader*. New York: St. Martin's Press, 1988.

Ortega y Gasset, Jose. "The Difficulty of Reading." Trans. Clarence E. Parmenter. *Diogenes* 28 (Winter, 1959): 1–17.

Ovid. *Metamorphoses*. Trans. Mary M. Innes. Middlesex, England: Penguin, 1955.

———. *The Metamorphoses*. Trans. Horace Gregory. New York: Viking Press [New American Library 5th reprint], 1958.

Poe, Edgar Allan. *Collected Works of Edgar Allan Poe: Tales and Sketches, 1843–1848*. Ed. Thomas Ollive Mabbott. Cambridge, Mass.: Harvard University Press, 1978, pp. 792–97.

———. "The Black Cat," *The Complete Illustrated Stories and Poems of Edgar Allan Poe*. Great Britain: Chancellor Press/Octopus Books, 1988, pp. 235–43.

———. The Imp of the Perverse," *The Complete Illustrated Stories and Poems of Edgar Allan Poe*. Great Britain: Chancellor Press/Octopus Books, 1988, pp. 439–45.

Poulet, Georges. "Criticism and the Experience of Interiority" in Macksey, *The Structuralist Controversy*, pp. 56–72.

Rajan, Gita. "A Feminist Rereading of Poe's 'The Tell-Tale Heart'," *Papers on Language and Literature* 24 (3) [Summer 1988]: 283–300.

Rancière, Jacques. *The Names of History*. Trans. Hassan Melehy. Minnesota: University of Minnesota Press, 1994.

de Saussure, Ferdinand. *Course in General Linguistics*. Trans. Wade Baskin. New York: McGraw-Hill, 1959, reprinted 1966.

Shakespeare, William. *The Tragedy of Macbeth*. Ed. Sylvan Barnet. New York: New American Library/Signet Classics, 1963.

Sussman, Henry. "A Note on the Public and the Private in Literature: The Literature of 'Acting Out'." *MLN* 104 (3) [April 1989]: 597–611.

Tompkins, Jane P., ed. *Reader-Response Criticism*. Baltimore: The Johns Hopkins University Press, 1980.

Vaihinger, Hans. *The Philosophy of "As If"—A System of the Theoretical, Practical, and Religious Fictions of Mankind*. Trans. C. K. Ogden. New York: Harcourt, Brace, & Co., 1924.

Valdes, Mario J. and Owen Miller, eds. *Identity of the Literary Text*. Toronto: University of Toronto Press, 1985.

Veeser, H. Aram, ed. *The New Historicism*. New York: Routledge, 1989.

Webster's Deluxe Unabridged Dictionary, Second Edition. New York: Dorset and Baber/Simon & Schuster, 1979.

Weiskel, Thomas. "The Logic of Terror," *The Romantic Sublime: Studies in the Structure and Psychology of Transcendence*. Baltimore: The Johns Hopkins University Press, 1976, pp. 83–106.

White, Hayden. *Metahistory*. Baltimore: The Johns Hopkins University Press, 1973.

———. New Historicism: A Comment," *The New Historicism*. Ed. H. Aram Veeser. New York: Routledge, 1989, pp. 293–302.

Williams, Michael J. S. *A World of Words: Language and Displacement in the Fiction of Edgar Allan Poe*. Durham: Duke University Press, 1988, pp. 36–38.

Witherington, Paul. "The Accomplice in 'The Tell-Tale Heart'," *Studies in Short Fiction* 22 (4) [Fall 1985]: 471–75.

BRETT ZIMMERMAN

Frantic Forensic Oratory:
Poe's "The Tell-Tale Heart"

I have no idea what Ezra Pound meant when he complained that Poe is "A dam'd bad rhetorician half the time" (qtd. in Hubbell 20). Perhaps he was referring to Poe's literary criticism, but what concerns me here is the rhetoric of one of Poe's murderous narrators, for John P. Hussey is certainly correct when he notes that "Poe created a series of rhetorical characters who try to persuade and guide their readers to particular ends" (37). Let us consider the protagonist of "The Tell-Tale Heart." It has been customary to see that tale as a *confession*, but it becomes clear that the narrator has *already* confessed to the murder of the old man who was his former living companion. The tale, then, is not so much a confession as a *defense*: "The Tell-Tale Heart" is actually a specimen of courtroom rhetoric—judicial, or forensic, oratory. This is not to say that he is necessarily arguing in a court of law; he may be speaking to his auditor(s) in a prison cell—but that he is telling his side of the story to someone (rather than writing to himself in a journal) is clear by his use of the word "you"; and that he is speaking rather than writing is clear by his exhortation to "hearken" (listen) to what he has to say. The important point is that his spoken account is forensic insofar as that means a legal argument in self-defense. To this end, the narrator has a considerable grasp of the techniques of argument but, like a damned bad rhetorician, he fails in his rhetorical performance even while striving des-

From *Style* 35, no. 1 (Spring 2001): 34–49. © 2001 by *Style*.

perately to convince. That does not mean that Poe himself is a damned bad rhetorician, for what John McElroy says of "The Black Cat" is equally true of "The Tell-Tale Heart": the story has "two simultaneous perspectives: the narrative and the authorial" (103). The author, Poe, puts various rhetorical figures of speech and thought, as well as argumentative appeals, into his narrator's explanations of the horrible events he has initiated, and then Poe sits back with his perceptive readers to watch the narrator fall short in his attempts at persuasion. The result is an irony that alert readers detect and a conviction—on my part, anyway—that Poe is a better literary craftsman than even some of his critical champions have realized.

Poe and the Tradition of Rhetoric and Oratory: His Time and Place

We cannot say for sure with which rhetorical handbooks Poe was familiar, but that he *was* familiar with some is shown by a remark he makes in "The Rationale of Verse": "In our ordinary grammars and in our works on rhetoric or prosody in general, may be found occasional chapters, it is true, which have the heading, 'Versification,' but these are, in all instances, exceedingly meagre" (14: 211). To be more particular, scholars attempting to demonstrate a nineteenth-century writer's familiarity with the rhetorical tradition often begin with the eighteenth-century Scottish divine and professor of rhetoric, Hugh Blair, whose *Lectures on Rhetoric and Belles Lettres* "went through 130 British and American editions between 1783 and 1911" (Short 177n). Hussey shows no diffidence at all in insisting that Poe's art is grounded "in the specific injunctions of the [rhetorical] handbooks," Blair's in particular. For *Eureka*, specifically, Poe needed appropriate personae for his narrator and a rigidly structured pattern or mold, for which he turned to the "classical address, again as Blair describes it, with six major sections: the Introduction (Exordium), Proposition and Division, Narration, Reasoning or Arguments, the Pathetic, and the Conclusion (Peroration)" (41). Although these divisions are centuries old and as such did not originate in *Lectures on Rhetoric and Belles Lettres*, Hussey makes a case for Poe's indebtedness to Blair by showing how the poet-cosmologist follows certain *dicta* expounded in the *Lectures*. Although he makes no attempt to prove his case, Donald B. Stauffer takes for granted that Poe took some of his ideas about style from Blair (4.54).

While Blair's rhetoric was most prevalent in Eastern colleges until 1828—in fact, "Until the middle of the nineteenth century it was one of the most widely used textbooks of rhetoric" (Thomas 204; see also Corbett 568)—other extant works were George Campbell's *Philosophy of Rhetoric* (1776), which achieved a circulation comparable to Blair's after 1830 (Thomas 204), Richard Whately's *Elements of Rhetoric* (1823), and Professor Samuel

P. Newman's *Practical System of Rhetoric* (1827), which would go through more than sixty editions (Matthiessen 203n). Another well-circulating work was Alexander Jamieson's *Grammar of Rhetoric and Polite Literature*, first published in 1818 and "in its twenty-fourth American edition by 1844" (Short 178n). Other works known in American colleges include Charles Rollin's *Belles Lettres*, John Stirling's *System of Rhetoric* (1733), John Holmes's popular *Art of Rhetoric Made Easy* (1739), John Mason's *Essay on Elocution and Pronunciation* (1748), John Lawson's *Lectures Concerning Oratory* (1758), John Ward's influential *System of Oratory* (1759), James Burgh's *Art of Speaking* (1761), Thomas Sheridan's *Lectures on Elocution* (1762), Joseph Priestley's *Course of Lectures on Oratory and Criticism* (1777), John Walker's *Elements of Elocution* (1781), John Quincy Adams's two-volume *Lectures on Rhetoric and Oratory* (1810), and William Enfield's *The Speaker* (1826). Less widely circulated were contributions to the teaching of oratory and rhetoric by American college professors, including Princeton's John Witherspoon, "whose lectures on rhetoric, delivered at the New Jersey college from 1758 to 1794, were posthumously collected and printed"; then there is *Lectures on Eloquence and Style*, by Ebenezer Porter, holder of the Bartlett Professorship of Sacred Rhetoric at Andover Academy from 1813 to 1831 (Thomas 205). He also produced *Analysis of the Principles of Rhetorical Delivery as Applied in Reading and Speaking* (1827). "one of the most widely used college elocutionary texts before 1850" (Thomas 207n2).

While John Quincy Adams and Joseph Priestley do indeed appear in Pollin's *Word Index to Poe's Fiction*, we find no reference there to any of the above texts (Blair is mentioned in *Exordium*)—and none appears in Killis Campbell's survey, "Poe's Reading." Still, it seems almost inconceivable that Poe would not have been familiar with at least some of these, especially when we consider that, as Kenneth Cmiel puts it, "From the seventeenth to the end of the nineteenth century, rhetoric saturated American culture" and was "critical to the school curriculum, pulpit, political forum, and court of law." Poe's career as a schoolboy and professional author fits, after all, between the years 1820 and 1860, "the golden age of American oratory" (592). Robert Jacobs calls oratory "the most admired form of Southern rhetorical expression in Poe's time" (76). "It was," says biographer Hervey Allen, "the age of the spoken word" (176). Indeed! In a brief history of American oratory from 1788 to 1860, Aly and Tanquary tell us that "speechmaking went on in the daily exercise of life in situations and under conditions that defy classification. And if no situation requiring speechmaking was at hand, then one was invented. The literary society, the 'bee,' the debating society, and the lyceum were largely given over to speechmaking in one form or another" (89).

It certainly looks as if speechmaking went on at Poe's childhood home, for his domestic environment and education were responsible for initiating

Poe's knowledge of rhetoric as both eloquence and persuasion. An early biographer, George Woodberry, tells us that, at the home of his foster parents, the Allans, Poe as a young boy was encouraged to give speeches to visitors: "his talent was to declaim"—an aptitude he had "perhaps by inheritance," both dead parents having been actors (15). A later biographer, James Harrison, confirms and elaborates by quoting a former acquaintance of Poe, Col. Thomas H. Ellis, who paid tribute to Poe in the *Richmond Standard* on May 7, 1881: "Talent for declamation was one of his gifts. I well remember a public exhibition at the close of a course of instruction in elocution which he had attended [. . .] and my delight when, in the presence of a large and distinguished company, he bore off the prize in competition with [. . .] the most promising of the Richmond boys" (1: 24; see also Quinn 84).[1] In fact, it is hard to imagine a precocious Virginia boy being *unaware* of rhetoric, given his environment: "Little Edgar's childhood and youth were passed in an atmosphere of sociability, open-air sports, oratory, and elocution. Patrick Henry, the great orator of the Revolution, lay in the neighboring churchyard of Old St. John's; Chief-Justice Marshall, the greatest of the justices of the Supreme Court, and John Randoph of Roanoke, celebrated for silver voice and stinging sarcasm, were familiar figures in Richmond streets; retired presidents like Jefferson, Madison, and Monroe" were also to be seen occasionally (1: 13). Biographer Jeffrey Meyers goes further—probably following Arthur Quinn (102)—speculating that Poe had met the author of "The Declaration of Independence," one of the most brilliant pieces of rhetoric ever penned by an American: "Every Sunday Mr. Jefferson regularly invited some of the students to dine with him at Monticello, and Poe must have met him on several social and academic occasions" (22).

Not only did the young Poe have the example of contemporary orators such as Jefferson ("Old Man Eloquent") constantly in front of him but his formal education acquainted him as well with the great rhetoricians of the past. When a young scholar in England, Poe attended John Bransby's school at Stoke Newington where he learned Latin, so important for a knowledge of ancient rhetoric. Back in America, in the English and Classical School of Richmond, Virginia, a barely adolescent Edgar "read the ordinary classical authors of the old preparatory curriculum" (Woodberry 19). Quinn is more specific, quoting the schoolmaster Joseph H. Clarke, who wrote in an 1876 letter, "When I left Richmond [. . .] Edgar's class was reading Horace and Cicero's Orations in Latin [. . .]" (83). At Jefferson's newly opened University of Virginia, Poe enrolled in the Schools of Ancient and Modern Languages, later to excel in French and, again, *Latin* (Norman 72). Harrison records that Poe impressed his associates with "his remarkable attainments as a classical scholar" (1: 48). As another biographer, Kenneth Silverman, notes, Poe also joined "the Jefferson Society, a debating club, [where] it was said, [he] 'grew noted as a debater'" (30). What better forum for the practice of rhetoric?

These scholarly achievements are reflected occasionally in Poe's writings, where we certainly find some references to rhetoric and oratory. In "Some Words with a Mummy," Poe provides a rather comical picture of modern oratorical gestures: "Mr. Gliddon [. . .] could not make the Egyptian comprehend the term 'politics,' until he sketched upon the wall, with a bit of charcoal, a little carbuncle-nosed gentleman, out at elbows. standing upon a slump, with his left leg drawn back, his right arm thrown forward, with the fist shut, the eyes rolled up toward Heaven, and the mouth open at an angle of ninety degrees" (6: 125). Poe would have known this cartoon orator to be partaking of the "mechanistic" concept of elocution, which was overwhelmingly popular in the 1800s. In other words, here Poe shows his awareness of the last of the traditional five parts of rhetoric: delivery. Mechanistic delivery concentrates on "the use of pitch, intensity, rate, and quality of the voice, as well as movements of hands, head, eyes, and other parts of the body" (Thomas 203). Vocal and physical communication was extremely important, and Walker's *Elements of Elocution* was one of the principle books devoted to the movement of the orator's body; Walker based his teaching "on observations of dance, musical, and theatrical performance" (Covino and Jolliffe 43). William Russell (see below) and Porter were both Walker adherents, but the most monumental book devoted to mechanistic oratory was Gilbert Austin's *Chironomia; or a Treatise on Rhetorical Delivery: Comprehending Many Precepts, Both Ancient and Modern, for the Proper Regulation of the Voice, the Countenance, and Gesture* (1806). Covino and Jolliffe say that Austin "grounded his teaching in a self-proclaimed scientific study of effective delivery" (see also Thomas 206). This book contains dozens of figures of gestures involving the hands, feet, and entire bodies (poses that would strike us as hilarious today and would get a modern speechifier laughed off the stage). Books published in nineteenth-century America that show Austin's influence, and that Poe may have known, include Increase Cooke's *The American Orator* (1819), Russell's *American Elocutionist* (1844), Rufus Claggett's *Elocution Made Easy* (1845), Merritt Caldwell's *A Practical Manual of Elocution* (1845), and C. P. Bronson's *Elocution; or Mental and Vocal Philosophy* (1845), in its fifth edition by 1845 (see Robb and Thonssen xviii). In the same oratorical tradition is Dr. James Rush's *Philosophy of the Human Voice*, "the greatest single influence upon the development of elocution in America. [. . .] The book was immediately popular, and [. . .] remained the supreme authority on voice through most of the nineteenth century" (Thomas 207). Relating oratorical animation to the histrionic tradition is Henry Siddon's *Practical Illustrations of Rhetorical Gesture and Action; Adapted to the English Drama* (1822). It is hard to imagine that the histrionic Poe would not have been attentive to issues of rhetorical delivery.

Poe also displays knowledge of rhetorical "dogma," both ancient and modern. In "The Purloined Letter," Dupin suggests to the narrator that "some color of truth has been given to the rhetorical dogma, that metaphor, or simile, may be made to strengthen an argument, as well as to embellish a description" (6: 47; see also 10: 143–44). And that Poe was knowledgeable about both ancient and modern rhetoric is shown by some remarks he makes in his Marginalia:

> We may safely grant that the *effects* of the oratory of Demosthenes were vaster than those wrought by the eloquence of any modern, and yet not controvert the idea that the modern eloquence, itself, is superior to that of the Greek. [. . .] The suggestions, the arguments, the incitements of the ancient rhetorician were, when compared with those of the modern, absolutely novel; possessing thus an immense adventitious force—a force which has been, oddly enough, left out of sight in all estimates of the eloquence of the two eras.

> The finest Philippic of the Greek would have been hooted at in the British House of Peers, while an impromptu of Sheridan, or of Brougham, would have carried by storm all the hearts and all the intellects of Athens.
> (16: 62; see the nearly identical remarks in a Poe review [10: 58–59])

Elsewhere in the Marginalia we find a reference to Cicero's speeches: "The best specimen of his manner [Professor Charles Anthon's] is to be found in an analysis of the Life and Writings of Cicero, prefacing an edition of the orator's Select Orations. This analysis [. . .] is so peculiarly Ciceronian, in point of fullness, and in other points, that I have sometimes thought it an intended imitation of the *Brutus, sive de Claris Oratoribus*" (16: 103). In fact, Poe reviewed Anthon's *Select Orations of Cicero* for the *Southern Literary Messenger* in January, 1837 (9: 266–68). In "The Man of the Crowd," the narrator refers to "the mad and flimsy rhetoric of Gorgias" (4: 134), the fourth-century Sicilian rhetorician and chief adversary of Socrates in Plato's *Gorgias*. The forensic oratory of Gorgias employed "highly musical forms of antithesis, involving isocolon, homoioteleuton, parison, paramoion and—above all—abundant paranomasia" (Cluett and Kampeas 33)—figures Poe himself uses on occasion in his own prose. Poe shows his familiarity with another ancient rhetor in his discussion of the mystical Ralph Waldo Emerson: "Quintilian mentions a pedant who taught obscurity, and who once said to a pupil 'this is excellent, for I do not understand it myself'" (15: 260). At any rate, Allen Tate, after acknowledging Poe's "early classical education" (and Christian upbringing), is certainly wrong when he goes on to say that Poe "wrote as if the experiences of these traditions had been lost" (49).

We do not have to be denouncing bitterly the King of Macedon or carrying on in the British House of Peers to engage in the art of persuasion, however, for we employ rhetoric every day of our lives, usually for the most ordinary of needs and unconsciously; nor do we need to have all our mental faculties in good working order to exploit rhetoric—as Poe demonstrates through the desperate narrators in his tales of criminal homicide. In, for instance, "The Tell-Tale Heart" and "The Imp of the Perverse," the mentally disturbed murderers want to convince their auditors of the *reasonableness* of their crimes—to make their audience understand that these things are comprehensible according to ordinary motives of human behavior and psychology. The profound *irony*, of course, is that these protagonists employ the traditional, the classical, language of reason (and primarily the Aristotelian appeal to *logos*) to justify and defend the actions of *unreason*. Readers should adopt the same stance of ironic detachment as Poe himself enjoys; that is, we should be aware of the discrepancy between his narrators' irrational actions, motives, and their techniques of rational argument, their forensic oratory. Like another American literary psychologist, Herman Melville, Poe recognized that victims of mental diseases do not appear to be psychologically ill all the time—that hysterical ravings and incomprehensible babblings do not always identify the insane (also the lesson in "The System of Dr. Tarr and Professor Fether" [especially 6: 72]). Poe would have appreciated Melville's psychoanalysis of John Claggart:

> Though the man's even temper and discreet bearing would seem to intimate a mind peculiarly subject to the law of reason, not the less in heart he would seem to riot in complete exemption from that law, having apparently little to do with reason further than to employ it as an ambidexter implement for effecting the irrational. That is to say: Toward the accomplishment of an aim which in wantonness of atrocity would seem to partake of the insane, he will direct a cool judgment sagacious and sound. These men are madmen, and of the most dangerous sort [. . .] (*Billy Budd* 76)

Like Melville's Ahab, Poe's madman in "The Tell-Tale Heart" particularly employs reason not only to carry out irrational acts but also to justify them. He behaves like an orator striving to convince an audience to take up a cause or like a defense-attorney advocating a point of view. We have to acknowledge that Poe's depraved rhetoricians—like Ahab, many of Shakespeare's evil characters, and the Satan of Milton's *Paradise Lost*—have fairly impressive powers of argument even while we recognize the absurdity of their attempts to justify themselves, or recognize at least the *pathos* of their attempts to explain the events in which they have played a role.

Frantic Forensic Oratory

Elsewhere (Zimmerman) I demonstrate that the killer in "The Tell-Tale Heart" is a paranoid schizophrenic, noting that symptoms of that disease include anxiety and argumentativeness (American Psychiatric Association 287).[2] These symptoms, especially his disposition to dispute, are manifested not only when he "arose and argued about trifles" (5: 95) but also throughout the narration. "The Tell-Tale Heart" is in fact an extended example of what classical Greek and Roman rhetors called *antirrhesis* (the rejection of an argument or opinion because of its error, wickedness, or insignificance). Obviously, the prisoner's captors have named his crime for what it is, the act of an anxiety-ridden madman; *this* is the argument that the narrator—illustrating another symptom of schizophrenia, lack of insight—rejects as erroneous, impertinent, absurdly false; this is the thesis to which he attempts to provide the antithesis. Acting as his own defense-lawyer, he is not concerned with the issue of his responsibility in the crime, with the quality of the evidence against him, with the nature of the law broken, or with determining the extent of harm done to the victim—all important issues in forensic oratory (see Corbett 137–38). That is, he is not concerned with *whether* something happened but with the *quality* of what happened: his motives—the causes of his murderous actions and his subsequent maneuverings. He wants to demonstrate, rhetorically, that they were the actions of a sane rather than an insane man—wants, therefore, to refute not the charge that he committed the crime but the charge that he is mad. In doing so he bases his argument on the topos of comparison, specifically the subtopic of *difference* ("I differ from homicidal madmen in several important respects").

As a specimen of courtroom oratory, "The Tell-Tale Heart" displays several parts of the classical speech: it begins, as it should, with an *exordium* or *prooemium* (introduction), which we might consider the first two paragraphs. Part of the introductory material is the *narratio*, a brief, clear statement of the case—the narrator knows that this is a principal component of forensic oratory. Speeches, however, do not always use or need every part of the classical division, and Poe's narrator omits a *partitio* (*divisio*—division of the issue into its constituent parts). He then combines the standard fourth and fifth sections—the *confirmatio* (one's strongest positive arguments) and *confutatio* (refutation of contrary viewpoints—his extended *antirrhesis*); these make up the bulk of the tale and are anticipated in the opening two paragraphs. It is telling that this speech lacks the final part of a classical oration, the *peroratio*—conclusion. Had the narrator been able to retain his initial tranquility, he might have been able to produce some closing remarks (a summary of his case and a terminal flourish), but by the end of the speech his forensic powers have degenerated into complete and utter frenzy: he succumbs to his schizophrenic symptoms again—specifically a violent mood swing comprised of anger and anxiety.

At the start, he knows that his audience has already determined what they think of him—knows that they are hostile and have labeled him a nervous "madman." He is aware, in other words, that his case is what Cicero would have called a "difficult" one (as opposed to being "honorable," "mean," "ambiguous" or "obscure") involving as it does an audience whose sympathies are alienated by the horrendous nature of his crime. Thus, the narrator uses his *exordium* as it is meant to be used: he attempts to win the good will of his auditors, at least to the extent that they are willing to hear him out patiently. While the rest of the speech is an appeal to *logos*, reason, at the beginning he must resort to an appeal to *ethos* in order to lessen the audience's hostility and make them more receptive. He begins, therefore, with *restrictio* in accepting *part* of their judgment: "True!—nervous—very, very dreadfully nervous I had been and am" (5: 88). He makes a concession (*paromologia*), and what better way to capture the audience's sympathies than by agreeing with their pronouncement, in effect congratulating them on their astuteness, their medical acumen. It is true that he qualifies their diagnosis with his rhetorical questions ("why *will* you say that I am mad?"; "How then am I mad?")—in this sense he is using what Richard Whately called the *introduction corrective* (see Corbett 284–85)—but he has already shown his good will (*eunoia*) toward his listeners by agreeing with at least part of their judgment. Corbett discusses the strategic usefulness of the concession as part of the ethical appeal: "The audience gets the impression that the person capable of making frank confessions and generous concessions is not only a good person but a person so confident of the strength of his or her position that he or she can afford to concede points to the opposition" (316).

Poe's clever forensic rhetorician uses other devices to "soften up," to *condition*, his audience. The first and second paragraphs of "The Tell-Tale Heart" also involve a device used often by Poe's narrators: *praeparatio* (preparing an audience before telling them about something done). Several Poe tales begin with short essays on various themes, concepts, that will be illustrated by the following narrative accounts; thus, the narrators prepare the audience to understand the specific cases to follow by illuminating the theories first. "The Murders in the Rue Morgue" commences with an essay on certain mental skills before we hear about their display by the amateur detective C. Auguste Dupin. "The Premature Burial" starts with several illustrations of untimely interment before we hear about how the narrator himself was apparently buried alive. "The Imp of the Perverse" begins with a short dissertation on that destructive and irresistible human impulse before the narrator provides three examples of it and finally his own case. I agree with Sandra Spanier (311), who quotes Eugene Kanjo with approval: "This essay-like introduction is not a failure of craft, as one critic contends, but a measure of Poe's craftiness" (41). This craftiness lies in Poe's use of the rhetorical tradition—here, in his employment of *praeparatio*. When used to preface a criminal confession, this device can make what would otherwise seem to be merely cold, hard, ugly, incriminating facts more understandable, even more acceptable—or, at least, less *un*acceptable. At the same time, most significantly, the forensic narrator combines the ethical appeal with the appeal to *pathos* (emotions): he attempts to enlist the sympathies of his hostile auditors by portraying *himself* as the real victim. He tries to weaken the charges against him by discoursing of his misfortunes, his difficulties: I *loved* the old man, but I was persecuted, hounded, harassed, and haunted day and night by his wretched Evil Eye (Sharon Crowley says "a rhetor's ethos may be a source of good will if she [. . .] elaborates on her misfortunes or difficulties" [176]).

In his use of *praeparatio*, the narrator in "The Tell-Tale Heart" differs from the Watson-like biographer of Dupin and the protagonists of "The Imp of the Perverse" and "The Premature Burial" in that he does not provide any general theories or other cases of his particular illness, but he *does* prepare us to understand it nevertheless. He wants us to recognize, first, that he suffers from overacute senses and, second, that the vulture eye of the old man, not hatred or greed (rather trite, uninteresting, normal motives), is what compelled him to commit his atrocity (here is also *expeditio*, if we can accept the term as meaning not just the rejection of all but one of various reasons why something should be done but also of why something *was* done). Also embedded within the larger trope, *praeparatio*, is *aetiologia*—giving a cause or reason for a result: "He had the eye of a vulture—a pale blue eye, with a film over it. Whenever it fell upon me, my blood ran cold; and so by degrees—very gradually—I made up my mind to take the life of the old man, and thus rid myself of the eye forever" (5: 88). Here the narrator employs another topos frequent in forensic oratory: the topos of relationship and its sub-topic, cause and effect. The pathetic irony in all this, of course, is that the narrator really believes his *aetiologia* to be reasonable, comprehensible, easily justifiable.

Poe maintains an objective distance with us and watches the ironic *aetiologia*. In fact, what characterizes most of the rhetorical devices in Poe's tales of criminal homicide is the conscious, the deliberate, *irony* with which he uses these techniques of argumentation. Overlapping with the ironic *aetiologia* is *necessum* (*dicaeologia*): defending one's words or acts with reasonable excuses; defending briefly the justice of one's cause. As with the *aetiologia*, what gives an interesting twist to the use of *necessum* in some of Poe's tales is the extent to which the narrators' auditors and we, the readers, might find the defense, the excuse, outrageously unconvincing and bizarre. The same is true of the use on the part of the "Tell-Tale Heart" narrator of what Cicero called *prae-munitio*—defending yourself in anticipation of an attack; strengthening your position beforehand: "If still you think me mad, you will think so no longer when I describe the wise precautions I took for the concealment of the body" (5: 92). Here the *praemunitio*, which is a normal component of the confirmation/refutation part of a classical oration, is pathetic, ironic, because clearly inadequate, outrageously unconvincing to anyone except the narrator—more generally, to anyone except those outside society's codes of moral behavior and lacking the conscience of the *superego*.

The bragging narrator, however, believes that he, as a man of superior powers (note his delusions of grandeur—another sign of schizophrenia), not only can plan and carry out the perfect crime, and conceal the evidence, but can also convince his prosecutors that his actions were entirely reasonable. "The Tell-Tale Heart" is an extended exemplification of *antirrhesis* but it is, as well, extended *consummatio* (*diallage*), a bringing together of several arguments to establish a single point: his sanity. Argument #1: I am not mad but suffer from overacute senses, especially of the auditory capacity ("And have I not told you that what you mistake for madness is but over acuteness of the senses?" [5: 91]). Argument #2: "Madmen know nothing. But you should have seen *me*. You should have seen how wisely I proceeded—with what caution—with what foresight—with what dissimulation I went to work" (5: 88). A lunatic, he believes, would be incapable of sagacity, caution, foresight, and ingenuity in planning and executing a murder ("would a madman have been so wise as this?" [5: 89]). Argument #3: "If still you think me mad, you will think so no longer when I describe the wise precautions I took for the concealment of the body."[3] Not only sagacity in execution but sagacity in concealment is also a sign of sanity, he believes.

His auditors, however, likely do not share the positive *slant* that he puts on his actions. After all, this shrewd forensic rhetorician seems to make use of what is sometimes considered a rather disreputable device: *paradiastole* (making the best of a bad thing; the euphemistic substitution for a negative word with something more positive). In his introduction to Machiavelli's *The Prince*, David Wootton calls chapters 16 to 18 of that work "a virtuoso exercise in *paradiastole*, the redescription of behavior in order to transform its moral significance" (xxxiv). For example, what we call hypocrisy in a ruler, Machiavelli would call *craftiness* or *expediency*; in other words, what most people consider a negative trait, Machiavelli considers positive. We see, then, how the device, a technique of argument, can involve essentially a Nietzschean revaluation of values. As part of his forensic oratory, the Machiavellian narrator in "The Tell-Tale Heart" seems to employ *paradiastole*, especially in the third paragraph. Consider his use of nouns and adverbs: "You should have seen how *wisely* I proceeded—with what *caution*—with what *foresight*—with what *dissimulation* I went to work! [. . .] Oh, you would have laughed to see how *cunningly* I thrust it in!" (5: 88–89; my italics). What we might call *perfidiously*, he calls *wisely*; what we might call *sneakiness*, he calls *caution*; what we might call *scheming*, he calls *foresight*; what we might call *treacherously*, he calls *cunningly*. Even the one word in that catalogue that has negative connotations, *dissimulation*, he would translate as *ingenuity*. Certainly his accusers, those whom he is addressing, have evaluated his conduct and might have expressed it thus: "We should have seen how perfidiously you proceeded—with what sneakiness—with what scheming—with what hypocrisy you went to work! Oh, we would have been appalled to see how treacherously you thrust in your head!" But the narrator, using *paradiastole*, has redescribed his behaviour, putting it in a positive light according to *his* twisted values and assuming that his audience would be persuaded to adopt those values also.

Let us summarize the rhetorical appeals, topoi, and devices that Poe's paranoid schizophrenic employs, within a classical arrangement, in order to win the skeptical audience to his point of view. We have seen that he employs four of the six parts of a classical oration. His *exordium* attempts to make the hostile audience more receptive to his point of view through *restrictio* and an initial, friendly concession (*paromologia*), part of his brief appeal to *ethos* (simultaneously, his introduction is of an inoffensively corrective nature in that he insists that his judges have misunderstood the nature of his illness and, hence, his case). Next, he continues his strategy of softening the auditors with *praeparatio*. His statement of the case (*narratio*), told in the plain style as it should be (according to Quintilian), also features *expeditio, aetiologia*, and *necessum*. The fourth and fifth parts of this forensic speech, the *confirmatio* and *confutatio*, begin with the third paragraph and employ *paradiastole, praemunitio, progressio, antirrhesis*, and *consummatio*. Additionally, the narrator's forensic oratory involves the topos of comparison (with its sub-topos of difference) and the topos of relationship (with its sub-topos of cause and effect); all these comprise a five-page appeal primarily to *logos*, reason—with a useful bit of *ethos* and *pathos* thrown in at the beginning.[4]

What is so tragic about the narrator's frantic forensic rhetoric, however, is his psychopathic inability to appreciate the moral gravity of his deeds, despite his—shall we say it?—otherwise brilliant capacity to construct a powerful piece of persuasion, of reasoning. Paige Matthey Bynum puts it this way: "Poe's narrator is maintaining a causal sequence—I can reason; therefore I am not insane—which Poe's audience had just discovered was false" (148). It is evident immediately to the reader, and increasingly as the narrative progresses, that the narrator is indeed clearly ill and, as John Cleman says, "The irony of ostensible sanity signaling insanity could not have been lost on Poe" (632). Let us narrow the focus from the broad and vague term *insanity* to the particular illness from which Poe's forensic orator suffers. His revaluation of values, his *paradiastole*, is really a manifestation of his schizophrenia, which, remember, refers to a split between thought and feeling: his thoughts of the grisly murder he committed are not accompanied by the feelings of disgust that mentally healthy people would feel. His feelings are of delight rather than disgust. That is why he is able to turn *perfidiously* into *wisely*, *sneakiness* into *caution*, *scheming* into *foresight*, *treacherously* into *cunningly*, and to define *dissimulation* as *ingenuity* rather than *hypocrisy*. We recognize this rhetorical revaluation of values as a sign of schizophrenia; the narrator does not.

Peroratio

Despite the glorification of oratory and rhetoric in Poe's time and place, in "The Tell-Tale Heart" we find Poe demonstrating that rhetoric can *fail*. Did Poe therefore distrust that ancient art of persuasion? As we know, contempt for and suspicion of rhetoric is a tradition at least as old as Plato, who, in his *Gorgias*, has Socrates liken that art to teaching a cook how to give poison a pleasing taste. This attitude certainly carried into the Renaissance: in Marguerite de Navarre's *Heptameron*, academics are rejected as good storytellers because "Monseigneur the Dauphin didn't want their art brought in, and he was afraid that rhetorical ornament would in part falsify the truth of the account" (69). In his essay "On the Education of Children," Montaigne writes of the ideal student who "knows no rhetoric, nor how, by way of preface, to *capture the benevolence of the candid reader*; nor has he any wish to do so. In fact, all such fine tricks are easily eclipsed by the light of a simple, artless truth. These refinements serve only to divert the vulgar" (77). Even Machiavelli dissociates himself from the tradition in the second paragraph of *The Prince*: "I have not ornamented this book with rhetorical turns of phrase, or stuffed it with pretentious and magnificent words, or made use of allurements and embellishments that are irrelevant to my purpose, as many authors do" (5). And Shakespeare, most obviously, shows through the many *linguistic Machiavellians* in his plays the necessity of qualifying Quintilian's definition of the rhetor as "a good man skilled at speaking." Poe, like Milton and Melville also, recognizes that *bad* men could speak well.

But I do not believe that Poe—the contemporary of Thomas Jefferson, Chief-Justice Marshall, John Randoph, Daniel Webster—held the rhetorical tradition in contempt. Like the Renaissance humanists cited above who claimed to despise rhetoric, he was trained in it and put it to good use. Yet, like them, he was wise enough to recognize how powerful a tool it could be and to hold it in suspicion. As well, he was simply fascinated by the ironic spectacle of the actions of unreason being justified through the linguistic tradition of reason—the *jarring collocation* of insanity employing the Aristotelian appeal to *logos*. Poe the Southerner may indeed have been trained in the classical tradition—the brilliant oratory, rhetoric, and logic of the wisest ancient Greeks and Romans—but he was also a student of the new science of abnormal psychology. Poe, the devotee of sweetness and light, gives in to the impulses of Dark Romanticism. A Poe narrator may strive to convince us that his mind is a Greek temple with its glorious friezes, fluted Doric columns, solid stylobates—but *we* know what kind of ruin it is. The classical man will give way: Cicero will succumb to the barbarian hordes of his psyche, Quintilian to the inner demons, Aristotle to the beast within.

Notes

1. That is worth repeating: *Poe took a course in elocution.* Thomas informs us that courses devoted to the delivery of speeches were developed at American colleges in the early 1800s. The teaching of speech came to be recognized "as a separate and distinct subject field":

> In 1806 John Quincy Adams was appointed to the Boylston Chair of Rhetoric and Oratory at Harvard. It was the first such appointment in the United States. Previously the subject had been taught by some tutor who also instructed in numerous other fields and was frequently not specifically prepared for teaching speech. But after Adams began his duties, other colleges established similar professorships. (196–97)

2. Note that schizophrenia refers to a split between thought and feeling, not to a split between personalities. Literary scholars seem especially prone to make this error.

3. We might also consider the narrative an extended example of *progressio*, building a point around a series of comparisons—in this case, between the narrator and a true "madman."

4. I have suggested in the first half of this essay that Poe was acquainted both with contemporary and classical rhetors. Many of the ancient terms I have been using (typically Greek)—certainly those naming the parts of an oration and the three appeals (*pisteis*)—could be found in both ancient and modern books. On the other hand, many of the names for the rhetorical figures are more likely to be found in the ancient texts, so I propose that Poe—who was, remember, classically trained—could have picked up such terms as *paradiastole*, *paromologia*, and *praeparatio* from them. Still, *that* proposal begs the question of whether Poe was even familiar with such esoteric terminology. In his review of Bulwer's *Night and Morning*, he demonstrates his awareness of the rhetorical name for personification: "Nor does the commonplace character of anything which he wishes to personify exclude it from the prosopopoeia" (10: 131; see also 10: 75). In "The Rationale of

Verse," he illustrates his knowledge of another fancy Greek term: "*Blending* is the plain English for *synoeresis*—but there should be *no* blending" (14: 231); Poe uses the adjective *synoeretical* in *Eureka* (16: 187). In his review of *The Dream, and Other Poems*, Poe displays his familiarity with the device *solecismus*: "Mrs. Norton will now and then be betrayed into a carelessness of diction; Mrs. Hemans was rarely, if ever, guilty of such solecisms" (10: 100). That Poe knew the esoteric name for personification, and that he knew the little known *synoeresis* and *solecism*, shows that he was indeed familiar with some of the classical terms for literary devices. Even if he did not know all the names for the figures I have identified at work in "The Tell-Tale Heart," these figures nevertheless *are there*. Thus, we can conclude either that Poe's classical background gave him the labels for these devices (*paradiastole*, *paromologia*, *praeparatio*, and so on), of which he made conscientious use for the rhetorical maneuverings of his characters, or that he did not know all the terms but had an *intuitive* understanding of the rhetorical strategies that they describe. Either way, he shows himself to be a master rhetorician, despite the rhetorical failings that he deliberately (and brilliantly) gives his narrators.

Works Cited

Allen, Hervey. *Israfel: The Life and Times of Edgar Allan Poe.* New York: Doran, 1927.

Aly, Bower, and Grafton P. Tanquary. "The Early National Period, 1788–1860." *A History and Criticism of American Public Address.* Ed. William Norwood Brigance. Vol. 1. 1943. New York: Russell, 1960. 55–110.

American Psychiatric Association. "Schizophrenia and Other Psychotic Disorders." *Diagnostic and Statistical Manual of Mental Disorders.* 4th ed. Washington, D.C.: American Psychiatric Association, 1994. 273–90.

Bynum, Paige Matthey. "'Observe How Healthily—How Calmly I Can Tell You the Whole Story': Moral Insanity and Edgar Allan Poe's 'The Tell-Tale Heart.'" *Literature and Science as Modes of Expression.* Ed. Frederick Amrine. Boston Studies in the Philosophy of Science 115. Boston: Kluwer, 1989. 141–52.

Campbell, Killis. "Poe's Reading." *University of Texas Studies in English* 5 (1925): 166–96.

Cleman, John. "Irresistible Impulses: Edgar Allan Poe and the Insanity Defense." *American Literature* 63 (1991): 623–40.

Cluett, Robert, and Rita Kampeas. *Grossly Speaking.* Toronto: Discourse, 1979.

Cmiel, Kenneth. "Rhetoric." *A Companion to American Thought.* Ed. Richard Wightman Fox and James T. Kloppenberg. Cambridge: Blackwell, 1995. 592–93.

Corbett, Edward P. J. *Classical Rhetoric for the Modern Student.* 1965. 3rd ed. New York: Oxford UP, 1990.

Covino, William A., and David A. Jolliffe. *Rhetoric: Concepts, Definitions, Boundaries.* Toronto: Allyn, 1995.

Harrison, James A. *Biography: The Complete Works of Edgar Allan Poe.* Ed. James A. Harrison. 1902. Vol. 1. New York: AMS, 1965.

Hubbell, Jay B. "Edgar Allan Poe." *Eight American Authors: A Review of Research and Criticism.* Rev. ed. New York: Norton, 1971. 3–36.

Hussey, John P. "Narrative Voice and Classical Rhetoric in *Eureka.*" *American Transcendental Quarterly* 26 (1975): 37–42.

Jacobs, Robert D. "Rhetoric in Southern Writing: Poe." *Georgia Review* 12 (1958): 76–79.

Kanjo, Eugene R. "'The Imp of the Perverse': Poe's Dark Comedy of Art and Death." *Poe Newsletter* 2 (1969): 41–44.

158 Brett Zimmerman

Machiavelli, Niccolò. *The Prince*. Trans. David Wootton. Indianapolis: Hackett, 1995.

Matthiessen, F. O. *American Renaissance: Art and Expression in the Age of Emerson and Whitman*. 1941. New York: Oxford, 1968.

McElroy, John Harmon. "The Kindred Artist; or, The Case of the Black Cat." *Studies in American Humor* 3 (1976): 103–17.

Melville, Herman. *Billy Budd, Sailor*. Ed. Harrison Hayford and Merton M. Sealts, Jr. Chicago: U of Chicago P, 1962.

Meyers, Jeffrey. *Edgar Allan Poe: His Life and Legacy*. New York: Scribner's, 1992.

Montaigne, Michele de. *Essays*. Trans. J. M. Cohen. New York: Penguin, 1978.

Navarre, Marguerite de. *The Heptameron*. Trans. P. A. Chilton. New York: Penguin, 1984.

Norman, Emma Katherine. "Poe's Knowledge of Latin." *American Literature* 6 (1934): 72–77.

Poe, Edgar Allan. *The Complete Works of Edgar Allan Poe*. 1902. Ed. James A. Harrison. 17 vols. New York: AMS, 1965.

Quinn, Arthur Hobson. *Edgar Allan Poe: A Critical Biography*. New York: Appleton, 1941.

Robb, Mary Margaret, and Lester Thonssen, eds. *Chironomia; or a Treatise on Rhetorical Delivery*, by Gilbert Austin. 1806. Landmarks in Rhetoric and Public Address. Carbondale: Southern Illinois UP, 1966.

Short, Bryan C. *Cast by Means of Figures: Herman Melville's Rhetorical Development*. Amherst: U of Massachusetts P, 1992.

Silverman, Kenneth. *Edgar A. Poe: Mournful and Never-Ending Remembrance*. New York: Harper Collins, 1991.

Spanier, Sandra Whipple. "'Nests of Boxes': Form, Sense, and Style in Poe's 'The Imp of the Perverse.'" *Studies in Short Fiction* 17 (1980): 307–16.

Stauffer, Donald Barlow. "The Language and Style of the Prose." *A Companion to Poe Studies*. Ed. Eric W. Carlson. Westport, Conn.: Greenwood, 1996. 448–67.

Tate, Allen. "Our Cousin, Mr. Poe." *Poe: A Collection of Critical Essays*. Ed. Robert Regan. Twentieth-Century Views. Englewood Cliffs, N.J.: Prentice-Hall, 1967. 38–50.

Thomas, Ota. "The Teaching of Rhetoric in the United States During the Classical Period of Education." *A History and Criticism of American Public Address*. Ed. William Norwood Brigance. 1943. Vol. 1. New York: Russell, 1960. 193–210.

Woodberry, George E. *Edgar Allan Poe*. 1885. New York: Chelsea, 1980.

Wootton, David. Introduction. *The Prince*. By Niccolò Machiavelli. Indianapolis: Hackett, 1995. xi–xliv.

Zimmerman, Brett. "'Moral Insanity' or Paranoid Schizophrenia: Poe's 'The Tell-Tale Heart.'" *Mosaic* 25 (1992): 39–48.

JOHN H. TIMMERMAN

House of Mirrors:
Edgar Allan Poe's
"The Fall of the House of Usher"

"The Fall of the House of Usher" is among those few stories that seem
to elicit nearly as many critical interpretations as it has readers. More recent
critical appraisals of the story have largely followed two directions: a reap-
praisal of the genre of the story as a Gothic romance[1] and a close attention
to Madeline Usher as a type of Poe's other female characters.[2] But the tale
presents the reader a multiplicity of problems that set it aside from Poe's
other stories. Madeline is as enigmatic as a new language and as difficult to
construe. While debates about Lady Ligeia have filled the pages of many
journals, it is not hard to understand why.[3] Her contrarian social role,
her purely gothic resurrection, and her defiant antithesis in character to
Rowena sharpen her person from the start. But Madeline? This sylph-like
creature, so attenuated and frail, seems to slip through the story like vapor,
all the more mysterious for that and for her incredible power displayed in
the conclusion.

Similarly, while the story is certainly Gothic in nature, here, too, we
find exceptions and qualifications. In the majority of Poe's Gothic tales the
narrative point of view is first person, and, significantly, the reader is also
placed inside the mind of this leading character-narrator who is only a step
away from insanity. In "Usher" we also have a creeping horror and the mental disintegration of the principal persona, but the story is in fact narrated

From *Papers on Language and Literature* 39, no. 3 (Summer 2003). © 2003 by Southern
Illinois University.

by an outside visitor (also representing the reader) who wants to find a way out of the horror. The only problem with this narrator is that, even having been given ample signs and warnings (as happens to Fortunato in "The Cask of Amontillado"), he is too inept to put the clues together. Poe has designed this deliberately, of course, for the reader is far more deductive than the narrator but has to wait for him to reach the extreme limit of safety before fleeing. However dull the narrator's mental processing, it is altogether better than being trapped in insanity.

One of the more penetrating of these studies of Gothic traits is G. R. Thompson's analysis of "The Fall of the House of Usher" in his *Poe's Fiction*. Thompson addresses the variations Poe creates with the Gothic tale by structuring a conflict between reason and irrationality. Particularly successful is his analysis of the decayed House mirroring Usher's mind so that "The sinking of the house into the reflecting pool dramatizes the sinking of the rational part of the mind, which has unsuccessfully attempted to maintain some contact with a stable structure of reality outside the self, into the nothingness within" (90). The analysis provides a lucid discussion of the process of that disintegration, of the dream-like qualities of Madeline as the devolution of the subconscious, and of the narrator's final infection by "Usher's hysteria." What Thompson does not explore, however, is an accounting for the loss of reason and what conclusion the reader may infer by the storm-struck house crumbling into the murky tarn.

To explore such issues, one must investigate beyond the confines of the tale proper, even beyond its generic home as a Gothic romance. The tale yields its full meaning as we turn to areas much overlooked in the study of this work; first, the influence of Poe's cosmology as set forth in other works but nonetheless pertinent, by his own telling, to his art; and, second, the historical context of his time when the effects of Enlightenment thinking of the prior century had not yet fully yielded (for Poe, at least) to the new spirit of Romanticism. The latter point in particular is crucial for an historicist appraisal of the story and of Poe, for it becomes evident that Poe did not reject Enlightenment thinking, that he was in fact suspicious of the newer Romanticism, and that at best he hoped for a tenuous harmony between the two. Keeping in mind such premises, we can observe the theory for unity, symmetry, and harmony emerging from *Eureka*, the aesthetic principles of the theory in his essays, and the application of those principles in a study of the conflict between Romanticism and Enlightenment in "The Fall of the House of Usher."

The casual treatment of Poe's cosmology no doubt springs from the conception that this is but one more entertaining hoax from the master trickster, somewhat akin to the elaborate architecture of "The Raven" described in "Philosophy of Composition." Undeniably, however, even Poe's most wildly

Gothic romances, his most mysterious tales of ratiocination, and virtually all his poems, spring from some "idea" of order, a principle that this world can try to twist and break but can never quite succeed. Basically, his cosmology rests upon the philosophical principle that the very apprehension of disorder assumes an agency of order. Those familiar with the works of Aristotle will recognize the argument immediately. The essentials of Poe's cosmology reside in his essay *Eureka*, and there, too, he relies upon Aristotelian premises.

Since the work is less familiar to contemporary readers, I preface a discussion of it with a brief chronology. In 1843 Poe published the "Prospectus of *The Stylus*," the literary magazine he hoped to launch in July of that year. In late 1847, he had completed the lecture "The Cosmogony of the Universe"[4] that would be the introduction to *Eureka*, but also a lecture (nearly two hours long) that he could use to raise funds for *The Stylus*. The lecture had limited use. The only event we are certain of was an appearance on January 17, 1848, at Society Library where only 60 people showed up, most of them journalists. Poe finally prevailed upon Putnam to publish the work, asking for a print run of 50,000 copies and receiving instead a run of 500. It appeared in early July 1848.[5]

There appeared to be good reason for caution. The narrative guise of the learned scholar adopted for the lengthy third section absolutely confounds the casual—or even the very literate—reader.[6] Elsewhere, the narrator moves from humble observer to snide satirist. In addition to the shifting narrative poses, the work itself is simply such a strange miscellany of facts and thoughts and extrapolations that it is nearly impossible to find an orderly, fruitful, and singular thesis emerging in it. Every issue seems to lead to an ever-widening gyre of new questions. Admitting that, however, the work still constitutes Poe's fundamental cosmological view, and it does remain central to understanding his aesthetic principles. That essential element of *Eureka*, at least, may be rather clearly and conveniently summarized.

Preceding all existence is a deity functioning like Aristotle's Prime Mover. Humanity, and all physical nature, exists because this Prime Mover willed it to exist. Poe states that "'In the beginning' we can admit—indeed, we can comprehend, but one *First Cause*, the truly ultimate *Principle*, the Volition of God" (237).[7] We have then, a fairly traditional view of God's creation *ex nihilo*, that is, he willed all things into being out of nothing more than his will. As with Aristotle (and also the Judeo-Christian tradition) God is that being beyond which one can go no further.

But here Poe throws some of his own twists into the proposition. If the creator being is that ultimate first cause, it must represent unity. All the created order is individuated; necessarily, therefore, its source is not chaos but unity. Poe speaks of this as "Irradiation from Unity"—the primary creative act. Moreover, "This primary act itself is to be considered as *continuous volition*" (237). This is to say that God's creative impulse continues through the creative order, including humanity, that he has willed into being.

We arrive at the old religious and philosophical conundrum. If willed into being by God, and out of nothing, then what constitutes both our individuation yet also our unity with this God? Judaism provides the earliest answer with the story of the Edenic fall, where because of an act of transgression the unity was partially severed and, according to the Kabbalistic myth of "God in Exile," God withdrew into mystery. Nonetheless, as God's creation, humanity was still *mindful* of God. Plato provides the first coherent philosophical accounting in the western world with his concept of the Ideal Forms being transmuted by the earthly stuff of humanity. Only humanity, however, possessed the quality of mind to apprehend the ideal.

Poe, on the other hand, insists upon an ongoing volitional act of God apprehended by intuition. The idea led to his notorious concept in "The Poetic Principle" that the task of the poet is "to apprehend the supernal loveliness" (*Essays* 77) of God's order and that the best way to do so is through sadness. Poe reflects "that (how or why we know not) this certain taint of sadness is inseparably connected with all the higher manifestations of true Beauty" (*Essays* 81). This leads Poe, then, to the idea that the most sad thing, and therefore the most beautiful, is the death of a beautiful woman. The result is a body of work littered with female corpses.

It remains difficult, even for the most earnest reader, to take "The Poetic Principle" altogether seriously. Yet, herein lie many of Poe's seminal ideas and aesthetic principles. Many of those ideas, moreover, relate directly to the cosmology of *Eureka*. One has to remember that Poe desires to startle the reader into an awareness of the divinity within, for, he insists, we are all part and particle of the divine.[8] Necessarily so, since God willed all things into being out of nothing. What then are we but particles of the divine itself? Therefore in all created order there resides what Edward Wagenknecht called "the Shadow of Beauty."[9] Poe describes it as such: "An immortal instinct, deep within the spirit of man, is thus, plainly, a sense of the beautiful" (*Complete Works* 14:273). Therefore, Poe concludes that, since we are willed into being *ex nihilo*, since we are thereby part and particle of the divine, and since the ongoing volition of the divine rests among its creation as a shadow of beauty, symmetry that mirrors this unity of the universe is the paramount aesthetic quality of the work. Poe argues that the sense of the symmetrical "is the poetical essence of the *Universal—of the Universe* which, in the supremeness of its symmetry, is but the most sublime of poems. Now symmetry and consistency are convertible terms; thus poetry and truth are one" (*Complete Works* 16:302).

Poe takes the issue one step further, however. If indeed all things are willed into being *ex nihilo*, then not only all humanity but also all matter is part and parcel with God. Such a view Poe expresses as his infamous "sentience theory" in "The Fall of the House of Usher."[10] In particular the theory exerts itself twice. When Usher reveals that he has not left the mansion in many years, he describes the effect that the "mere form and substance" of the mansion has had upon him: "An effect which the *physique* of the gray walls and turrets, and of the dim tarn into which they all looked down, had, at length, brought upon the *morale* of his existence" ("Usher" 403).[11] Later, after Usher's rhapsody of creative expressions, the narrator and Usher fall into a conversation on "the sentience of all vegetable things" (408). Remembering Usher's description of this, the narrator describes the preternatural interconnectedness of mansion and family, and concludes, in Usher's terms, that "The result was discoverable . . . in that silent, yet importunate and terrible influence which for centuries had moulded the destinies of his family, and which made *him* what I now saw him—what he was" (408).[12]

Careful readers of Poe will quickly understand that this use of a mental landscape is nothing new to Poe. It appears most prominently, perhaps, in the poetry. In "Ulalume" for example, the weird and otherworldly geographical landscape is nothing more than an objectification of the narrator's own mind. But so too it appears repeatedly in the short stories, particularly in the descriptions of the ornate and convoluted furnishings of a room ("Ligeia," "Masque of the Red Death") that mirror the mind of the narrator. In no other work, however, has Poe structured this sentience, or interconnectedness, between the physical world and the mental/psychological world more powerfully and tellingly than in "The Fall of the House of Usher."[13]

On the basis of his cosmological and aesthetic theories, Poe thereby constructs his architecture of mirrors to prop the movement of the story. Several studies have probed the pattern of mirror images, usually relating them to the rationality/irrationality of Usher or the physical/psychological tension between him and Madeline. Indeed, it falls beyond the space or provision of this essay to list them all, but in order to demonstrate the functions of pairing and splitting that the mirror images provide, a few central patterns may be noted.

The most evident, but eerily complex, of course, is the House of Usher itself. Roderick himself tells the narrator that over the centuries the mansion and the family had been so bonded as to become identified as one. Moreover, the diminishment of the Usher family, through years of inbreeding to this one lonely brother and sister, precisely parallels the physical collapse of the house, standing far apart from civilization as it does in some distant, lonely tract of country. The pairing between Roderick and the mansion is sustained in the careful detailing of descriptions, as the narrator observes first the one, then the other, and discerns unnerving similarities.

Although paired in matters of neglect and in physical description, both the Ushers and the mansion are undergoing a simultaneous process of splitting. The house is rent by a zigzag fissure that threatens its stability. In his letter to the narrator, Roderick admits to "mental disorder" that threatens his stability.[14] Similarly, the brother and sister are paired—not only by heritage but also by being fraternal twins. They, too, however, are simultaneously splitting apart, Madeline into her mysterious cataleptic trance and Roderick into an irrationally surrealistic world of frenzied artmaking.

Many other mirror images accumulate in the story. The house is mirrored by its image in the tarn and collapses beneath its waters at the close. Roderick's painting of the underground burial vault—at which the narrator marvels "If ever mortal painted an idea, that mortal was Roderick Usher"—preternaturally and prophetically mirrors Madeline's escape from the vault. The light with no apparent source in the painting may be referenced to Lady Ligeia's exclamation on the Conqueror Worm. "O Divine Father," Ligeia exclaims in a line that could be taken from *Eureka*, "Are we not part and parcel in Thee? Who—who knoweth the mysteries of the will with its vigor? Man doth not yield himself to the angels, *nor unto death utterly*, save only through the weakness of his feeble will" ("Ligeia" 319). Surprisingly with her glacial, ghostly demeanor prior to her entombment, Madeline possesses just such a will also.

"The Haunted Palace" provides another artistic mirror image. The work precisely traces the devolution of the House of Usher from a palace governed in orderly fashion by "Thought's Dominion" to a den of disorder in which demons flicker about like bats—except that these demons are in Usher's mind. An interesting submotif of the poem is the transition from spirits moving "To a Lute's well-tunèd law" to forms moving fantastically "to a discordant melody." With the demise of some structured order, artforms rampage into dissonance and cacophony.

This process of devolution forms the centering thesis of Gillian Brown's innovative study, "The Poetics of Extinction." Drawing upon Charles Lyell's *Principles of Geology* (1830–1833), in which he argues the diminishment and passing of "organic beings" over vast periods of time, Brown finds a model for the disintegration of both the House and lineage of Usher. The value of the essay resides in Brown's crisp demonstration of the relationship between the devolution of environment and humanity, predicated on Lyell's theory. As we have seen, moreover, that close interconnectedness between the physical and psychological, the external environment and the internal mind, is amply supported by *Eureka*, as well as by Poe's essays and art. Nonetheless one questions to what end this devolution exists in the fiction. Is it simply that all things pass away? Nothing could be further from Poe's writings, with their tenacious, almost frenzied grip upon the great mind that endures, as *Eureka* has it. Beyond anything Poe sought the physical incarnation of Hippocrates's incantation in his *Aphorisms: Ars longa, vita brevis*. To complete the careful construction of the story into an imaginative architecture that endures, however, one final set of mirror images bears scrutiny.

In order to create something of a mental theater that draws out the suspense of the story, Poe constructed a conflation of such images at the ending. To put Roderick's mind at ease, the narrator reads to him from "Mad Trist" by Sir Launcelot Canning.[15] Every step of Ethelred to force the entrance to the hermit's dwelling has its mirror in Madeline's clangorous escape from the dungeon. Meanwhile, a storm descends upon and envelops the mansion, mirroring the swirling collapse of Usher's rationality. Here, too, in the mirror of the storm and Roderick's mind, we find a clear use of the sentience theory.

Yet, the reader somehow feels dissatisfied if only construing the story as a clever construction of Poe's cosmology in his sentience theory. However carefully structured, the pairings and splittings of the mirror images point suggestively to a larger pattern than mere aesthetic architecture. Many directions to this larger significance have been offered.[16] It may be profitable, however, to relate the story to a larger conflict that Poe had been struggling with for some time: how to balance Romantic passion with Enlightenment order. By virtue of his work in the Gothic tale itself, many readers are quick to place him without qualification in the Romantic camp. But it is a conflict that Poe had struggled with previously that does, in fact, inhabit *Eureka* and comes to bear most forcefully in "The Fall of the House of Usher."

Although literary scholars generally date the Enlightenment era from 1660 (as a departure from the Renaissance) to 1798 (with the publication of *Lyrical Ballads*), all acknowledge the artificiality of such dating. All such periods consist of attitudes, ideas, and cultural dynamics that precede and postdate the era. Benjamin Franklin's fervid belief in perfectibility of self[17] gave way to romantic dissolution in order to feel life more passionately. Moreover, one could convincingly argue that the conflict between Enlightenment, with its heroic grandiosity of the mind, and Romanticism, with all its disheveled passions, continue in full force. Perhaps the conflict was only more heightened at Poe's particular point in literary history.

The Enlightenment presupposed the primacy of human reason, the ethical template of formal order, and the lifestyle of staid decorum. It may be argued that Poe's short stories eclipse reason by the supernatural, disrupt ethical values by gothic disorder, and blast decorum by the weird and grotesque. The argument would be wrong, for Poe sought nothing less than the delicate symbiosis between the two—and the key quality of symbiosis is in the mutual benefit one to another.

That Poe had struggled with the national literary shift from Enlightenment to Romantic thinking is evident long before 1839.[18] And while many of the early nineteenth-century writers embraced Romanticism passionately as the full outlet for an intuitive, imaginative, and story-driven art, Poe was by far more reserved. In his "1836 Letter to B___" Poe refers to the Lake Poets in quite derogatory terms: "As I am speaking of poetry, it will not be amiss to touch slightly upon the most singular heresy in its modern history—the heresy of what is called very foolishly, the Lake School" (*Essays* 6–7). The heresy of which Poe speaks, specifically in reference to Wordsworth, is that didactic poetry is seen as the most pleasurable. While admiring Coleridge's great learning, despite all that learning Poe is quick to point out his "liability to err." As for Wordsworth, "I have no faith in him" (*Essays* 8). Truly, the "Letter to B___" ends in a gnarled fist of contradictions (of Coleridge, Poe says he cannot "speak but with reverence"), and his attempt to define poetry is, in his own words, a "long rigmarole." But shot through the essay resides the governing belief that intellect and passion work together in art.

Such also became the central argument of "The Philosophy of Composition," a much better known, much clearer, but not necessarily more credible work. Here Poe lays his famous rational grid upon the composition of a poem of irrationality—"The Raven." For example, he states his (predetermined) scheme for rhythm and meter: "The former is trochaic—The latter is octometer acatalectic, alternating with heptameter catalectic repeated in the refrain of the fifth verse, and terminating with a tetrameter catalectic" (*Essays* 21). Poe's "The Rationale of Verse," moreover, might well be called one of the preeminent Enlightenment documents of the Romantic era. Surely, there were poets of Poe's time who followed fairly rigid verse forms, yet none of them that I am aware of would likely ever claim such an ornate, intellectual concept prior to the poem's composition. The fact is all the more telling in that the elegy, "The Raven," corresponds in many ways with "The Fall of the House of Usher," the singular exception being that in the former we are placed inside the disintegrating mind of the narrator while in the latter the narrator gives us some objective distance from the disintegration.

While "The Raven" remains one of the best known works in the western tradition generally, a second of Poe's elegies, "Ulalume," is perhaps of more critical importance to understanding the balancing act Poe was attempting between the Enlightenment and the Romantic. Upon a casual reading the poem seems archetypally romantic. We find the narrator wandering a strange landscape that ultimately is a mirror to his inner torment, if not his mind itself (his companion is Psyche). Similarly the time is more of a psychic state rather than the announced month of October with its withering and sere leaves. Into the groaning realms, he walks with Psyche his soul. Why? To what end? To discover the full meaning of the event for which they had traveled here the year prior.

The heightened, fantastic elements of the poem intensify through-out. The lonely season, the "dank tarn of Auber" (line 6), the unsettled and threatening landscape—all the essentials of the Gothic are here. Further-more, supernatural figures enter—the ghouls who feed on the dead but also heavenly figures. The quarter moon rises, like twin horns hung in the sky. With it appears the figure of Astarte, Phoenician goddess of fertility and passion whose symbol is the twin horns of the bull. She is the consummate romantic figure, representing the outpouring of creative passion. The narra-tor observes that "She is warmer than Dian" (39), a reference to the Roman goddess of chastity and order. Strangely, and in spite of Psyche's caution to fly, the narrator trusts Astarte to lead him to the truth. Essentially, we have the old Appollonian-Dionysian conflict between order and impulse played out with two female goddesses—appropriate to the elegy for Virginia. In this case, and with the maddening desire to confront whatever lies at the end of his journey, the narrator insists,

> Ah, we safely may trust to its gleaming,
> And be sure it will lead us aright—
> We surely may trust to its gleaming
> That cannot but guide us aright.... (67–70)

Astarte, the goddess of passion, the fuel for the romantic flame, does in this poem lead him to the burning encounter with the fact of Ulalume's death. In this poem, Poe appears to recognize the enormous creative potential in romantic passion; yet, he remains wary of it, cautions that once unleashed it has the capacity to consume someone entirely.

This tension is similar to that which Poe takes to "The Fall of the House of Usher." Few other authors struggled as powerfully with that tension and with maintaining a balance between the analytic intelligence and the creative fancy. The possible exception is Nathaniel Hawthorne, whose "Rappaccini's Daughter" can very profitably be read as a clash between the coldly analytic Enlightenment man (Rappaccini) and the Romantic man (Baglioni). In "The Fall of the House of Usher" one notices the conflict already in the first para-graph, a masterpiece of prose poetry. The narrator possesses the initial ratio-nal distance from the scene, reporting to the reader what he sees and feels as he approaches the mansion. The organic form with which he reports his findings, however, allows the reader intuitively to grasp the sense of insuf-ferable gloom. In the initial sentence, heavy, sinking, *o* and *u* vowels droop like sullen rain. The pacing of the sentences, with relatively brief, stumbling phrases in very long, heavy sentences, enhance the effect.[19]

The carefully ordered architectural grid Poe places upon the story, including the escalation of mirror images, is similar to the (purportedly)

careful ordering of his poems. In this story, however, the balance between
Enlightenment and Romantic itself is situated at the heart of the story.
Roderick himself is emblematic of Romantic passion, while Madeline is
emblematic of Enlightenment. Their genesis, as fraternal twins, is unified—
a perfectly mirrored complementarity—but the story unveils their splitting
to mutual destruction.

This way of viewing the relationship between brother and sister is not
customary, to be sure. The common view is that the narrator, coming from
outside the palace of horrors, represents rational order. An example of this
view appears in Jack Voller's study of the sublime in Poe's tale, in which he
states that "The narrator is associated with the rescuing force of reason. . . .
Although he strikes few readers as cheerful, the narrator is suited to his
task . . ." (29). Yet, it is hard to find the narrator exercising anything like
a force of reason. In the main, his role is limited to some musing observations, a rather slow study in horror, and a hopeless inefficiency to do much of
anything about the divisive destruction of the tenants of the House, which
seems to be precisely Poe's point. When Romantic passion and Enlightenment order divide, their mutual destruction is assured.

Madeline therefore becomes abstracted to little more than a mental evanescence—Enlightenment at its extreme, out of touch with reality.
When the narrator first sees her passing in the distance, he is filled with
unaccountable dread, so otherworldly she appears. She is, Roderick discloses, simply wasting away of some illness with no known etiology. At
the very same time, Roderick diverges in the opposite direction. While
Madeline disappears into a vaporific mist, Roderick flames into an unre-
stricted creative power, full of unrestrained, raw passion. He becomes the
fiery polar to Madeline's cold abstraction. The narrator describes his successive days with Usher and his artmaking thus: "An excited and highly
distempered ideality threw a sulphurous luster over all" ("Usher" 405).
Usher thereby enters a creative mania, churning out songs, paintings, and
poems against the coming dark.

That is precisely the point Poe makes in this tale. When split apart,
as they are here, Enlightenment thinking becomes all cold, analytic, and
detached; Romanticism, on the other hand, blazes into a self-consuming
passion. Aesthetically and ideally they ought to be mirrors to each other,
working in a complementary fashion to serve art. When split from each
other, they become mutually self-destructive. Preternaturally charged with
his Romantic instincts, Roderick hears, above the storm, the approaching
footsteps of Madeline. She enters, falls upon her brother, and together they
die. The splitting pairs have conjoined once again, but tragically this time.
The separation had gone to the extreme, disrupting the sentient balance,
destroying both. As the narrator flees, the house itself parallels the act of

Roderick and Madeline, first splitting apart along the zigzag fissure and then collapsing together into the tarn.

If *Eureka* teaches us the design of unity, and the essays teach us Poe's efforts to integrate intellectual order into his aesthetics, then it may be fairly said that "The Fall of the House of Usher" is a cautionary tale, warning of a way Poe would not have artists go. While he did exult in the freedoms of the Romantic imagination, he was also highly suspicious of it. He needed, and called for, the orderliness of design inherited from the Enlightenment to contain that imagination. Without that synchronous working, as "The Fall of the House of Usher" demonstrates, both are doomed.

NOTES

1. Perhaps the most helpful study of this sort is Gary E. Tombleson's "Poe's 'The Fall of the House of Usher' as Archetypal Gothic: Literary and Architectural Analogs of Cosmic Unity" (*Nineteenth-Century Contexts* 12.2 [1988]: 83–106). Tombleson locates the place of the story—both its traditional and innovative elements—within the tradition dating to Walpole's *The Castle of Otranto, A Gothic Story* (1764). Also helpful is Stephen Dougherty's "Dreaming the Races: Biology and National Fantasy in 'The Fall of the House of Usher'" (*Henry Street* 7.1 [Spring 1988]: 17–39). Of particular interest, and with a revealing twist on interpreting the story, is Mark Kinkead-Weekes' "Reflections On, and In, 'The Fall of the House of Usher.'" Kinkead-Weekes argues that the story is "not merely Gothick, but rather a 'Gothick' which at every turn signals a consciousness of its own operation" (17). This pattern includes, furthermore, an awareness of the writer of the Gothic.

2. See, for example, Cynthia S. Jordan's "Poe's Re-Vision: The Recovery of the Second Story" (*American Literature* 59.1 [Mar. 1987]: 1–19). Jordan sets forth the ways by which Poe differs from Hawthorne and pays close attention to such stories as "Berenice," "Morella," and "Ligeia," in addition to "The Fall of the House of Usher." In "'Sympathies of a Scarcely Intelligible Nature': The Brother–Sister Bond in Poe's 'The Fall of the House of Usher'" (*Studies in Short Fiction* 30 [1993]: 387–396), Leila S. May discusses the issue of the female persona with an interesting twist, arguing that the story represents Poe's vision of social destruction with the breakup of family structures in mid-19th century. That the relationship between Roderick and Madeline is aberrant goes without saying, but May provides insufficient evidence of a social meltdown at this time or support for Poe's holding this view.

3. It is nearly impossible to keep track of all the articles and dissenting opinions that "Ligeia" has engendered. In Poe's mind, at least, the story was his best to date. To Philip Pendleton Cooke he wrote, "'Ligeia' may be called my best tale" (9 August 1846 *Letters* 2:329). Readers don't always agree with authors on such matters. The story is, nonetheless, a fascinating document for Poe's revision process. In *The Collected Works of Edgar Allan Poe*, volume 2, Thomas Mabbott discusses these at some length.

4. Technically, a "cosmogony," the term Poe uses, is concerned with the origins and the evolution of the universe. A "cosmology," the more fitting term here, deals with the universe in total relativity—from the origin to the acts and consequences of all life in the universe. As we will see, Poe's theory clearly points in the latter direction.

5. For helpful discussion of the relationship between the lecture and *Eureka* see Burton R. Pollin's "Contemporary Reviews of *Eureka*: A Checklist" (*Poe as Literary Cosmologer: Studies on "Eureka"—A Symposium*. Hartford, CT: Transcendental Books, 1975. 26–30) in addition to standard biographies.

6. Frederick Conner demonstrates the plethora of contradictions and fallacies in the third section in his "Poe's *Eureka*" (*Cosmic Optimism: A Study of the Interpretation of Evolution by American Poets from Emerson to Robinson*. New York: Octagon, 1973. 67–91).

7. Quotations from *Eureka* are from volume 16 of the Harrison edition of *The Complete Works*. Page numbers refer to this volume. More recently, Richard P. Benton has edited a new edition of *Eureka* with line numbers, a compendium essay, and a bibliographic guide (Hartford, CT: Transcendental Books, 1973). The text is quite difficult to find, however, while the Harrison edition is in nearly every library.

8. Poe made this point in a number of places, perhaps most forcefully in his 2 July 1844 letter to James Russell Lowell: "But to all we attach the notion of a constitution of particles—atomic composition. For this reason only we think spirit different; for spirit, we say, is unparticled, and therefore is not matter. . . . The unparticled matter, permeating and impelling all things, is God. Its activity is the thought of God—which creates. Man, and other thinking beings, are individualizations of the unparticled matter" (*Letters* 1:257). Humanity is a part or extension of God. Since it is the nature of God to create, humanity's closest affinity to the Deity lies in its creativity. To express its godliness humanity must create in its own unique, but divine, method.

9. Wagenknecht puts it as such: "For though the Shadow of Beauty may float unseen among us, we can never make much contact with it in human experience unless it can somehow be made to impregnate the stuff of human life . . ." (151). It is precisely the task of the poet to make that "impregnation."

10. One should not be deterred from spotting similarities in cosmology by the fact that *Eureka* was published nearly a decade (1848) later than "The Fall of the House of Usher," which first appeared in *Burton's Gentleman's Magazine*, September 1839. The fundamental beliefs pulled together in *Eureka* were ones that Poe had been developing in part for years and in *Eureka* tried to systematize as a whole.

11. All quotations from "The Fall of the House of Usher" and "Ligeia" are from volume 2 of Mabbott's authoritative edition and will be cited as "Usher" and "Ligeia."

12. In his "Sentience and the False Deja vu in 'The Fall of the House of Usher,'" John Lammers makes a distinction critical to understanding Poe. Sentience, he points out, is a matter of shared awareness:

> Since the word "sentience" can mean "feeling with awareness" or "feeling without awareness," since everyone believes that plants at least have "feeling without awareness," and since Usher's theory is unusual because only four writers in the history of the world have agreed with him, then the meaning of "sentience" here must be the unusual one—"feeling with awareness or consciousness." In short, Usher believes that all vegetation has a mind. (21)

This view comports precisely with the "volitional" act of creation appearing in *Eureka*. For another discussion of sentience, see David L. Coss's "Art and Sentience in 'The Fall of the House of Usher'" (*Pleiades* 14.1 [1991]: 93–106).

13. For a consideration of the disintegrating mind of Usher, see G. R. Thompson's *Poe's Fiction*, 87–97. Thompson's views have been contested by many. See, for example, Patrick F. Quinn's "A Misreading of Poe's 'The Fall of the House of Usher'" (*Critical Essays on Edgar Allan Poe*. Ed. Eric W. Carlson. Boston: G. K. Hall, 1987. 153–59). In a study of "Ligeia" and "The Fall of the House of Usher," Ronald Bieganowski observes that "Reflected images double the intensity of beauty" (186).

14. Earliest published forms of the story use the term "pitiable mental idiosyncrasy" here. See *s*2:398. For a lengthier discussion of the house and the "divided mind," see Jack G. Voller's "The Power of Terror: Burke and Kant in the House of Usher."

15. In an unusual twist on Poe's notorious ending, Kinkead-Weekes views it as an ironic, comedic scene in which the affected superiority of the narrator is destroyed (30–31).

16. Several of these different interpretations explore the conflict between the natural and the supernatural, such as E. Arthur Robinson's "Order and Sentience in 'The Fall of the House of Usher'" (*PMLA* 76.1 [Mar. 1961]: 68–81) and David Ketterer's *The Rationale of Deception in Poe* (Baton Rouge: Louisiana State UP, 1979). Several studies explore the subconscious or the conflict between image and reality in the story. Representative here are Sam Girgus's "Poe and the Transcendent Self" (*The Law of the Heart*. Austin: U of Texas P, 1979. 24–36) and Leonard W. Engel's "The Journey from Reason to Madness: Edgar Allan Poe's 'The Fall of the House of Usher'" (*Essays in Arts and Sciences* 14 [1985]: 23–31).

17. "It was about this time I conceived the bold and arduous project of arriving at moral perfection. I wished to live without committing any fault at any time. . . . As I knew, or thought I knew, what was right and wrong, I did not see why I might not always do the one and avoid the other" (Franklin 1384).

18. For a more detailed analysis of Poe's relation with the English Romantics and the part they played in his aesthetics, see my article, "Edgar Allan Poe: Artist, Aesthetician, Legend" (*South Dakota Review* 10.2 [Spring 1972]: 60–70).

19. For linguists with an interest in quantitative rhetoric, the first paragraph is a treasure trove. Just dealing with the baseline figures, the first four sentences are 60, 22, 32, and 81 words in length, for an average of 49, an extraordinary average. But the proliferation of short phrases and clauses works as interior counterpart.

WORKS CITED

Bieganowski, Ronald. "The Self-Consuming Narrator in Poe's 'Ligeia' and 'Usher.'" *American Literature* 60.2 (May 1988): 175–87.

Brown, Gillian. "The Poetics of Extinction." *The American Face of Edgar Allan Poe*. Ed. Shawn Rosenheim and Stephen Rachman. Baltimore: Johns Hopkins UP, 1995. 330–44.

Franklin, Benjamin. *The Autobiography*. New York: The Library of America, 1987.

Kinkead-Weekes, Mark. "Reflections On, and In, 'The Fall of the House of Usher.'" *Edgar Allan Poe: The Design of Order*. Ed. A. Robert Lee. London: Vision Press, 1987: 17–35.

Lammers, John. "Sentience and the False Deja Vu in 'The Fall of the House of Usher.'" *Publications of the Arkansas Philological Association* 22.1 (Spring 1996): 19–41.

Poe, Edgar Allan. *Collected Works of Edgar Allan Poe*. Ed. Thomas Ollive Mabbott. 3 vols. Cambridge: Belknap Press of Harvard U, 1969–.

———. *The Complete Works of Edgar Allan Poe*. Ed. James Harrison. 17 vols. New York: T. Y. Crowell, 1902.

————. *Essays and Reviews*. Ed. B. R. Thompson. New York: Modern Library, 1984.

————. *The Letters of Edgar Allan Poe*. 2 vols. Ed. John Ward Ostrom. Cambridge, MA: Harvard UP, 1948.

Thompson, G. R. *Poe's Fiction: Romantic Irony in the Gothic Tales*. Madison: U of Wisconsin P, 1973.

Voller, Jack G. "The Power of Terror: Burke and Kant in The House of Usher." *Poe Studies* 21.2 (1988): 27–35.

Wagenknecht, Edward. *Edgar Allan Poe: The Man Behind the Legend*. New York: Oxford UP, 1963.

RICHARD KOPLEY

A Tale by Poe

The relationship of Roger Chillingworth to Arthur Dimmesdale is succinctly intimated in one of Hawthorne's 17 November 1847 notebook entries: "A story of the effects of revenge, in diabolizing him who indulges in it" (8:278, see also 8:27). Scholars have linked the diabolized doctor to three clusters of previous writings: those works that involve or relate to the devil (John Milton's *Paradise Lost*, John Bunyan's *Pilgrim's Progress*, and versions of Faust); those works that concern psychological probing (accounts of Francis Cheynell's torment of William Chillingworth, accounts of William Prynne's torment of Archbishop Laud, William Godwin's *Caleb Williams*, and James Malcolm Rymer's *Varney the Vampire*); and those works that involve murder (accounts of the murder of Sir Thomas Overbury and accounts of the murder of Captain Joseph White).[1] The three clusters reinforce the burden of the critical tenth chapter of *The Scarlet Letter*: a satanic figure, probing the psyche of a guilty man, commits a spiritual murder. However, none of the sources in these clusters seems to be the immediate prompt for Chillingworth's intrusion upon the sleeping Dimmesdale and his discovery of Dimmesdale's secret. That incident may find its model in a work by Hawthorne's one peer in the short story in 1840s America, Edgar Allan Poe.

* * *

From *The Threads of* The Scarlet Letter: *A Study of Hawthorne's Transformative Art*, pp. 22–35, 125–130. © 2003 by Rosemont Publishing & Printing Corp.

Nathaniel Hawthorne highly respected the fiction of Poe. In the fall of 1842, he acknowledged as much in his short story "The Hall of Fantasy," including Poe in a select company of poets and writers in the Hall of Fantasy "for the sake of his imagination" (although threatening him with "ejectment" for his criticism) (10:636).[2] And Hawthorne wrote to Poe on 17 June 1846, "I admire you rather as a writer of Tales, than as a critic upon them. I might often—and often do—dissent from your opinions, in the latter capacity, but could never fail to recognize your force and originality, in the former" (16:168). Poe's May 1842 *Graham's Magazine* review of *Twice-Told Tales*—a review acknowledging "force" and "originality," but incorrectly accusing Hawthorne of plagiarism (*Complete Works* 11:104–13)—must have particularly antagonized Hawthorne.[3] Yet Poe's literary artistry clearly impressed him.

George Ripley's already-quoted early review of *The Scarlet Letter* stimulates inquiry into the possibility of a Hawthorne debt to Poe. The 1 April 1850 critique notes several parallels between the work of Hawthorne and that of Poe: "the same terrible excitement . . . the same minuteness of finish—the same slow and fatal accumulation of details, the same exquisite coolness of coloring, while everything creeps forward with irresistible certainty to a soul-harrowing climax." Then Ripley qualifies his observation, noting Hawthorne's softening of the supernatural. Although he quotes amply from *The Scarlet Letter*, he does not go on to identify a specific related Poe tale.[4] Nevertheless, Ripley's general observation clearly provides encouragement for a consideration of Hawthorne's possible reliance on Poe.

Scholars have occasionally engaged in this consideration. Arlin Turner rightly stated, "similarities in details and in method [in the stories of Hawthorne and Poe] indicate that [Hawthorne] possibly came in some measure under Poe's influence." However, the relationships that Turner suggests are not developed. Maurice Beebe nicely elaborated parallels in setting and characters between Hawthorne's novel *The House of the Seven Gables* (1851) and Poe's short story "The Fall of the House of Usher" (1839), but he did not argue for Hawthorne's indebtedness. Millicent Bell intimated that Hawthorne borrowed for "The Birthmark" (1843) from Poe's "The Oval Portrait" (1842), and Joel Pfister concurred, but the case is still not altogether conclusive.[5] The initial considerations are suggestive, though, and there remains a wide field for further inquiry. Such inquiry is rewarded: evidence suggests a strong, but hitherto unrecognized, correspondence between *The Scarlet Letter* and Poe's classic short story "The Tell-Tale Heart."

* * *

Hawthorne would have read "The Tell-Tale Heart" when it was first published, in January 1843. The story appeared in the first number of James

Russell Lowell's literary magazine, *The Pioneer*, a monthly periodical that Hawthorne would have had reason to anticipate—Lowell had solicited a contribution.[6] And on 17 December 1842, Hawthorne sent Lowell a piece for *The Pioneer*, the aforementioned "The Hall of Fantasy," which would appear in the second number (15:663). On 4 January 1843, Hawthorne's wife Sophia Hawthorne wrote admiringly about "The Hall of Fantasy" to her sister-in-law Louisa Hawthorne, and added, "James [Russell] Lowell . . . has sent us the first [number of *The Pioneer*], but that has nothing of Nathaniel's" (15:667). However, that number had Lowell's highly commendatory review of Hawthorne's *Historical Tales for Youth*. And that first issue of the magazine featured, too, Poe's intense tale of murder and guilt, "The Tell-Tale Heart"—a work praised by Lowell, who referred to the author's "powerful imagination."[7] Hawthorne would surely have read this issue of *The Pioneer* with interest, and with particular interest Poe's remarkable contribution.

Contemporary response to the first publication of "The Tell-Tale Heart" was emphatic, if we judge from the second number of Lowell's magazine, which offered comments on Poe's tale in three reprinted reviews of *The Pioneer*'s first number. It was probably Horace Greeley who wrote in a New York *Tribune* review—with a mixture of admiration and distaste—that "The Tell-Tale Heart" was "a strong and skilful, but to our minds overstrained and repulsive analysis of the feelings and promptings of an insane homicide." A critic asserted in a Boston *Bay State Democrat* review that the tale was "an article of thrilling interest." And N. P. Willis remarked in his *Brother Jonathan* review—with unmixed admiration for Poe's tale—that "Mr. Poe's contribution is very wild and very readable, and that is the only thing in the number that most people would read and remember."[8] Doubtless Hawthorne would have shared the views of the anonymous critic and Willis, especially in light of his own favorable comment on Poe's imagination in "The Hall of Fantasy," the lead-off piece in that second number of *The Pioneer*. Hawthorne would have been much engaged by the tale's dark theme and its guilt-wracked protagonist.

And he would surely have been fascinated by the tale's indebtedness to works familiar to him—Daniel Webster's speech to the jury at the Joseph White murder trial, Shakespeare's *Macbeth*, and his own biographical sketch, "Thomas Green Fessenden." Our perceiving Hawthorne's probable recognition of some of the origins of "The Tell-Tale Heart" permits greater insight regarding his attraction to Poe's story.

* * *

As T. O. Mabbott has observed, in writing "The Tell-Tale Heart" Poe relied critically on Daniel Webster's prosecutorial speech regarding John

Francis Knapp, who was accused (and found guilty) of participating in a conspiracy responsible for the murder of Captain Joseph White, a crime that took place on 6 April 1830 in Salem, Massachusetts. Webster imagined the very deliberate murderer, Richard Crowninshield Jr., entering the room of the sleeping "old man," striking his helpless victim, and later, unable to contain his guilt, confessing his deed. Webster identified the story as "a new lesson for painters and poets," and Poe, probably reminded of the speech by quotations from it in a Mary Rogers article in the *Brother Jonathan* of 21 August 1841, clearly took the lesson: "The Tell-Tale Heart" concerns just the sequence of events described (*Collected Works* 3:789–91).[9]

Webster's published speech, a synthesis of the summations that the famous lawyer had made at the two trials of John Francis Knapp, appeared in Salem in late 1830 in the *Appendix to the Report of the Trial of John Francis Knapp*.[10] This celebrated speech would have been known to Hawthorne, who was a resident of North Salem at the time of the murder and that of the trials (August to December 1830). Scholars have noted that Hawthorne might even have heard Webster speak at the trials.[11] Certainly Hawthorne would have heard much about the sensational murder and the trials—and he wrote a letter to his cousin John S. Dike in September 1830 concerning, in part, the convicted John Francis Knapp and his accused brother Joseph and their family (15:206–9). He also referred to the White murder in two subsequent letters, one of these to his younger sister Maria Louisa and the other to Dike (15:214, 217). Furthermore, Hawthorne recurred to that murder in later years—in 1837, he wrote in his notebook about a cabinet in the Essex Historical Society containing old portraits, clothes, manuscripts, and "[t]he club that killed old Jo. White" (23:177);[12] in 1847, he imagined a story based on the Committee of Vigilance that had been created to find the murderers of Captain White (8:279); and in 1852, he listed the birth of Joseph White, adding, "Murdered, more than fourscore years afterwards, in Salem" (8:550). Hawthorne's son-in-law George Parsons Lathrop connected the Joseph White murder with the alleged guilt of Clifford Pyncheon for the death of his uncle, in *The House of the Seven Gables*; also, David S. Reynolds linked the Knapp brothers with Roger Chillingworth. F. O. Matthiessen specifically related the Webster speech to the murder of Judge Pyncheon, and Margaret Moore has recently linked Webster's dramatic speech to Reverend Dimmesdale's urge to confess.[13] Certainly Hawthorne would have recognized what Mabbott termed "the chief inspiration" for "The Tell-Tale Heart" (*Collected Works* 3:789).[14]

And Hawthorne would also very probably have recognized an important indebtedness in "The Tell-Tale Heart" to an even more famous work concerning the murder of an old man in his bed—Shakespeare's *Macbeth*. At the very center of Poe's story, his narrator directs a ray of light upon the old man's veiled eye—what he terms "the damned spot" (*Collected Works* 3:795). As Richard Wilbur has noted, Poe thus alludes to the guilt-ridden Lady Macbeth, who, in the renowned sleepwalking scene, apostrophizes the blood she perceives on her hand, "Out, damn'd spot! Out, I say!" (5.1.35). Hawthorne had alluded to *Macbeth* in an 1839 letter to Sophia ("Hurley-Burley," 15:316 [see *Macbeth* 1.1.3]) and in the 1842 story "The Lily's Quest" (the stream stained with a murderer's blood, 9:446 [see *Macbeth* 2.2.57–60]), and he had alluded specifically to Lady Macbeth's words in her sleepwalking scene in his 1835 travel piece, "Sketches from Memory" ("all the perfumes of Arabia," 11:299 [see *Macbeth* 5.1.50–51].[15] It is interesting to add that Hawthorne would read Shakespeare to his wife in 1844 (16:13), and she would allude to *Macbeth* in a letter in 1845 (regarding Una's "murthered" sleep, 16:109 [see *Macbeth* 2.2.33]). And he would later teach his children passages from Shakespeare, and his son Julian would readily draw on *Macbeth* (regarding an older woman's "golly locks" [see *Macbeth* 3.4.49–50]).[16] As he read "The Tell-Tale Heart" in January 1843, Hawthorne would surely have been struck not only by its reliance on Daniel Webster's speech, but also by its allusion to Shakespeare's *Macbeth*.

Finally, Hawthorne would very likely have recognized another important source for Poe's "The Tell-Tale Heart"—his own essay, "Thomas Green Fessenden." Scholars have noted Poe's occasional reliance on Hawthorne: Seymour Gross has suggested that Poe revised "Life in Death" (soon to be "The Oval Portrait") because of his reading Hawthorne's "The Birthmark" (appearing in the third number of *The Pioneer*, in March 1843); Robert Regan has maintained that in writing "The Masque of the Red Death" Poe drew on "The Legends of the Province House" in *Twice Told Tales* (second edition, 1842)—"Howe's Masquerade," "Lady Eleanore's Mantle," "Edward Randolph's Portrait," and "Old Esther Dudley"; and D. M. McKeithan has confirmed Regan with regard to "Howe's Masquerade" and "Lady Eleanore's Mantle" and has linked Poe's "The Oval Portrait" with Hawthorne's "The Prophetic Pictures."[17] Consistent with these views is the view that Poe's writing of "The Tell-Tale Heart" was influenced by his reading of Hawthorne's 1838 sketch of Fessenden. This point requires brief elaboration.

Poe lived in New York City from January 1837 through mid-1838. Having worked as the editor of Richmond's distinguished monthly magazine, the *Southern Literary Messenger*, from August 1835 through January 1837—and probably seeking similar employment in New York—he announced his presence at the celebrated 30 March 1837 Booksellers' Dinner by toasting "The Monthlies of Gotham—Their Distinguished Editors, and their vigorous Collaborateurs." Notably, he had, at that time, a library including "magazines bound and unbound."[18] Of all the American magazines then published, the *American Monthly Magazine* would have particularly commanded his attention—he had termed it in January 1837 a periodical "for whose opinions we still have the highest respect" (*Complete Works* 9:273), and he would write in October 1846 that that magazine "[is] one of the best journals we have ever had" (*Complete Works* 15:121). Edited by Park Benjamin, the *American Monthly Magazine* featured in the May 1837 issue an account of the Booksellers' Dinner; in the June 1837 issue Poe's tale, "Von Jung, the Mystific"; and in the July 1837 issue the unsigned Hawthorne tale, "Incidents from the Journal of a Solitary Man."[19] Moreover, the periodical offered in the November 1837 issue Benjamin's review of *The Token* for 1838, where the editor referred to his "admiration of the genius of NATHANIEL HAWTHORNE," alluding to his remark in a review of *The Token* for 1837 that Hawthorne was a "man of genius." The December 1837 issue included Benjamin's announcement that "A valued friend" would soon write a "biographical sketch" of the recently deceased editor and poet Thomas Green Fessenden, and the January 1838 issue provided that sketch of Fessenden, signed by that "valued friend," that "man of genius," Nathaniel Hawthorne.[20] Poe would probably have been very curious about Hawthorne at this time and perhaps somewhat competitive with him; he surely would have seen Hawthorne's sketch of Fessenden in the *American Monthly Magazine* and read the piece with interest.[21]

And Poe might well have already heard significantly of Fessenden—especially during his 1827 stay in Boston. Then looking for "employment on any of the large journals," Poe would very likely have known of "the most widely circulated agricultural journal in New England," Fessenden's *New England Farmer*, the office of which was located at 52 North Market Street, opposite Faneuil Hall.[22] Pertinently, Fessenden listed his *New England Farmer's Almanack, for 1828* for sale at one bookstore in Boston—Bowles and Dearborn, located at 72 Washington Street, only a few blocks from Faneuil Hall. Poe would have come upon this bookstore since it was between the offices of the *North American Review* and *United States Literary Gazette* at 74 Washington Street and the office of Calvin F. S. Thomas, the printer of his 1827 *Tamerlane and Other Poems*, at 70 Washington Street.[23] Probably Bowles and Dearborn would have sold, too, the *New England Farmer* itself. Especially noteworthy in that periodical, in light of the "*scarabaeus*" of Poe's prize-winning 1843 tale "The Gold-Bug," is the 31 August and 7 September 1827 front-page article titled "Remarks on the Scarabaeus Roseus, or Rose-Bug." (It should be added that Poe joined the army while he was living in Boston, and in late October 1827 his battery was sent to Sullivan's Island, in the harbor of Charleston, South Carolina, an island that he would later use as the setting for "The Gold-Bug.")[24] The evidence is primarily circumstantial but quite suggestive—it does seem reasonably likely that Poe would have heard significantly of Fessenden in 1827. If he had, then Hawthorne's 1838 Fessenden piece would have held even greater meaning. And perhaps, too, it would have been an even more probable work from which Poe might borrow.

Hawthorne had lived with Fessenden in 1836 and had clearly been devoted to him; he declared towards the close of his Fessenden sketch his affection for the senior editor.[25] In this regard, we should recall, in Poe's "The Tell-Tale Heart," the murderous narrator's notoriously asserting, "I loved the old man" (*Collected Works* 3:792) and his identifying the old man's disturbing features as his filmy eye and his beating heart. We may well be struck, then, by Hawthorne's feelingly stating of Fessenden, "On my part, *I loved the old man*, because his *heart* was as *transparent* as a fountain" (23:106–7; emphasis added). The great probability that Poe read this statement in the *American Monthly Magazine* and the identity of the assertion of love in Hawthorne and in Poe suggest Poe's debt to Hawthorne. Furthermore, Poe's ironic treatment of that assertion in "The Tell-Tale Heart" is strengthened by an inversion of Hawthorne's explanation. I would propose that even as Poe, in *The Narrative of Arthur Gordon Pym*, inverted the Isaiahan prophecy of the peace of Jerusalem—"not one of the stakes thereof shall ever be removed, neither shall any of the cords thereof be broken" (Isaiah 33:20)—to convey the destruction of Jerusalem—natives pull "cords" attached to a line of "stakes," causing a landslide (*Collected Writings* 1:184–85)[26]—so, too, did Poe, in "The Tell-Tale Heart," invert the cause for Hawthorne's love for the old man—Fessenden's *transparent* heart—to serve as the provocation of the narrator's hostility to the old man—his victim's *filmy* eye, his *veiled* eye. I would propose, too, that Poe further inverted that transparent heart by creating a secret-bearing heart, a tell-tale heart. According to this view, Hawthorne's statement of love in the Fessenden sketch was both acknowledged and subverted by Poe. Arguably, in "The Tell-Tale Heart," the beloved editor Thomas Green Fessenden became Poe's stern foster father John Allan.

In his November 1847 review of Hawthorne, Poe specifically remembered the March 1838 *American Monthly Magazine* review of Hawthorne (probably by Park Benjamin) (*Complete Works* 13:142)—it seems wholly plausible, therefore, that when he wrote "The Tell-Tale Heart" in 1842, Poe would have remembered the January 1838 *American Monthly Magazine* sketch of Fessenden by Hawthorne. Perhaps Poe had a copy of the January 1838 issue of the magazine—whether "bound or unbound"—in his possession or at least accessible; very likely he had Hawthorne's unabashedly expressive language in mind.

Reading "The Tell-Tale Heart," Hawthorne would surely have recognized its debt to the Webster speech, Shakespeare's *Macbeth*, and his own Fessenden sketch. As engaged by the work as he would have been given its authorship, its characterization, and its thematics, he would have been even more beguiled by the work because of its genesis.

It is relevant to add that after Hawthorne's story "The Birth-Mark" was published in the third and final number of *The Pioneer* (March 1843), Henry Wadsworth Longfellow (also mentioned in the "Hall of Fantasy" [10:635]) praised the work to Hawthorne in a letter of 19 March 1843, and then admonished, "But you should have made a Romance of it, and not a short story only. But more of that on Tuesday." On Tuesday, 21 March 1843, Hawthorne dined with Longfellow in Cambridge (8:368) and undoubtedly learned more of Longfellow's assessment. Perhaps the two writers also discussed *The Pioneer*'s inclusion of "The Tell-Tale Heart"—especially since that tale opened with a stanza from Longfellow's "A Psalm of Life" (*Collected Works* 3:792). In any case, as Hawthorne considered the suggestion that he write a romance, he would still have had Poe's recently-published work, "The Tell-Tale Heart," fresh in his mind.[27]

And Hawthorne may have had occasion to encounter "The Tell-Tale Heart" again. Although it was not reprinted in Poe's 1845 *Tales* (a copy of which Hawthorne owned [16:158]), it did appear in the 23 August 1845 issue of the *Broadway Journal*—the same issue in which Poe offered a paragraph of comment on Hawthorne as a "prose poet" deserving greater financial success (*Collected Writings* 3:225). But regardless of whether Hawthorne saw the *Broadway Journal* publication of "The Tell-Tale Heart," he would not likely have forgotten the work's intensity or its familiar origins. Clearly he could well have had Poe's memorable tale of guilt in mind in late September 1849 as he "began work in earnest" on *The Scarlet Letter*. And he would soon have had an unexpected but compelling reason to call to mind the Poe tales he admired: on 7 October 1849, Poe died. And then followed the broad press consideration of Poe's life and work.[28] There is ample reason to infer that Hawthorne would have had reason to think of "The Tell-Tale Heart" as he wrote his first novel.

* * *

Evidence for Hawthorne's use of Poe in that novel is a clear pattern of parallels between "The Tell-Tale Heart" and *The Scarlet Letter*. In Poe's story, for seven nights at "about midnight" a young man "thrust[s]" his head inside the "chamber" of a sleeping "old man" with an "Evil Eye," and opens a lantern "cautiously (for the hinges creaked)" and shines it upon this "Evil Eye" (*Collected Works* 3:792–93). On the eighth night, the young man is "more than usually cautious in opening the door" of the room of the "old man," but the sound of the young man's chuckling startles his sleeping victim, who is therefore "lying awake" (*Collected Works* 3: 793–94). The young man opens his lantern "stealthily" and shines it upon the "Evil Eye," then jumps into the room and kills the "old man" because of his "Evil Eye" and his loudly beating heart (*Collected Works* 3:794–95). In Hawthorne's novel, an "old man" (1:129, 131, 137, 139, 141, 167, 169, 172, 174, 175, 179, 194, 195, 224, 229, 252, 253, 256, 260) with an "evil eye"—the physician Roger Chillingworth— seeks something "far worse than death" (1:196): the violation of the guilty heart of the adulterous young minister, Arthur Dimmesdale. In the critical tenth chapter of *The Scarlet Letter*, "The Leech and His Patient," Poe's story is approximated by Hawthorne's presentation of a related figurative event and a similarly related literal one. Initially, Hawthorne writes that Chillingworth, as he probes for Dimmesdale's secret, "groped along as stealthily, with as cautious a tread, and as wary an outlook, as a thief entering a chamber where a man lies only half asleep,—or, it may be, broad awake" (1:130). Hawthorne adds, "In spite of his premeditated carefulness, the floor would now and then creak." And just as Poe's "old man" sensed "the unperceived shadow" of "Death" (*Collected Works* 3:794), so, too, does Dimmesdale "become vaguely aware" of "the shadow of [Chillingworth's] presence" (1:130).[29] The figurative becomes literal when Chillingworth, this "old man" with an "evil eye," actually enters "at noonday" the room of the sleeping young man, lays "his hand upon [the minister's] bosom," "thrust[s] aside the vestment," and discovers the scarlet letter on Dimmesdale's breast—the sign of the minister's secret guilt (1:138). Chillingworth has trespassed, causing a spiritual exposure "far worse then death." Poe's intruder had taken a life; Hawthorne's intruder thinks he has taken a soul.

In "The Tell-Tale Heart," after the murder of the old man, Poe's intruder "smile[s] gaily" (*Collected Works* 3:795), but soon thereafter, in great agony, confesses his deed (*Collected Works* 3:797). In *The Scarlet Letter*, after the violation of the minister, Hawthorne's intruder is in "ecstasy" (1:138), and although Chillingworth does not acknowledge his guilt, Dimmesdale earlier asked the diabolical doctor a question that recalls the confession of the narrator in "The Tell-Tale Heart": "Why should a wretched man, guilty, we will say, of murder, prefer to keep the dead corpse buried in his own heart, rather than fling it forth at once, and let the universe take care of it?" (1:132). And Dimmesdale does eventually, after great agony, confess his deed (1: 254–55).

In both Poe's story and Hawthorne's novel, the heart is "tell-tale." The imagined, perhaps projected beating of the buried heart of the murdered old man provokes Poe's narrator's confession of murder (*Collected Works* 3:797); and the evident stigma, the *A* upon Dimmesdale's chest, emerging from the minister's "inmost heart" (1:258–59), indicates his sin of adultery. In both works, a heart reveals the heart's secret.[30]

Appropriately, Hawthorne relied in chapter 10 of his novel on the Shakespearean play to which Poe alluded in "The Tell-Tale Heart," *Macbeth*. The "air-drawn lines and figures of a geometrical problem" (1:129)—to which Chillingworth's view of the elements of his investigation is compared—recall Lady Macbeth's speaking to Macbeth of "the air-drawn dagger which you said / Led you to Duncan" (3.4.61–62). Clearly Shakespeare's "charm" was "firm and good," and Poe and Hawthorne honored it in their allusive creations.

George Ripley's general comment may be applied specifically: Poe's "The Tell-Tale Heart" and Hawthorne's *The Scarlet Letter* do both possess a "terrible excitement," a "minuteness of finish," a "slow and fatal accumulation of details," a "coolness of coloring," and a "soul-harrowing climax." But they share more than that. Poe's tale and chapter 10 of Hawthorne's novel share language—"old man," "awake," "chamber," "creak," "shadow," "cautious," "stealthily," and "thrust"—and the "old man" in both tale and novel possesses the "evil eye." Furthermore, "The Tell-Tale Heart" and the tenth chapter of *The Scarlet Letter* share a dramatic situation (anticipated figuratively, then rendered literally in that tenth chapter): at twelve o'clock, one man enters the room of another man, asleep or awakened, and assaults him, causing death or a violation thought worse than death. Also, tale and novel share the crucial theme of man's sinfulness, guilt, and need for confession. Significantly, chapter 10 of *The Scarlet Letter* specifically mentions a tormented murderer's need to confess his crime. Furthermore, in both the short story and the novel, a seemingly supernatural heart lays open man's sin. And both works feature a covert reference to the murder of the sleeping Duncan in *Macbeth*.[31]

As Hawthorne borrowed, he also transformed. Ripley notes that Hawthorne softened the supernatural of Poe; we may note other modifications here. Even as Poe had inverted elements of "Thomas Green Fessenden" for "The Tell-Tale Heart" and Hawthorne inverted elements of *Macbeth* and the Webster speech (notably, the relative ages of murderer and victim) for *The Scarlet Letter*, so, too, did Hawthorne invert elements of "The Tell-Tale Heart" for his novel. Hawthorne switched the young man and the old man— the former became the sleeper and the latter the intruder. And he switched the time, as well—midnight became noon. Furthermore, he modified the motive of the intruder—the narrator's desire to alleviate his nameless terror became Chillingworth's desire to determine definitively his wife's lover. And he modified the nature of the helpless victim—the terrified old man in "The Tell-Tale Heart" became the remorseful minister in *The Scarlet Letter*. Hawthorne also refashioned the heart in Poe's story—the provocative heart of the old man in "The Tell-Tale Heart" became the object of the scrutiny of the old man in *The Scarlet Letter*. And Hawthorne adapted the murder in Poe's work to his own purpose, spiritualizing that murder, turning it into the violation of "the sanctity of a human heart" (1:195)—a violation that he considered, in his short story "Ethan Brand," the "Unpardonable Sin" (11:90, 94, 98–99; see also 8:251). Unlike the sin of murder in Poe's story, this sin in Hawthorne's novel is never confessed—though Dimmesdale does confess his adultery and duplicity.

Finally, and, crucially, Hawthorne transformed the damnation of Poe's work to the salvation of his own. Poe's narrator in "The Tell-Tale Heart" had "heard many things in hell" (*Collected Works* 3:792) and had presumably developed his horror of the old man's "Evil Eye" because of its knowledge of his damnation—he later states of his burial of the old man, "no human eye— not even *his*—could have detected anything wrong" (*Collected Works* 3:796). Trying to destroy the condemning eye—that "damned spot"—through murder, the narrator only increased his own damnation. His painful confession suggests momentary escape, but there is no evidence of redemption or salvation. The narrator is as damned at the tale's close as he had been at its beginning—indeed, if possible, even more so. In contrast, the investigation of Dimmesdale in chapter 10 of *The Scarlet Letter* has a salvific purpose, which Hawthorne acknowledges immediately before and after that chapter. Before chapter 10, Hawthorne writes that "[t]his diabolical agent [Chillingworth] had the Divine permission, for a season, to burrow into the clergyman's intimacy, and plot against his soul" (1:128); after that chapter, Hawthorne writes that "Providence" was "using the avenger and his victim for its own purposes, and, perchance, pardoning, where it seemed most to punish" (1:139–40). And Dimmesdale does eventually confess, thankful to his "afflictions," his "agonies" (1:256–57)—including Chillingworth's burrowing into his own suffering—for permitting his "victory" (1:255). Dimmesdale defeats Chillingworth's "evil eye," acknowledging instead "God's eye" (1:255).

When Poe alluded in his December 1844 "Marginalia" to his (erroneous) May 1842 claim in his review of *Twice-Told Tales* that Hawthorne had used "William Wilson" for "Howe's Masquerade," he stated that he was "honored in the loan" and added that "[Hawthorne's] handling is always thoroughly original" (*Complete Works* 16:43). One imagines that in light of his response to an imagined borrowing, an actual borrowing (suggested by parallels between "The Tell-Tale Heart" and *The Scarlet Letter* in language, plot, setting, theme, and literary touchstone) would have led Poe again to be "honored in the loan." And the noted transformations of the former work in the latter would have confirmed him in his opinion that Hawthorne's "handling" was "always thoroughly original."

In view of the telling parallels identified, including parallels in language, we may consider "The Tell-Tale Heart" to be an important source for Hawthorne's writing of Chillingworth's discovery of Dimmesdale's secret—a significant addition to the cluster of works about murder (*Macbeth*, the Overbury accounts, the Webster speech) on which Hawthorne relied for chapter 10 of his novel. We may infer that by recalling these works, as well as those in the clusters concerning the devil and psychological probing, Hawthorne was well prepared to write of Chillingworth's assault upon Dimmesdale. We may extrapolate from this instance and, returning to the figure of our title, infer that as Hawthorne fashioned *The Scarlet Letter*, he bore in mind threads from other literary and historical narratives—threads relevant to his planned character development, theme, and plot—so as to strengthen his imaginative effort. Still, to preserve the desired hue of his fabric, he toned down individual threads. As Hawthorne stitched these threads, more or less evidently, into his narrative, he deepened the work and challenged his readers.

Arlin Turner wrote that Hawthorne "had one prevailing method of expanding each idea—a method involving what we may call the catalogue or procession." In the case of *The Scarlet Letter*, Turner added, that catalog consists of scenes involving Hester Prynne and Arthur Dimmesdale. Turner noted, too, that Hawthorne relied on his life experiences and his reading.[32] We may advance this point by returning to the term "catalog." Ironically, even as Hawthorne dramatized the idea of secret guilt in *The Scarlet Letter* in a catalog of scenes, he elaborated each scene with the help of a catalog of secret sources—or clusters of secret sources. Yet Hawthorne was—as he advised his readers to be—"true" (1:260)—he offered detail (primarily language) through which the sources "may be inferred." And not adultery, but artistry, is revealed. Although one scholar has asserted that "[Hawthorne's] sources are not readily traceable, because they appear in his ideas and effects but hardly ever in his phrasing," this statement is not accurate.[33] In fact, some of Hawthorne's sources may be traceable especially because of his phrasing—or at least his wording—as his allusions to "The Tell-Tale Heart" in *The Scarlet Letter* make apparent.

We may return to our primary figure—as Hawthorne stitched, he borrowed others' threads that would inspire him and enhance his handiwork. He allowed these threads to fade, but not so much as to preclude identification. Hawthorne could sew with subtlety and dexterity; he could reveal faintly. Indeed, Hester's "delicate and imaginative skill" (1:81) was also his own.

* * *

It seems fitting to close this chapter by noting that even after he wrote *The Scarlet Letter*, Hawthorne continued to rely on Poe. Hawthorne's phrasing in *The House of the Seven Gables* reveals his debt. And it wasn't only "The Fall of the House of Usher" that he employed in that novel.

In chapter 20, "The Flower of Eden," Holgrave shows to Phoebe, in the reception room of the Pyncheon house, a miniature of the dead Judge Pyncheon—the corpse itself is seated in the next room. Holgrave does not say how Judge Pyncheon died, although the repeated descriptions of the suspicious "Gri*malkin*" (2:247, 281, 298; emphasis added) near the death scene suggest that *kin* of *Maule* may have been responsible. (Perhaps the name's earlier use for the witch's familiar—"Graymalkin"—in *Macbeth* [1.1.9] encourages conjecture regarding murder.)[34] In any case, Holgrave tells Phoebe (truthfully or not) that he had heard that Judge Pyncheon was missed, and *"A feeling which I cannot describe—an indefinite sense of some catastrophe*, or consummation—impelled me to make my way into this part of the house, where I discovered what you see [the dead Judge]" (2:303; emphasis added). Hawthorne's language with regard to this House of the Dead corresponds closely with Poe's language in his tale of a Ship of the Dead, the Death Ship, the Flying Dutchman, a vessel whose men had been punished for some terrible crime: the award-winning tale, "MS. Found in a Bottle." Although Hawthorne may have read the story in the 1850 Griswold edition of Poe, it is also possible that he read the work in *The Gift for 1836*—after all, both Hawthorne's "Howe's Masquerade" and Poe's "William Wilson" may well have been drawn from Washington Irving's "An Unwritten Drama of Lord Byron," which appeared in *The Gift for* 1836. And it was in that gift-book that "MS. Found in a Bottle" was first reprinted.[35]

Holgrave's *"A feeling which I cannot describe—an indefinite sense of some catastrophe"* may be linked backward to the language of Poe's narrator as he sees the dead crew and captain on the Death Ship: *"An indefinite sense of awe*, which at first sight of the navigators of the ship has taken hold of my mind, was perhaps the principle of my concealment"; *"A feeling for which I have no name*, has taken possession of my soul" (*Collected Works* 2:140–41; emphasis added). The correspondences in phrasing are unobtrusive yet unmistakable. By alluding to Poe's tale about the Death Ship, Hawthorne underscored the presence of the dead in the Pyncheon house, increased the sense of mystery and possible discovery, and again paid tribute to Edgar Allan Poe. As he relied on "The Tell-Tale Heart" in *The Scarlet Letter*, so, too, did he rely on "MS. Found in a Bottle" for *The House of the Seven Gables*. "For the sake of [Poe's] imagination"—especially with regard to crime and guilt—Hawthorne employed Poe's fictions in his own, sewed Poe's threads into his own fabric.

Notes

I am pleased to note that an earlier version of this chapter appeared in the Autumn 1995 issue of *Studies in American Fiction*.

1. For sources for Chillingworth in the three identified clusters, consider the following scholarly works. Regarding Milton's *Paradise Lost*, see Stewart, Introduction, lii–liii; Matthiessen, *American Renaissance*, 305–8; and Abel, "Devil in Boston." Regarding Bunyan's *Pilgrim's Progress*, see Matthiessen, 273, and David E. Smith, *John Bunyan*, 62–66. Regarding versions of Faust, see Stein, *Hawthorne's Faust*. For Cheynell's torment of Chillingworth, see Maes-Jelinek,

"Roger Chillingworth," and for Prynne's torment of Laud, see Isani, "Hawthorne and the Branding." For comment on Godwin's *Caleb Williams*, consult Scheuerman, "Outside the Human Circle"; for discussion of Rymer's *Varney the Vampire*, see Autrey, "Source." Reid considers the murder of Sir Thomas Overbury (*Yellow Ruff*), and David S. Reynolds treats the murder of Captain Joseph White (*Beneath the American Renaissance*, 250–51). A possible literary source for Chillingworth that does not fall into any one of the three clusters is Edmund Spenser's *The Faerie Queen*, characters from which may have suggested the doctor's appearance (Stewart, Introduction, lii–liii; "Hawthorne and *The Faerie Queen*," 200–201). A possible historical source is one of Hawthorne's Salem enemies, Richard Saltonstall Rogers (Julian Smith, "Hawthorne and a Salem Enemy").

2. Scholars have tried to date the composition of "The Hall of Fantasy" by attending to Hawthorne's comments on his contemporaries in the first version of that story. Harold P Miller, considering when Henry Wadsworth Longfellow returned to the United States from England, suggested the time of composition as November 1842 ("Hawthorne Surveys," 228). Buford Jones, focusing on the time of Bronson Alcott's return from Europe, viewed the story as written "between 1 September and 20 October" ("Hall of Fantasy," 1430). The editors of the first volume of Hawthorne's letters, also noting Longfellow's return, asserted that "The Hall of Fantasy" was "probably written in October or early November" of 1842 (*Centenary Edition*, 15:662n). John J. McDonald, attending to Hawthorne's knowledge of Longfellow's return, posits the time of composition as "16 November to 17 December 1842" ("Old Manse Period Canon," 23).

Poe quoted Hawthorne's comment about him from "The Hall of Fantasy" in the *Saturday Museum* biography, published on 25 February 1843 and 4 March 1843; see Pollin, "Poe's Authorship," 165.

3. Quotations from Edgar Allan Poe's work are cited in the text with short titles.

4. Ripley, Review of *The Scarlet Letter*, 158–59. For the quoted excerpts in the novel, see Cameron, "Literary News." For a portion of the review, see Ripley, "[Gothic, the Supernatural, the Imagination]." For Ripley's mixed evaluation of Poe, see his Review of *The Works of the Late Edgar Allan Poe*.

5. Turner, "Hawthorne's Literary Borrowings," 558; Beebe, "Fall of the House of Pyncheon"; Millicent Bell, *Hawthorne's View*, 81, 182; Pfister, *Production of Personal Life*, 43–44. Alfred H. Marks contended that Hawthorne satirized Poe in "Egotism; or, the Bosom Serpent" ("Two Rodericks and Two Worms"). Arlin Turner suggested that Hawthorne satirized Poe in "P's Correspondence" (*Nathaniel Hawthorne*, 159), though Poe's notice of the work does not indicate that he saw himself in it (*Collected Writings* 3:88–89).

6. Lowell's fiancée Maria White wrote to Caroline King on 4 October 1842, "James has gone to Portland today to engage John Neill [Neal] as a contributor [to *The Pioneer*] and will go this week to Concord to see Hawthorne and obtain his services." See Maria White Lowell to King. (Published by permission of the Schlesinger Library, Radcliffe Institute, Harvard University.) For a description of the manuscript of this letter, see Loewentheil and Edsall, *Poe Catalogue*, 56. Caroline King was later the author of *When I Lived in Salem*. Perhaps Lowell visited the Hawthornes by himself at this time; certainly he did visit them with Maria on 2 November. (See Maria White Lowell to Sarah Shaw.) Further consideration of Lowell's time at the Hawthornes and the Lowell-Hawthorne relationship is offered in chapter 2.

7. Writing in his review of Thomas Middleton's plays of the feeling of "*bodily remorse*" after one commits murder, James Russell Lowell states in a footnote, "This *bodily* feeling is painted with a terrible truth and distinctness of coloring in Hood's 'Dream of Eugene Aram,' and with no less strength by the powerful imagination of Mr. Poe, in his story of the 'Tell-tale heart,' on page 29 of the present number" ("Plays of Thomas Middleton," 37 n). (Poe later acknowledged this praise—see *Letters*, 1:221.) Poe mentions Thomas Hood's "The Dream of Eugene Aram" in August 1845 (*Collected Writings* 3:202); he also mentioned Edward Bulwer-Lytton's *Eugene Aram* in December 1835 (*Complete Works* 8:95) and April 1841 (*Complete Works* 10:132). Hawthorne reviewed Hood's *Poems* in May 1846, though without treating "The Dream of Eugene Aram" ("Simms's *Views and Reviews*; Hood's *Poems*," 23:239–41). Although Hood's poem has an affinity with "The Tell-Tale Heart" and *The Scarlet Letter*, parallels are not strong enough to suggest its having served as a source.

8. James Russell Lowell, ed., *Pioneer*, inner wrappers of second issue.

9. In writing "The Tell-Tale Heart," Poe also relied on Charles Dickens's "The Clock-Case: A Confession Found in a Prison in the Time of Charles the Second" for the placement of the chair over the buried body and the murderer's difficulty in looking in the eye of his victim (Krappe, "Possible Source"; *Collected Works* 3:790). And he referred to a variety of biblical verses with several of the phrases in the story (including Psalms 113:6 and Philippians 2:10 with "I heard all things in the heaven and in the earth" [*Collected Works* 3:792]; Exodus 20:21, Deuteronomy 4:11, and 5:22 with "thick darkness" [*Collected Works* 3:793]; and John 13:1 with "The old man's hour had come!" [*Collected Works* 3:795]). All citations to the Bible here and hereafter are to the King James Version.

10. See *Appendix*, 31–62. Webster's speech was reprinted in his *Speeches and Forensic Arguments*, 450–89.

11. Mellow, *Nathaniel Hawthorne*, 291; Moore, *Salem World*, 165–66.

12. Reference to the weapon that killed Joseph White was not made in the first appearance of the notebook entry in the Hawthorne edition (8:155) because the copy-text was Sophia Hawthorne's version of the notebook, and she must have deleted the phrase (8:155; see also 8:701). She apparently shared a sensitivity regarding the White murder with Caroline King, who destroyed her own writing on the subject because it was "indiscreet" (*When I Lived in Salem*, 9). The full notebook entry was first published in Nathaniel Hawthorne, *Hawthorne's Lost Notebook*, 42.

One wonders if Hawthorne knew that the ship *Mary and Eliza*, which his father Nathaniel Hathorne had commanded in 1804, had been owned by Joseph White. (See Hoeltje, "Captain Nathaniel Hathorne," 346.)

13. George Parsons Lathrop, *Complete Works*, 3:9; David S. Reynolds, *Beneath the American Renaissance*, 251; Matthiessen, *American Renaissance*, 214–15; Moore, *Salem World*, 164.

14. Interesting Hawthorne–Webster links might be added. Hawthorne referred to the Whig view of Webster as "a disreputable character" in 1838 (15:230) and termed him "a majestic brute" in 1845 (8:258). Still, Hawthorne served as recording secretary of the Salem Lyceum when Webster spoke about the United States Constitution in 1848 (16:244–45), and historian and Whig leader William H. Prescott appealed for Webster's assistance regarding Hawthorne's imminent loss of his position at the Salem Custom House in 1849. Forwarding Prescott's letter, Webster wrote to William M. Meredith, secretary of the treasury, "I suppose it will

be for the best to leave Mr. Hawthorne where he is, for the present" (See Cameron, "New Light," 4, and Mellow, *Nathaniel Hawthorne*, 296). But according to J. C. Derby, Webster wrote to Prescott, "How can you, a Whig, . . . do such a thing, as to recommend the continuance in office, of a man of the politics of Hawthorne?" (Derby, *Fifty Years*, 327). For a comparison of Hawthorne's negative view of Webster (allegedly revealed in "The Great Stone Face") with his wife's positive view, see Julian Hawthorne's *Nathaniel Hawthorne and His Wife*, 1:476–81. For a listing of several letters by Sophia Hawthorne touching on Daniel Webster, see McDonald, "Guide," 282–83. For a treatment of the possible relationship of *The Scarlet Letter* to the Fugitive Slave Law, notoriously supported by Daniel Webster, see Korobkin, "Scarlet Letter of the Law."

15. Arlin Turner's doctoral dissertation, "Study of Hawthorne's Origins," provided the second and third of these Hawthorne links to *Macbeth*, 68–69. Turner also notes a passage in Hawthorne's *The Marble Faun* that is suggestive of the sleepwalking scene. A connection between "Young Goodman Brown" and *Macbeth* is suggested by Frank Davidson, "Young Goodman Brown," 69. An excellent discussion of "The Tell-Tale Heart" and *Macbeth* is offered by Wilbur, "Poe," 6–8.

16. Julian Hawthorne, *Hawthorne Reading*, 122.

17. Gross, "Poe's Revision," 18–20; Regan, "Hawthorne's 'Plagiary,'" 284–92; McKeithan, "Poe and the Second Edition," 257, 262–68.

18. For Poe's toast, see Thomas and Jackson, *Poe Log*, 243. For Poe's library, see Stoddard, *"Put a Resolute Hart to a Steep Hill,"* 26.

19. Park Benjamin had been editor of the *New England Magazine* and publisher there of fifteen Hawthorne stories; however, Hawthorne may have been irritated because Benjamin had broken up his collection "The Story-Teller" (see "Fragment, to Elizabeth P. Peabody," 18:89; see also Adkins, "Early Projected Works," 132–33). For further background on Benjamin, see Hoover, *Park Benjamin*; for additional considerations of Hawthorne and Benjamin, see Turner, "Park Benjamin," and Gilkes, "Hawthorne." During different portions of Poe's stay in New York City in 1837 and 1838, Benjamin was assisted by Charles Fenno Hoffman, Robert Montgomery Bird, and Robert M. Walsh (Chielens, *American Literary Magazines*, 19).

20. Benjamin, Review of *The Token* (1838), 487; Review of *The Token* (1837), 407. For the review of the 1837 *Token*, see Idol and Jones, *Nathaniel Hawthorne, Contemporary Reviews*, 15. For the anticipation of Hawthorne's essay on Fessenden, see Benjamin, "Thomas Green Fessenden." Lowell may have had Benjamin's original comment in mind when he referred to Hawthorne as "a man of acknowledged genius," Review of *Historical Tales for Youth*, 42. Benjamin's expression of admiration for Hawthorne in 1837 seems to anticipate Herman Melville's famous dedication to *Moby-Dick* (1851): "IN TOKEN OF MY ADMIRATION FOR HIS GENIUS, This Book is Inscribed To NATHANIEL HAWTHORNE" (*Writings*, 6:vii).

21. Other items in the *American Monthly Magazine* of this period also merit mention. For example, the April 1837 issue included Park Benjamin's review of Thomas Green Fessenden's satirical poem *Terrible Tractoration* (previously reviewed by Hawthorne in the *American Magazine of Useful and Entertaining Knowledge* [23:230–34]), and the December 1837 issue featured William Austin's short story, "Martha Gardner; or, Moral Re-action" (considered by Brook Thomas to have an affinity with *The House of the Seven Gables* [*Cross-examinations of Law and Literature*, 51–52]).

22. Regarding Poe's employment goal, see Thomas and Jackson, *Poe Log*, 79. For the description of the *New-England Farmer*, see McCorison, "Thomas Green Fessenden," 14.

23. See [Advertisement for Bowles & Dearborn]; [Boston Map]; and the Boston directory for 1827. The Bowles & Dearborn bookshop is discussed by Mary E. Phillips (*Edgar Allan Poe*, 1:295–99), but with erroneous information regarding Poe's supposed trip to London before his stay in Boston. Bowles & Dearborn published the *United States Literary Gazette* and the *Christian Examiner*, as well as various books. The printer of Fessenden's *New England Farmer's Almanack*, for 1828 was John B. Russell, later the printer of the first edition of Hawthorne's *Twice-Told Tales*.

24. Thomas and Jackson, *Poe Log*, 83.

25. It is interesting to note that Hawthorne's future sister-in-law, Elizabeth Palmer Peabody, had stayed with the Fessendens in 1822—his future wife Sophia Peabody had written, "I am *very* glad to hear you are at Mr. Fessenden's where you are so pleasantly situated." See Sophia Hawthorne to Elizabeth Palmer Peabody, 2 November 1822. (Published by permission of the Berg Collection of English and American Literature, The New York Public Library, Astor, Lenox and Tilden Foundations.)

26. See Kopley, "*Very* Profound Under-current," 148–49; and *Narrative of Arthur Gordon Pym of Nantucket*, xxv, 239 n.

27. For Longfellow's advice in his 19 March 1843 letter to Hawthorne, see Longfellow, *Letters*, 2:519. Poe's other contributions to *The Pioneer* were "Lenore" (February 1843) and "Notes upon English Verse" (March 1843), where he offered scansion of Longfellow verses. Hawthorne's positive attitude toward Poe in early 1843 may be suggested by his responsiveness to Poe's invitation to contribute a story and a portrait to the *Stylus*. On 17 April 1843, both Lowell and Sophia Hawthorne reported Hawthorne's acceptance of the invitation (Poe, *Complete Works* 17:142; Sophia Hawthorne to Maria Louisa Hawthorne, 17 April 1843). See also her letter to her mother, Mrs. Elizabeth Palmer Peabody, 20 April 1843.

28. The dating of Hawthorne's beginning work "in earnest" on *The Scarlet Letter* is offered by Larry J. Reynolds in "*The Scarlet Letter* and Revolutions Abroad," 57. A discussion and listing of the obituaries of Poe and memorial pieces about Poe appearing in the year after his death are provided by Pollin, "Posthumous Assessment."

29. The variorum edition of Poe, edited by T. O. Mabbott, (*Collected Works*) offers the 1850 *Works* text of "The Tell-Tale Heart," with variants from the *Pioneer* and *Broadway Journal* texts of the story identified at the base of the page. None of the material quoted here varies from the *Pioneer* text except for the word "Death," which was, in *The Pioneer*, "death." (See James Russell Lowell, *Pioneer*, 30.) Mabbott does not list the lower-case variant.

30. Another Poe work that might have reinforced for Hawthorne the idea of the revelatory heart is the "Marginalia" installment in the January 1848 issue of *Graham's Magazine*, which gave the title of the unwritable true autobiography as "My Heart Laid Bare" (*Collected Writings* 2:322–23). Poe writes that "The paper [of this autobiography] would shrivel and blaze at every touch of the fiery pen" (*Collected Writings* 2:323); Hawthorne writes in "The Interior of a Heart" that Dimmesdale, confessing obliquely from the pulpit, had thought that "the only wonder was, that

they [his congregants] did not see his wretched body shrivelled up before their eyes, by the burning wrath of the Almighty!" (1:143–44).

31. For a formal link between "The Tell-Tale Heart" and *The Scarlet Letter*, see chapter 4.

It is interesting to recall Edward Stone's observation ("More on Hawthorne and Melville," 66) that Herman Melville wrote in *Moby-Dick*, "For all men tragically great are made so through *a certain morbidness*" (Melville, *Writings*, 6:74; Stone's emphasis) even as Hawthorne had written in chapter 10 of *The Scarlet Letter*, "Yet Mr. Dimmesdale would perhaps have seen this individual's character more perfectly, if *a certain morbidness*, to which sick hearts are liable, had not rendered him suspicious of all mankind" (1:130; Stone's emphasis). It is certainly possible that Melville was influenced by this Poe-permeated chapter of Hawthorne's novel. Furthermore, Starbuck's looking at the sleeping Ahab, that "Terrible old man!" whose closed eyes looked toward the "tell-tale" (6:235), may recall to us Poe's "The Tell-Tale Heart." And the association of *Moby-Dick* with Poe's tale becomes even stronger when we note that the monomaniacal Ahab—linked (by "half-slouched hat" [6:161] and swinging cabin light [6:235]) with the evil-eyed, guilty Jonah (6:43–45)—speaks of dismemberment (6:168).

Another debt to Poe's "The Tell-Tale Heart" seems present in chapter 11 of Frederick Douglass's 1845 *Narrative of the Life of Frederick Douglass*. Douglass writes of an angry Master Hugh Auld, "He raved, and swore" (73), recalling Poe's writing, as the narrator of "The Tell-Tale Heart," "I raved—I swore!" (*Collected Works* 3:797). Furthermore, Douglass writes that by "working steadily," he was able to allay suspicion of his imminent flight north—indeed, his master "thought I was never better satisfied with my condition than at the very time during which I was planning my escape (74). Similarly, Poe's narrator asserts, "I was never kinder to the old man than during the whole week before I killed him" (*Collected Works* 3:792). Douglass was living in Lynn, Massachusetts, when Poe's tale appeared in *The Pioneer* in January 1843. He was, of course, involved in Boston's abolitionist movement, as was the editor of *The Pioneer*, James Russell Lowell. Douglass probably read Poe's work and later alluded to it as he wrote his own story. This is not so surprising for, as J. Gerald Kennedy has pointed out, Poe and Douglass shared a defiant attitude toward paternalistic authority. (See "Trust No Man," 228.)

32. For the comment on Hawthorne's "prevailing method of expanding each idea," see Turner, "Hawthorne's Methods," 305; for elaboration of this view regarding *The Scarlet Letter*, see 307, 309–12.

33. Abel, "Immortality vs. Mortality," 570.

34. That Matthew Maule's descendant Holgrave was the murderer of Judge Pyncheon has been argued in Cox, "'Who Killed Judge Pyncheon?'"

35. Thornton, "Hawthorne, Poe, and a Literary Ghost," 151–52.

Chronology

1809	Born in Boston on January 19 to itinerant actors Elizabeth Arnold Hopkins Poe and David Poe Jr. Father abandons the family while Edgar is an infant.
1811	Elizabeth Poe dies on December 8 in Richmond, Virginia. John Allan, a Richmond importer, and his wife, Frances, take in Edgar, while his brother and sister each end up in different locations.
1815–1820	Travels with the Allans to England and Scotland, where John Allan hoped to expand his business. Attends boarding school in London, 1818 to 1820. Family returns to Richmond in 1820.
1824	Writes earliest extant verse.
1825	Meets and becomes romantically involved with Sarah Elmira Royster. John Allan inherits considerable wealth and property from his uncle, William Galt.
1826	Attends University of Virginia but does not return after the winter break.
1827	Goes to Boston, where he enlists in the army. Publishes first book of poetry, *Tamerlane and Other Poems*.
1829	While stationed in Virginia, Poe hires a substitute and is discharged from the army. Frances Allan dies. Publishes *Al Aaraaf, Tamerlane, and Minor Poems*.

1830	With Allan's help, attains an appointment to West Point and enrolls in May. Allan remarries and ends his relationship with Poe.
1831	Court-martialed and expelled from West Point for neglecting classes and drills. Publishes *Poems: Second Edition*. Moves to Baltimore, where he lives in poverty with his grandmother; his aunt, Maria Clemm; his cousin, Virginia; and Poe's brother, William Henry Leonard Poe, who dies August 1.
1832	*The Saturday Courier*, a Philadelphia magazine, publishes five stories Poe submitted as entries in a contest. John Allan writes Poe out of his will.
1834	John Allan dies.
1835	Grandmother dies. Poe begins writing for T. W. White's fledgling *Southern Literary Messenger*, then moves back to Richmond with his aunt and cousin to edit the magazine. Contributes stories and often-scathing book reviews to the publication.
1836	Marries his thirteen-year-old cousin, Virginia Clemm, in May.
1837	Moves the family to New York City, after he is either fired by White or resigns.
1838	Moves to Philadelphia. Publishes *The Narrative of Arthur Gordon Pym*.
1839	Becomes coeditor of William E. Burton's *Gentleman's Magazine*. First 25 stories are published as *Tales of the Grotesque and Arabesque*.
1840	Leaves *Gentleman's Magazine*.
1841	Hired as an editor of *Graham's Magazine*.
1842	Virginia contracts tuberculosis. Resigns from *Graham's*.
1843	Travels to Washington, D.C., to win a government job and raise subscriptions for his planned magazine.
1844	Moves to New York City. Works as an editorial assistant at the *New York Evening Mirror*.
1845	Becomes coeditor of the *Broadway Journal* and later its proprietor. Publishes *Tales* and *The Raven and Other Poems*.
1846	*Broadway Journal* folds. Moves with family to Fordham, New York. Suffers severe illness when Virginia's health declines.

1847	Virginia dies in January. Poe is depressed and ill for most of the year and writes little.
1848	*Eureka* is published. Engaged to Sarah Helen Whitman; she breaks the engagement. Probably attempts suicide by overdose of laudanum.
1849	Negotiates with E.H.N. Patterson to establish the *Stylus*. Proposes to Sarah Elmira Royster Shelton. Falls into a coma. Dies on October 7 and is buried in Baltimore.

Contributors

HAROLD BLOOM is Sterling Professor of the Humanities at Yale University. He is the author of 30 books, including *Shelley's Mythmaking*, *The Visionary Company*, *Blake's Apocalypse*, *Yeats*, *A Map of Misreading*, *Kabbalah and Criticism*, *Agon: Toward a Theory of Revisionism*, *The American Religion*, *The Western Canon*, and *Omens of Millennium: The Gnosis of Angels, Dreams, and Resurrection*. *The Anxiety of Influence* sets forth Professor Bloom's provocative theory of the literary relationships between the great writers and their predecessors. His most recent books include *Shakespeare: The Invention of the Human*, a 1998 National Book Award finalist, *How to Read and Why*, *Genius: A Mosaic of One Hundred Exemplary Creative Minds*, *Hamlet: Poem Unlimited*, *Where Shall Wisdom Be Found?*, and *Jesus and Yahweh: The Names Divine*. In 1999, Professor Bloom received the prestigious American Academy of Arts and Letters Gold Medal for Criticism. He has also received the International Prize of Catalonia, the Alfonso Reyes Prize of Mexico, and the Hans Christian Andersen Bicentennial Prize of Denmark.

DANIEL HOFFMAN is part of the emeritus faculty in the English department at the University of Pennsylvania. He has published many volumes of poetry, and his critical studies include *Faulkner's Country Matters* and *Form and Fable in American Fiction*.

WALTER STEPP has been a professor of English at Nassau Community College, Garden City, New York. In addition to critical assessments of Poe, he has also written on Henry James.

GITA RAJAN is an associate professor of English at Fairfield University. She coauthored *New Cosmopolitanisms: South Asians in the U.S.* and coedited *Postcolonial Discourse and Changing Cultural Contexts*, among other works.

HENRY SUSSMAN is a professor of comparative literature at the State University of New York at Buffalo. Among his studies in literary criticism and critical theory are *The Aesthetic Contract: Statutes of Art and Intellectual Work in Modernity* and *Psyche and Text: The Sublime and the Grandiose in Literature, Psychopathology, and Culture*.

PAIGE MATTHEY BYNUM has taught at the University of North Carolina at Chapel Hill and is coauthor of *Lawrence Durrell: Comprehending the Whole*. He has been a speaker at the annual meeting of the Poe Studies Association.

SHAWN ROSENHEIM has taught at Williams College. He is the author of *The Cryptographic Imagination: Secret Writing from Edgar Allan Poe to the Internet*.

JOHANN PILLAI is chair of the general education department and an associate professor at Eastern Mediterranean University, Cyprus.

BRETT ZIMMERMAN is an assistant professor at York University in Toronto. He has authored *Edgar Allan Poe: Rhetoric and Style* and *Herman Melville: Stargazer* and also has published book reviews, opinion pieces, and magazine and journal articles.

JOHN H. TIMMERMAN teaches American literature at Calvin College. He has authored or edited numerous essays and books, such as *A Nation's Voice: An Anthology of American Short Fiction* and *Other Worlds: The Fantasy Game*.

RICHARD KOPLEY is a professor of English at Penn State University's DuBois campus. He is the editor of *Poe's Pym: Critical Explorations*, wrote the introduction and annotations for the Penguin edition of Poe's novel *The Narrative of Arthur Gordon Pym*, and has worked on other publications as well. He is a past president of the Poe Studies Association.

Bibliography

Burwick, Frederick L. "Edgar Allan Poe: The Sublime and the Grotesque." *Prism(s): Essays in Romanticism* 8 (2000): 67–123.

Cantalupo, Barbara. "Interview with Daniel Hoffman (April 2002)." *Edgar Allan Poe Review* 3, no. 1 (Spring 2002): 95-112.

Cleman, John. "Irresistable Impulses: Edgar Allan Poe and the Insanity Defense." *American Literature: A Journal of Literary History, Criticism, and Bibliography* 63, no. 4 (December 1991): p. 623–640.

Dameron, J. Lasley. "Poe and Twain: Cooper Reviewed and Revised." *Mississippi Quarterly* 53, no. 2 (Spring 2000): 197–207.

Davis, Robert Con. "Lacan, Poe, and Narrative Repression." *MLN* 98, no. 5 (December 1983): 983–1005.

Dern, John A. "Poe's Public Speakers: Rhetorical Strategies in 'The Tell-Tale Heart' and 'The Cask of Amontillado.'" *Edgar Allan Poe Review* 2, no. 2 (Fall 2001): 53–70.

Ehrlich, Heyward. "Poe in Cyberspace: Electronic Guides to Printed and Online Research." *Edgar Allan Poe Review* 4, no. 2 (Fall 2003): 93–97.

Frank, F. S. "Neighborhood Gothic: Poe's 'Tell-Tale Heart.'" *The Sphinx: A Magazine of Literature and Society* 3, no. 4 (1981): 53–60.

Freedman, William. *The Porous Sanctuary: Art and Anxiety in Poe's Short Fiction.* New York: Peter Lang, 2002.

Gillikin, Patricia. "Applying Models of Masculine and Feminine Sexuality: Narrative Patterns in Poe and Gilman." *Proceedings of the Philological Association of Louisiana* (1992): 61–66.

Gruesser, John C. "Madmen and Moonbeams: The Narrator in 'The Fall of the House of Usher.'" *Edgar Allan Poe Review* 5, no. 1 (Spring 2004): 80–90.

Hayes, Kevin J. *The Cambridge Companion to Edgar Allan Poe*. Cambridge, England: Cambridge University Press, 2002.

Hoffman, Daniel. "Returns from the Grave: The Spirit of Poe in Contemporary Fiction." *Edgar Allan Poe Review* 5, no. 1 (Spring 2004): 6–15.

Hovey, Kenneth Alan. "'These Many Pieces Are Yet One Book': The Book-Unity of Poe's Tale Collections." *Poe Studies/Dark Romanticism* 31, nos. 1–2 (1998): 1–16.

Hughes, John. "Poe's Resentful Soul." *Poe Studies/Dark Romanticism* 34, nos. 1–2 (2001): 20–28.

Irwin, John T. "Knight's Gambit: Poe, Faulkner, and the Tradition of the Detective Story." In *William Faulkner: Six Decades of Criticism*, edited by Linda Wagner-Martin, 355–75. East Lansing, Mich.: Michigan State University Press, 2002.

Kennedy, J. Gerald, ed. *A Historical Guide to Edgar Allan Poe*. Oxford: Oxford University Press, 2001.

Magistrale, Tony, and Sidney Poger. *Poe's Children: Connections between Tales of Terror and Detection*. New York: Peter Lang, 1999.

Merivale, Patricia, and Susan Elizabeth Sweeney, eds. *Detecting Texts: The Metaphysical Detective Story from Poe to Postmodernism*. Philadelphia: University of Pennsylvania Press, 1999.

Mücke, Dorothea E. von. *The Seduction of the Occult and the Rise of the Fantastic Tale*. Stanford, Calif.: Stanford University Press, 2003.

Neiworth, James. "International Poe Bibliography: 1998-2000." *Poe Studies/Dark Romanticism* 35 (2002): 38–65.

Peeples, Scott. *The Afterlife of Edgar Allan Poe*. Rochester, NY: Camden House, 2004.

Perry, Dennis R. *Hitchcock and Poe: The Legacy of Delight and Terror*. Lanham, Md.: Scarecrow Press, 2003.

Phinney, Kasey. "Image Robbing: Speech and Identity in 'The Tell-Tale Heart' (Selected Papers, 1999 Conference, Society for the Interdisciplinary Study of Social Imagery, March 11–13, 1999, Colorado Springs, Colorado)." In *The Image of America in Literature, Media, and Society*, edited by Will Wright and Steven Kaplan. Pueblo, Colo.: Society for the Interdisciplinary Study of Social Imagery, University of Southern Colorado, 1999.

Pitcher, Edward W. "The Physiognomical Meaning of Poe's 'The Tell-Tale Heart.'" *Studies in Short Fiction* 16 (1979): 231–233.

Polk, Noel. "Welty, Hawthorne, and Poe: Men of the Crowd and the Landscape of Alienation." *Mississippi Quarterly* 50, no. 4 (Fall 1997): 553–565.

Rainwater, Catherine. "Edgar Allan Poe (1809–1849)." In *Writers of the American Renaissance: An A-to-Z Guide*, edited by Denise D. Knight. Westport, Conn.: Greenwood, 2003. p. 300–307.

Renza, Louis A. "Edgar Allan Poe, Henry James, and Jack London: A Private Correspondence." *Boundary 2* 27, no. 2 (Summer 2000): 83–111.

_____. "Never More in Poe's Tell-Tale American Tale." *Edgar Allan Poe Review* 4, no. 2 (Fall 2003): 22–40.

Robinson, E. Arthur. "Poe's 'The Tell-Tale Heart.'" *Nineteenth-Century Fiction* 19, no. 4 (March 1965): 369–78.

Stockholder, Kay. "Is Anybody at Home in the Text? Psychoanalysis and the Question of Poe." *American Imago* 57, no. 3 (Fall 2000): 299–333.

Tucker, B. D. "'The Tell-Tale Heart' and the 'Evil Eye.'" *Southern Literary Journal* 13, no. 2 (Spring 1981): 92–98.

Vines, Lois Davis. *Poe Abroad: Influence, Reputation, Affinities.* Iowa City: University of Iowa Press, 1999.

Weaver, Aubrey Maurice. "And Then My Heart with Pleasure Fills. . . ." *Journal of Evolutionary Psychology* 9, nos. 3-4 (August 1988): 317–320.

Whalen, Terence. *Edgar Allan Poe and the Masses: The Political Economy of Literature in Antebellum America.* Princeton, N.J.: Princeton University Press, 1999.

Wright, Thomas. "Edgar Allan Poe's Tales of the Grotesque and Arabesque." In *American Writers Classics, I,* edited by Jay Parini, 339–358. New York: Thomson Gale, 2003.

Zimmerman, Brett. "'I Could Read His Prose on Salary, but Not Jane's': Poe's Stylistic Versatility." *Language and Discourse* 5 (1997): 97–117.

_____. 'Moral Insanity' Or Paranoid Schizophrenia: Poe's 'The Tell-Tale Heart'. *Mosaic: A Journal for the Interdisciplinary Study of Literature* 25, no. 2 (Spring 1992): 39–48.

Acknowledgments

Daniel Hoffman, *Poe Poe Poe Poe Poe Poe Poe,* pp. 205–232, "Grotesques and Arabesques." Originally published, Garden City, New York: Doubleday & Company, Inc., 1972. Baton Rouge: Louisiana State University Press, 1998. © 1972 by Daniel Hoffman.

Walter Stepp, "The Ironic Double in Poe's 'The Cask of Amontillado." From *Studies in Short Fiction* 13, no. 4 (Fall 1976). (c) 1977 by Newberry College. Reprinted with permission.

Gita Rajan, "A Feminist Rereading of Poe's 'The Tell-Tale Heart.'" From *Papers on Language & Literature,* vol. 24, no. 3 (Summer 1988): 283–300. © 1988 by the Board of Trustees, Southern Illinois University.

Henry Sussman, "A Note on the Public and the Private in Literature: The Literature of 'Acting Out.'" From *Modern Language Notes* 104:3 (1989), 597–611. © The Johns Hopkins University Press. Reprinted with permission of The Johns Hopkins University Press.

Paige Matthey Bynum, "'Observe how healthily—how calmly I tell you the whole story': Moral Insanity and Edgar Allan Poe's 'The Tell-Tale Heart,'" pp. 141–152. From *Literature and Science as Modes of Expression,* Frederick Amrine, ed. Norwell, MA: Kluwer Academic Publishers, 1989. © 1989 by Kluwer Academic Publishers, with kind permission from Springer Science and Business Media.

Shawn Rosenheim, "Detective Fiction, Psychoanalysis, and the Analytic Sub-lime," pp. 153–176. From *The American Face of Edgar Allan Poe,* Shawn Rosenheim and Stephen Rachman, eds. © 1995 The Johns Hopkins University Press. Reprinted with permission of The Johns Hopkins University Press.

Johann Pillai, "Death and Its Moments: The End of the Reader in History." From *Modern Language Notes* 112:5 (1997), 836–875. © The Johns Hopkins University Press. Reprinted with permission of The Johns Hopkins University Press.

Brett Zimmerman, "Frantic Forensic Oratory: Poe's 'The Tell-Tale Heart.'" From *Style* 35, no. 1 (Spring 2001): 34–49. © 2001 by *Style.* Reprinted with permission.

John H. Timmerman, "House of Mirrors: Edgar Allan Poe's 'The Fall of the House of Usher.'" From *Papers on Language and Literature* 39, no. 3 (Summer 2003). © 2003 by Southern Illinois University. Reprinted with permission.

Richard Kopley, "Chapter 1: A Tale by Poe" and notes, pp, 22–35, 125–130. From *The Threads of The Scarlet Letter: A Study of Hawthorne's Transformative Art.* © 2003 by Rosemont Publishing & Printing Corp.

Every effort has been made to contact the owners of copyrighted material and secure copyright permission. Articles appearing in this volume generally appear much as they did in their original publication with few or no editorial changes. In some cases, foreign language text has been removed from the original essay. Those interested in locating the original source will find the information cited above.

Index